Building Law
for Students

Consulting Editor
C.R. Bassett, BSc., FCIOB, FFB

Building Law for Students

Second Edition

Anne Galbraith, LLB (Dunelm)

Newnes
An imprint of Butterworth–Heinemann Ltd
Linacre House, Jordan Hill, Oxford OX2 8DP

🍂 PART OF REED INTERNATIONAL BOOKS

OXFORD   LONDON   BOSTON
MUNICH   NEW DELHI   SINGAPORE   SYDNEY
TOKYO   TORONTO   WELLINGTON

First published 1989
Second edition 1991

British Library Cataloguing in Publication Data
Galbraith, Anne
  Building law for students.
  1. England. Law for construction industries
  I. Title
  342.41

ISBN 0 7506 0302 X

Printed and bound in Great Britain by
Redwood Press Limited, Melksham, Wiltshire.

Contents

Preface

Despite the widely held view that the law stands still, the truth is often quite the opposite. If our law is to serve the needs of society, it must be adaptable and constantly responsive to changing needs. Of course, not everyone welcomes change: 'Change is not made without inconvenience', wrote Hooker four hundred years ago. How wise he was!

One of those inconveniences is that books on such broad-ranging material as that covered in *Building Law for Students* inevitably become out of date quite quickly. In less than two years, we have seen major changes in the fields of negligence, statutory nuisance, planning, the courts, contract, employment law, company law – and no doubt there is more to come.

But take comfort. Washington Irving commented in the nineteenth century that 'there is a certain relief in change' – and that is definitely the case in some of the new law incorporated into this edition. Some considerable simplification and clarification of the law regarding liability for pure economic loss in negligence has resulted from the decision of the House of Lords in Murphy *v.* Brentwood District Council. Of course, one cannot help but fear that something more complex may be developing just around the corner – as Irving did go on to say that 'it is a comfort to shift one's position and be bruised in a new place'.

Not only have I sought to incorporate changes to the law in this edition, but also I have taken the opportunity of a new edition to re-order some material. I have tried as far as possible to take account of comments from my colleagues, some of whom have used the book as a student text, and for those suggestions I am most grateful.

Anne Galbraith

Preface to the first edition

One of Shakespeare's characters suggests, 'Let's kill all the lawyers' – but perhaps we should hesitate to follow this advice. A mass of complex law governs construction activities: contracts may fall through; planning permission may be refused; workers may be injured on site; buildings may collapse or prove to be defective; traffic may be halted by construction work; strikes may occur; building contractors may become insolvent; an inspector may issue a Prohibition Notice. In such circumstances, legal advice given in good time may prove to be very cost effective in the long term.

The aim of this book is to present a clear and readable account of those areas of the law that are of principal relevance to 'built environment' subjects – building construction, planning, surveying, architecture, quantity surveying – and to alert both student and practitioner to situations that may have a legal dimension.

No book on building law can cover in detail all the diverse topic areas, and no building student can become a legal expert with no need of lawyers. However, it makes sense in any field of activity to be armed with a basic knowledge of the appropriate legal framework. Mistakes can be expensive in terms of losses incurred, physical injury, suffering and distress, and damage to reputation. Using the law to fulfil a 'planning' function can usefully prevent or minimize such costly errors.

In some areas of law the rules are derived from the cases, which are real disputes between real parties. These cases not only determine what the rules should be, but also flesh out our understanding of how those rules will work in practice. In some of the topic areas covered by this book frequent reference is made to such cases, as the rules would be meaningless or non-existent without them. In other areas, Parliament has chosen to provide a framework of laws in statutory form. It has sometimes proved possible to examine that framework with far less reference to case law. This does not mean that the cases have no role to play in those areas. It simply means that the 'bare bones' of the statutory framework provide a straightforward foundation from which students can proceed with confidence to more detailed specialist texts where necessary.

In order to provide coverage of as many relevant aspects of the law as possible, treatment of some topic areas has necessarily had to be brief. Where possible, examples have been chosen which are relevant to the construction industry, the aim being to make the book as readily digestible as possible by the non-lawyer. Inevitably, laws which govern so many people and so much diverse activity can be complex. The temptation will often be to leave the complexities for the professional lawyer, but the consequences of ignoring the law can be expensive. Remember, ignorance is *not* bliss. 'Ignorance of the law excuses no man': so wrote John Seldon in the sixteenth century. No doubt in these days of non-discrimination, he would include 'woman' in this warning!

My thanks are due first to Mrs Ann Baldwin, who cheerfully typed the manuscript; to my long-suffering colleagues, several of whom have given their help and moral support in abundance; and finally to my family, who must often have doubted whether a finished product would ever emerge.

Anne Galbraith

Table of statutes

Regulations

Table of cases

1

The nature of law

Introduction

Any society quickly finds that it needs rules or laws to enable it to function smoothly. Consider the results if you had decided to drive to work today on the right instead of the left. People need to be able to live and go about their business in certainty, knowing that they can expect others to abide by the same rules. It is probably true that most people obey most of the rules most of the time. They may not have any precise knowledge of the actual rules which they are obeying, but that precise knowledge only becomes important when disputes arise or problems have to be solved.

As society evolves and becomes more complex, the number of laws increases and the types of laws become more sophisticated. Initially people need laws to protect their person or their property. Some rules accord with basic ideas of morality, e.g. not killing or not stealing but it is not essential for all the rules to have a moral base. For instance, when we create a rule for motorists that they must drive on the left the rule commands obedience simply because it is necessary and certain.

Although certainty is an important principle in any legal system, the rules of law should also aim to achieve justice. This is sometimes accomplished by giving a discretion. Some areas of English law are subject to discretionary principles known as equity. It should be remembered that laws are equally binding even if they are thought to be unjust. The remedy then is to seek to reform the law, not to violate it.

Sanctions

If a law is disobeyed, there must be some effective means by which it can be enforced. This may be described as a sanction and could take the form of a fine, imprisonment, an award of damages or an injunction, which is an order of the court forbidding certain actions or behaviour. Although such sanctions may deter people from breaking the law, in fact the reasons for obeying the law may be far more complex. A person may obey the law because he fears the disapproval or hostility of others, or because he believes in the 'rightness' of the rule, or because he sees obedience of the law as a duty he owes as a citizen.

Divisions of the law

It should be noted that all the contents of this book relate to English law. Although it is appropriate to talk about the British Constitution it should be remembered that Scotland has a different system of law to England. Whereas some of the rules are common to both countries, there are still significant differences. These are most apparent in areas like the system of land holding and in the structures and procedures of the courts.

English law may be sub-divided in a number of ways. A simple division would be into criminal and civil law. It is quite common for the layman to believe that the bulk of our law consists of criminal law. This inevitably results from the publicity given in the media to major criminal cases. In this sense the law is like an iceberg – the criminal law is the part seen above the water and the civil law is the mighty bulk that lies below. The state has an interest in preserving our society and upholding law and order, and it makes criminal laws to secure those objectives. A person who infringes those laws commits a criminal offence for which he can be prosecuted by the state. The principal objectives of the criminal law may, therefore, be seen to be to deter and to punish. The civil law protects rights and creates obligations between individuals, although sometimes those individuals will be large public corporations, government departments, local authorities etc.

There is no simple way to classify civil law, but it may be subdivided into the law of contract, the law of tort (i.e. civil wrongs), the law relating to property and the law relating to persons. The rules of civil law must deal with matters as diverse as contracts for the sale of goods, actions for damages for negligence, planning applications and compulsory purchase, divorce, tenancy, creation of companies, contracts of insurance, making a will, money lending, recovery of debts, defective workmanship and unfair dismissal.

Language of the law

Every profession has its language or jargon, which is often a convenient shorthand method of communication between people engaged in that profession. With its long history, the language of the law is especially rich as it frequently uses Latin expressions such as *res ipsa loquitur* (the facts speak for themselves,) or *caveat emptor* (let the buyer beware). Different terminology applies to criminal and civil law. In criminal proceedings a person is arrested, charged with an offence and prosecuted in summary or indictable proceedings by a prosecutor. If the accused person is found guilty he will be sentenced and punished. If he is found not guilty he will be acquitted. In a civil action a plaintiff sues a defendant. If the defendant is found to be liable he may be ordered to pay damages or an order of the court such as an injunction may be made against him. Where the terminology is correctly used it is possible to tell whether a case concerns criminal or civil law.

Although it is convenient to break down the mass of English law into sub-divisions for the purposes of study, it should be realized that these various divisions of the law are not mutually exclusive. It is possible for one set of facts to give rise to both civil and criminal liability. The simplest example is the motorist who drives carelessly and injures a pedestrian. A motorist may both be prosecuted in criminal proceedings for an offence under the Road Traffic Acts and be sued in civil proceedings by the injured pedestrian hoping to recover compensation. Similarly, an employee injured at work may wish to bring civil proceedings against his employer to recover damages where the employer has been negligent in caring for the employee's safety. Arising out of the same set of facts, the Health and Safety Executive may prosecute the employer for breaches of the Health and Safety at Work Act 1974.

Making the law

Unless some catastrophic event like a war or a revolution occurs, which may cause a country to adopt a completely new system of law, the law-making processes will have developed over a period of centuries. Many of the rules of English law which are still in force are of considerable antiquity. Laws do not become ineffective merely because they are very old. Indeed some old rules have been used very imaginatively by the judges in the courts to create principles relevant to modern life.

In the early stages of law making, custom will usually play a large part. As the needs of a society become more sophisticated, custom as a source of law tends to be superseded by more formal sources. Local custom may still be upheld as a valid part of the law where it can be shown that the custom is reasonable and certain and has been continued without interruption since time immemorial. For practical purposes this normally means that the custom must be shown to have existed during living memory. Occasional examples still come before the courts.

The two main sources of law in our system today are legislation (laws made or approved by Parliament) and judicial precedents (binding decisions of the judges). Both of these sources of law must now take account of the fact that the United Kingdom is a member of the European Community.

The UK and the European Community

The UK joined the European Community in 1972. The legal power for its membership is contained in the European Communities Act 1972. There had been previous abortive attempts to join the Community. Even when our membership became a reality, doubts were expressed which were sufficient to prompt a unique referendum in 1975 which confirmed the view that the UK should stay in the Community. Since our entry other countries have joined, most recently Spain and Portugal.

Many of the doubts about joining the Community related to the loss of sovereignty which would result. To what extent would it be true to say after 1972 that Parliament is supreme? At the time many people in the UK believed that our first loyalties lay with the Commonwealth and that inevitably membership of the European Community would result in a diminution of those ties.

The European Community operates through a number of institutions, principally the Council of Ministers, the Commission and the European Assembly or Parliament. There is also a Council of Europe which consists of heads of government and foreign ministers who meet several times a year. The Council is not recognized by any of the treaties creating the Community but because of the stature of the persons who attend it is obviously very significant. Vital issues like the size of our financial contribution to the European budget are thrashed out in the Council.

Additionally there is a Council of Ministers composed of one representative of each member state, who will usually be the Foreign Minister. This is the principal decision-making body and member states hold its presidency in turn. Usually the Council of Ministers takes decisions based on the proposals put forward by the Commission. The Commission is the executive arm of the Community. Its members become Commissioners, each with responsibility for a specific aspect of work of the Community, for example agriculture. The Commission initiates legislation, usually after consulting the Civil

Service of the various member states. In deciding on its response to the Commission's proposals, the Council will have consulted the European Assembly. The Assembly has been a directly elected body since 1979. The UK has eighty-one Euro MPs who are elected on a party political basis. Once elected the Euro MPs sit in political, not national, groupings. The principal role of the Assembly is to give its opinion to the Council of Ministers.

Both the Council of Ministers and the Commission can make regulations which have direct force in the UK. In other cases where they issue 'directives' or 'decisions', our own Parliament must usually implement the rules for this country, although then it may have some discretion about the method of implementation. The European Communities Act 1972 provides that the various Community Treaties shall have effect in UK law and that decisions of the European Court are applicable in UK courts. Where relevant, therefore, Community law prevails over UK law.

This thorny question of 'supremacy' has caused much argument. One view is that European law is supreme and takes precedence over domestic legislation. In joining the European Community, the argument runs, the United Kingdom conceded that the British Parliament can no longer pass inconsistent legislation. A counter argument has always insisted that what Parliament has accepted – in the European Communities Act 1972 – it could also reject. Recent cases, however, confirm that the former view is correct. In *R. v. Secretary of State for Transport, ex parte Factortame Ltd*, the European Court of Justice indicated that where there is a national rule in conflict with a Community rule, the national rule becomes inapplicable. Cases involving equal pay and sex discrimination have been a rich field for development of these principles (see page 168).

New legislation

Law-making authority is vested in the Crown and Parliament, although the role of the Crown is now almost entirely formal. Our complex modern society requires rule-making techniques which are capable of coping with economic, social and welfare problems. Parliament, consisting of the House of Lords and the House of Commons, is said to be supreme, but in practice its ability to make rules must be viewed subject to a number of limitations. By virtue of the European Communities Act 1972 a new element of European Community law was introduced into our system. European Community law takes precedence over the national law of any member state. This, therefore, imposes a limit on the ability of Parliament to make whatever laws it wishes. If English law is found to conflict with European Community law the Community law will prevail. Other factors which would limit the power of Parliament are the existence of an opposition party, or parties, whose duty is to seek to curb or limit government proposals; Parliamentary question time which is held daily, when ministers, including the Prime Minister, must justify their activities; the two chamber system whereby the House of Lords can at least delay the passing of legislation; and public opinion, pressure groups, freedom of speech and publicity through the media. Once laws are enacted by Parliament the interpretation of those laws is carried out by the judges in the courts. If Parliament has passed a law which is seen to be too harsh or too extensive in its application it may be possible for the judges, by restrictive interpretation of the words of the statute, to limit the scope of the new rule.

Acts of Parliament, which can also be called statutes, contain the main laws made by Parliament, acting in its legislative role. Until the statute or Act has passed through all its stages in both Houses and received the royal assent, it is referred to as a Bill.

The inspiration for new legislation may come from a number of sources. A new government will have made manifesto commitments and will have outlined its own policies. During its first year or so in office it will be keen to push through those changes which were outlined in its election manifesto. Inevitably this source of new legislation becomes comparatively less significant as the government's term of office, a maximum of five years, progresses. Each of the major government departments will have a programme of legislation which it would like to introduce. Parliamentary time is at a premium and this may well produce competition between departments. Where a small measure is needed a department may seek to persuade a private member who has won a high place in the private members' ballot to introduce a bill on its behalf.

New laws may also be needed to implement recommendations of the Law Commission, a body established in 1965 to review the law with a view to its systematic development and reform. Occasionally the government of the day sets up Royal Commissions or other special committees of enquiry. These are usually established to investigate one specific topic area and they will be disbanded once their reports are published. Many of these reports gather dust and do not result in their recommendations being implemented in legislation. In other cases the recommendations may be implemented in their entirety. One such example was the Robens Report on Health and Safety which very quickly became the Health and Safety at Work etc. Act 1974. There is a limited scope for individual politicians to introduce private members' bills, by which means small changes may be introduced into our law. Occasionally new laws will be required to meet a sudden emergency and, where necessary, Parliament can act with considerable speed. It is possible for an Act of Parliament to pass through all its stages in both houses and receive the Royal Assent in a day if necessary.

Once an idea for a piece of legislation has been accepted by the Legislation Committee of the Cabinet there will usually follow an intensive period of deliberation and consultation. Parliamentary Counsel (the draftsmen of the Bills) will then be required to draw up the Bill clause by clause. Many Bills will be significantly redrafted before they are enacted in their final version. The problems which beset the draftsmen include the lack of precision of our language; trying to reconcile many conflicting demands; attempting to cover situations which can be envisaged but which have not yet arisen in practice; and pressure of time. Not surprisingly many Acts of Parliament are subsequently found to create interpretive difficulties which must be resolved in the courts.

Acts of Parliament begin life as bills, which may be either public, private or private member's bills. Public bills comprise the vast majority passed in each parliamentary session. An example of a private bill may be one promoted by a local authority to authorize some activity specifically in its own local area. Private member's bills provide the limited opportunity available in each parliamentary session for an MP to introduce some proposals for change in the law on a topic of his choice. Public bills are usually introduced by government departments, and may be introduced in either House. The likelihood is that most of these public bills will be passed. A government, particularly one with a large majority, has an effective stranglehold on procedures in Parliament. Non-controversial bills are often introduced in the House of Lords but all money bills must be introduced in the Commons.

The normal procedure in both Houses is that when the bill is introduced it will have its first reading. Normally the sponsors of the bill present it in dummy form at the table of the House and one of the clerks reads out the title. The bill is then deemed to have been read for the first time. It is next ordered to be printed and published, and a date fixed for the second reading. Its second reading is the occasion for a parliamentary debate on the principles of the bill. The bill is not considered clause by clause at this stage. There will be a vote at the end of the debate and the bill could be rejected at this stage. Assuming that the bill is not lost it is then referred to a committee, to undergo its committee stage. It will usually go to a standing committee of between sixteen and fifty members, chosen to reflect the relative strength of the political parties in the House, and having regard to the special qualifications, concerns and interests of the MPs in question. These standing committees usually sit in the morning, and they will consider the bill in detail, examining it clause by clause, trying to produce a result which is unambiguous. The committee will also deal with proposed amendments to the bill. Where a bill is of major constitutional importance, the committee stage may be taken in a Committee of the Whole House. However, the drawback of this system is that, while it sits as a committee, no other business can be conducted by the House.

Many of the amendments proposed to the bill at the committee stage may be put down by the minister in overall charge of the bill himself. These proposed amendments may reflect afterthoughts by him or his officials, or they may be the result of concessions to outside pressure groups. Once the committee stage is completed, the bill is then reported back to the House (the report stage) when the changes introduced in committee will be outlined. There is then a third reading of the bill, often done immediately after the report stage is concluded, and the debate on the third reading may culminate in a vote.

Where the measures proposed are controversial, both the government and the opposition will be anxious to have as many of their supporters voting as possible, and each may have issued a three line whip, which is an instruction to their supporters to attend and vote in accordance with instructions. The whip system is the means by which political parties control and organize their members in Parliament. There is a system of whipping in the Lords, but its principal importance is in relation to the activities of the House of Commons. The name comes originally from the world of hunting. The whipper-in is a hunt official charged with the control of the hounds. The word has now transferred itself to the Parliamentary context. A whip in Parliament is a person whose job it is to give information to his party members and to maintain discipline among them.

Once the bill successfully passes all its stages in both Houses, it receives the Royal Assent and becomes an Act of Parliament. It takes effect from the date on which it receives Royal Assent, or from the date of commencement set out in the Act itself, or from a date to be fixed in the future. Power to fix that date will usually by given to an appropriate minister. The Act then remains in force until it is repealed. Repeals are effected by exactly the same process. It is usual to refer to the Act by its short title, for example, the Sale of Goods Act 1979, or the Occupiers' Liability Act 1984. Unless the Act states to the contrary, it will apply throughout the UK.

Nowadays Acts of Parliament follow a fairly standard pattern.

Before setting out any of the main text there is a preamble which establishes the purpose of the Act. For example, the Drought Act 1976 begins: 'an Act to confer fresh powers to meet deficiencies in the supply of water due to exceptional shortage of rain and for connected purposes.' The main text is then divided into sections and sub-sections and, if appropriate, the whole Act will be set out in parts. Where the Act contains detailed lists, these will often be contained in a schedule to the Act. Most modern Acts have sections which deal with definitions, repeals, date of commencement and area of operation. The definition section in an Act of Parliament is important because within it, the draftsman of the Act can set out the precise meaning of a word for the purpose of that Act only. This can be of considerable help to a judge when he subsequently needs to interpret the exact meaning of the legislation. The repeals section will indicate which earlier Acts or regulations or parts of Acts and regulations have been repealed by the present Act.

Pressure groups

It is undoubtedly true today that in drawing up and seeking to implement its legislative programme, no government can afford to ignore the views of pressure groups. Joining a pressure group is one of the ways in which individuals have an opportunity to influence government decisions and future legislation. There are two main types of pressure groups – interest groups, where the group exists primarily to promote the interests of its own members (for example the Automobile Association or the National Farmers Union or the various trade unions) and cause groups, which are usually formed for the purpose of lobbying for a specific cause (for example Help the Aged, The National Society for the Prevention of Cruelty to Children and the Committee for Nuclear Disarmament).

The word 'lobbying' means influencing members of the legislature. The word itself derives from the practice of people meeting their MPs in the lobby of the House of Commons. The process of lobbying can be extended over a very long period and requires considerable energy, organization and resources to carry it out effectively. A large organization may employ professional lobbyists to pursue its cause.

The government of the day is likely to be influenced by pressure groups for a number of reasons – the pressure group may well be expert within its particular field or the government may need active cooperation from the members of the pressure group in order to implement its policies. Some pressure groups are immensely wealthy, and can promote their cause by advertising and other forms of publicity, while other pressure groups are powerful in terms of the significant proportion of the community which they represent.

Pressure groups can seek to exercise influence in a number of ways and at a number of points in the legislative process. Before any legislation is introduced, members of pressure groups may be represented on advisory bodies connected with appropriate government departments. If legislation is proposed, consultation with appropriate groups will frequently take place before a bill is introduced. A pressure group will always be working to advertise and promote its cause, possibly by liaising with sympathetic MPs, even when no immediate legislation is proposed. Once a bill has been introduced, MPs sympathetic to particular causes may participate at the detailed committee stage, when numbers of amendments to a bill may be proposed. At that point, the pressure group will wish to stay in touch with its 'tame' MPs. Even after an Act has been passed, a watching and monitoring role can be played by pressure groups who may seek changes by regulations if an Act is seen to have loopholes. Much of the success of a pressure group may depend on making and maintaining good personal contact with MPs, peers who sit regularly in the Lords, civil servants and ministers.

Delegated legislation

It can easily be seen that pressure on parliamentary time is so great that all the rules necessary in a complex modern society cannot be made in the laborious and time consuming way previously outlined. It is therefore common for Parliament to lay down a framework in an Act (an 'enabling Act') and then grant power to some other person or organization to make the detailed regulations. For example, by s.15 of the Health and Safety at Work etc. Act 1974, the Secretary of State has power to make regulations for any of the general purposes of that Act.

Delegated legislation can take one of three forms:

1 *Orders in Council* – where the rule-making power is vested in the Privy Council. This is normally confined to emergency situations and was much used during the Second World War.
2 *Statutory instruments* – this is the form commonly used when ministers make regulations by virtue of delegated powers.
3 *Bye-laws* – made by local authorities or other public bodies (e.g. British Rail) under powers granted to them by Parliament.

Although delegated legislation can be seen to be necessary and to have some advantages as a rule-making technique, there must be adequate control of the process. The advantages include:

- *Speed* – where there is an emergency or a temporary or rapidly changing situation.
- *Flexibility* – out-dated rules can be more easily changed.
- *Expertise* – consultation with outside bodies may harness the experience of technical and other experts.

Despite these advantages, it will be realized that rule making by these methods gives great power to persons who have not been elected. Critics of delegated legislation would argue that it vests too much power in the hands of the executive, and that scrutiny and control of the process are vital. That control may come through the procedures themselves, for example by delegating powers on strict terms to prevent abuse, or by subjecting any regulations proposed to an affirmative resolution procedure of one or both Houses of Parliament, or by requiring prior consultation with an advisory body.

If the power which had been granted is exceeded, control can be exercised by the application of the *ultra vires* principle. This would require a person aggrieved by the abuse of power to claim in court that the rule maker has acted outside the scope of his authority i.e. that his action has been *ultra vires*. If so found by the court, the *ultra vires* action will be declared to be void i.e. of no legal effect. Parliament itself is aware of the danger of abuse of power and has established a select committee of statutory instruments, usually known as the Scrutiny Committee, to act as a watchdog. Parliament might pass only ninety Acts of Parliament in any one year, yet in the same period more than 3000 Statutory Instruments might be made, so the potential size of the problem can be seen.

Statutory interpretation

When an Act of Parliament comes into force it may cause disputes as to its true meaning. The written word is not an exact form of communication and it will ultimately be the duty of the judges, when cases arise on disputed points in an Act, to determine the 'intention of Parliament'.

Faced with such a problem, the judge starts by looking at the Act itself. Most Acts contain a definition section, in which words will be given a specific meaning for the purposes of that Act only. For example in s.14 of the Unfair Contract Terms Act 1977, definitions are given of the words 'business', 'goods' and 'notice', thereby giving those words a specific and restricted meaning confined to that Act. 'Business' is defined there as including a profession and the activities of any government department or local or public authority.

Where no definition is given within the Act itself, a judge may take the meaning of a word from a dictionary, but if he does so, he must bear in mind the principle expressed in Latin, *'noscitur a sociis'* which means 'a word is known by the company it keeps'. The meaning of a word may well be governed by the context in which it is used, e.g. in the phrase used in another Act, 'interest, annuities or other annual payments', the word 'interest' means annual interest. The judge may also turn to the Interpretation Act 1978 which gives meanings for standard phrases and expressions like day, week and month. And again, the word or phrase in question may have been interpreted and applied in an earlier case heard by the court, so that the present judge would be obliged by the rule of judicial precedent to accept that meaning in the case before him.

Assuming that these aids do not solve the problem, the judge may then adopt one of the following approaches to the question:

1   *The literal approach* – this approach dictates that words should be given their ordinary, plain and natural meaning, even if this produces an absurd result. Judges favouring this approach take the view that it is then Parliament's responsibility to put the situation right by amending the law. In using this approach, two general rules of construction should be remembered:

   (a) The *euisdem generis* rule – when specific words are followed by general words, the general words must be read in the light of the specific words. For example, 'on a pond, lake, river, canal or other water'. By applying this rule, these words would be read to include a reservoir but not the open sea. It is clearly intended by the specific words to confine the stretches of water to inland water.

   (b) The rule *'expressio unius est exclusio alterius'* – if one thing is specifically mentioned in the Act, the Act is presumed not to apply to another e.g. some sections of an Act may refer to the seller and the buyer. A subsequent section mentioning only the seller is presumed not to apply to the buyer.

The literal approach to interpretation is not favoured by some judges. One judge has said: 'When a defect appears a judge cannot simply fold his hands and blame the draftsman.'

2   *The golden rule* – this allows the judge to interpret so as to avoid the absurdity, or to avoid a result which is inconsistent with the Act itself or common law principles. This approach was used in *Re Sigsworth*, in a case where a man claimed his mother's property, despite having murdered her. Under the Act which governed the distribution of her property, this ought to have been shared amongst her children. The son was the only child. The judge held

that the common law rule that a murderer cannot benefit from the person he has murdered, prevailed over the clear words of the Act.

3   *The mischief rule* – another approach adopted where the judge looks to see which defect of the law is intended to be corrected by the Act and then interprets to correct the defect.

A simple example from a case may illustrate some of the problems of interpretation faced by judges. In a case concering single payments under the old Supplementary Benefit scheme, a claimant requested a single payment to help towards the purchase of wallpaper to redecorate her lounge and kitchen. The wording of the appropriate regulation required that payments could only be made in respect of expenses of *essential* internal redecoration. The court had to consider what was the meaning of the word 'essential'. It was not defined anywhere in the Supplementary Benefits Act 1976 or the relevant Regulations and it fell, therefore, to be given its ordinary meaning in everyday use. When a dictionary was consulted, the *Shorter Oxford English Dictionary* gave two rather differing meanings of the word 'essential'. It can mean 'material' or 'important' in the sense of 'your work is essential to the success of this project', or it can mean 'indispensably requisite', as for example, 'water is an essential ingredient of a cup of tea'. Relying on the stricter meaning of the word, the benefit officer had refused a single payment. On appeal to the tribunal, however, the judge favoured the less strict interpretation of the word. He was guided in doing so by the fact that the same word 'essential' was used elsewhere in the Regulations, where its meaning tended to be 'material' and 'important' rather than 'indispensably requisite'.

No one instructs a judge as to which of these approaches he should use. It is clear that the process of interpreting and applying Acts of Parliament gives considerable power to the judges. But their role in the law-making process is not limited to the interpretation of statutes because the other principal source of law is judicial precedent (binding decisions of the judges).

Judicial precedent

When a judge gives his decision in a case before him, this has two elements:

1   The actual decision affecting the parties, e.g. he finds X to be liable and that X must pay damages to Y of £1000,
2   The principles of law which have caused the judge to arrive at that decision.

Where the case concerns facts or situations which are comparable with earlier cases heard by the courts, the judge will normally apply the principles from the earlier cases. In one well-known case, a soft-drinks manufacturer was held to be liable to the ultimate consumer who had suffered physical harm by drinking a bottle of the manufacturer's ginger beer which was contaminated by the remains of a decomposed snail. If, on a future occasion, a court hears a case brought by a person made ill by eating a pie containing a dead mouse, the same principles can be applied. By analogy these principles may be extended further. The principle in the 'ginger beer' case was actually applied to a later case where a person contracted dermatitis because of wearing underpants where chemicals had been left in the material during their manufacture.

Although many systems of law in practice apply this principle of deciding cases in the same way as previous cases of a similar nature, the English system goes further. The judge is bound by the earlier decisions, hence the system is often referred to as the system of binding precedent. One difficulty presented by this technique lies in finding the actual part of the case which is binding. When a judge gives a decision, his legal reasoning, when set out in the law reports, can be several pages long. Much of what he says may relate to why he rejected other arguments put to him by counsel, or what would have influenced him if the facts had been slightly different. These parts of his judgement are not binding in later cases. They are 'said by the way' or in legal terms, '*obiter dicta*'. The judge in a later case must search to find the rule of law upon which the decision is based, properly called the '*ratio decidendi*'.

The process of identifying the ratio is a vital part of the training of a lawyer. In each case the first step is to establish the material facts. For example, Mrs Smith, a mother of four aged forty-five, knocked down and injured Mr Brown last Friday. The accident was caused because Mrs Smith had gone to sleep at the wheel. The only material facts here are that a motorist injured a pedestrian by driving negligently. Once the material facts have been established, if they correspond with the material facts of an earlier decision, the judge will usually be bound by the earlier case. However, a judge is normally only bound by decisions given in a court superior to his own. This allows the system to be flexible (as it is open to a higher court, on appeal, to overrule or reverse his decision) but certain (as it obliges lower courts to follow the decisions of higher courts). The structure of the courts is considered in Chapter 2.

Advantages and disadvantages of the system of precedent

One of the greatest advantages of the system of binding precedent is that the rules have evolved from real-life cases and are, therefore, essentially practical. Again, the 'binding' feature of the system makes it reasonably certain. However, two major criticisms are often levelled against the system. The first is that it creates a bulky system of very detailed rules which requires the production, at considerable expense, of large numbers of law reports to enable the previous cases to be checked and quoted. A more significant problem is that the system can be very uncertain, due to the powerful role played by the judges. Consider the case where a judge is faced with a precedent which in theory is binding on him, but which he prefers not to apply. There is a technique called 'distinguishing' one case from another which may allow him to avoid applying the earlier decision. The judge is allowed to distinguish (and therefore not apply) any case where the material facts are not the same as in the case before him. When this technique is properly used it allows the law to be flexible. When improperly used it results in hair-splitting distinctions, which can leave two apparently conflicting decisions reported in the casebooks.

So that the system of binding precedent can function effectively there must be a well-organized procedure for reporting cases and there must be an established hierarchy of the courts. Generally, lower courts are bound by their own previous decisions and by those of higher courts.

If a person is dissatisfied with the outcome of his case he may have grounds for appeal. The final court of appeal in the English system is the House of Lords. Until 1966, even the House of Lords was bound by its own previous decisions, but it was then announced that: 'Their Lordships propose to modify their present practice, and while treating former decisions of this House as normally binding, to depart from a previous decision when it appears right to do so.' The most recent example of such a departure can be seen in Murphy v. Brentwood D. C. in 1990 (see page 212).

Applying a precedent

Examples taken from actual cases demonstrate how the case law system works. To see how the normal processes of applying a precedent operate, look first at a case from 1932, *Donoghue v. Stevenson*. A manufacturer of ginger beer which was marketed in an opaque bottle was held to be liable to the ultimate consumer of the drink in the tort of negligence. (A tort is a civil wrong.) The consumer had become ill on discovering the remains of a decomposed snail in the bottle. If this precedent had subsequently been confined by judges to sets of facts involving drinks sold in opaque bottles its value as a precedent would have been very limited. However, in 1936, another court seized the opportunity to extend the scope of the precedent. In the case of *Grant v. Australian Knitting Mills*, the plaintiff, Dr Grant, had purchased a pair of long woollen underpants, manufactured by the defendants. He contracted a severe form of dermatitis after wearing them, shown to have been caused by excessive amounts of sulphur which had not been successfully washed out during the manufacturing process. Were the defendants liable? The judges examined the Donoghue case, and extracted from it the following statement of principle:

> A manufacturer of products which he sells in such form that he intends them to reach the ultimate consumer with no reasonable possibility of intermediate examination, and where the absence of reasonable care in the preparation of the products will result in injury to the consumer, owes a duty to the consumer to take reasonable care.

Undoubtedly a manufacturer of underpants must realize that potential customers cannot carry out scientific tests to measure sulphur levels before purchasing, and the courts had no difficulty in applying the Donoghue principle. If the court in the Grant case had thought the principle was unsound, it could have sought to distinguish the two cases on the ground that the material facts were not similar. For example, the snail case concerned goods to be consumed internally, whereas the underpants case concerned goods to be worn externally. Such fine distinctions could have been justified if the earlier precedent had been unpopular for any reason, but the law develops best when the scope of a sound principle is gradually extended.

Common law and equity

The expression 'common law' is frequently used and can have a number of meanings. It may mean the law which is common throughout England. Indeed the phrase was originally used in that sense to distinguish it from local rules and customs. The expression may also mean rules developed through precedents, rather than created by Acts of Parliament. It may further be used to mean rules which are not derived from equity. An unusual system emerged in England between the twelfth century and 1875 whereby a completely separate system of courts developed, administering quite separate rules – the principles of equity. These rules were usually developed to meet situations where the common law had no remedy to offer or where the common law was in some way deficient or unjust. The equitable principles are discretionary in nature and, since 1875, have been administered side by side with the rules of common law. If the two sets of rules should ever conflict, the principles of equity will prevail.

2

Settlement of disputes

In any situation where things go wrong, causing a dispute or conflict between people or organizations, the parties involved may think of turning to the 'law' for a remedy or a solution. So if you have bought faulty goods, or want to claim against a motorist who has damaged your car, or are owed money and want to recover the debt, you may wish to take proceedings in the courts against the relevant party. It would be wrong to think only of the courts when considering the settlement of disputes. Some measures of self-help can be very effective, and in other cases the parties may prefer the privacy of arbitration proceedings. Sometimes legislation has provided that a forum other than the courts is more appropriate for the settlement of disputes, for example those cases where any rights must be pursued through specialized tribunals. There are also occasions where a dispute reveals no cause of action capable of being pursued through the courts, and in those cases it may be that conciliation procedures or intervention by the Ombudsman may be more appropriate. The scope of these various procedures is considered separately.

Self-help

Where a dispute arises between parties, it may be possible to settle matters by negotiation without the need to go to court. For example, in the law of trespass the person in possession of land can ask the trespasser to leave, and if he does not do so, may then use a reasonable amount of force to eject him. What is reasonable will vary with the circumstances of each case. More specialized examples of self-help can be found in the rules relating to set-off and lien. Set-off can occur where one party owes money to another, and is in turn owed money by that other. So if A owes B £10, and B owes A £5, then A may set-off the £5 he is owed by B and thereby reduce the amount he must pay to B.

A lien is the right of a person in possession of goods which belong to someone else to retain them until some demand, usually a demand for payment, has been met. This remedy can be particularly useful to people such as garage owners who have carried out expensive repairs on a vehicle. They can hold on to the vehicle, i.e. exercise their right of lien, until their bill is paid.

These are legally recognized forms of self-help, but less formal methods may be equally effective. Large numbers of pressure groups now exist which may support individuals who have grievances or who are involved in disputes. The power of the press and the media can sometimes achieve more than the use of formal legal procedures. Moreover, the intervention of an advice agency may be sufficient to prompt the other party to a dispute to resolve matters without resorting to court action.

Court procedures

If proceedings in court become necessary, it will quickly be realized that there is an elaborate system of courts, both civil and criminal. However, the vast majority of cases are disposed of by the inferior, or lower, courts at first instance. In criminal law, for example, more than 90 per cent of all cases are dealt with by the Magistrates Courts.

Courts of first instance are where cases are first heard. The complicated system of courts in England results from their haphazard development over hundreds of years. In an attempt to rationalize the system and concentrate courts in the places where they were most needed, major reforms of the system took place in 1970 and 1971. The present structure can be seen in Figure 1 where possible rights of appeals are indicated by the arrows.

Figure 1 shows that the House of Lords is the highest court of appeal for both civil and criminal cases in our English legal system. It is also the final court of appeal for civil cases from Scotland. The court can sit with a minimum of three judges, but cases are usually heard by five Lords of Appeal in Ordinary. One judge will be appointed from Scotland and another from Northern Ireland. Other judges who may sit in the House of Lords are the Lord Chancellor, any ex Lord Chancellors, the Master of the Rolls and other peers who have held

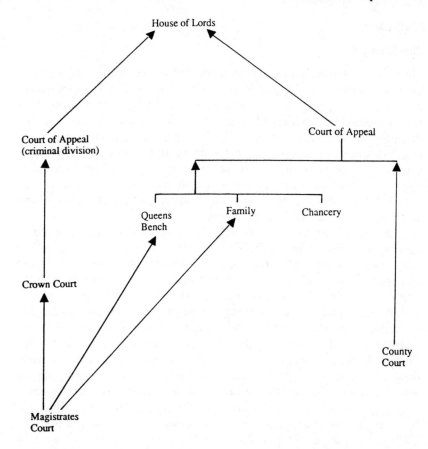

Figure 1   *Court procedures structure*

high judicial office. Hearings of the court take place in the House of Lords at Westminster and all cases coming before the court will involve points of law of general public importance. Leave of the court below is necessary before an appeal can be brought. Not surprisingly, only a very small proportion of cases can reach this level of the court structure, not least because of the expense involved. In Figure 1, courts which principally hear criminal cases are shown on the left side. Whereas some courts have exclusively criminal jurisdiction, for example the Court of Appeal Criminal Division, other courts have a mixed jurisdiction to hear both civil and criminal cases, for example, the Magistrates Courts. Others hear only civil cases, for example the County Courts.

Civil cases

The County Court

The Country Court is a local court involved with settling civil disputes between individuals. However, one of those individuals may be a large company or public corporation or a nationalized industry. It is sometimes said that when it becomes necessary to use a court to settle a dispute, this is a sign of failure. The failure is on the part of the parties to compromise or reach some satisfactory settlement between themselves. It is often much more satisfactory to accept some kind of compromise rather than embark on litigation (bringing an action to the court). Litigation involves stress, expenditure of time and money and uncertainty about the final outcome.

The jurisdiction of the County Court was previously limited to claims worth less than £5,000. Changes introduced by the Courts and Legal Services Act 1990 mean that, in future, there will be a more flexible system for allocating work between the County Court and the High Court. The County Court is a local court, and to commence an action there, one of the following conditions must be satisfied: either the defendant must reside in the district; or the defendant must carry on business in the district; or the cause of action must have arisen in the district. Cases are started by giving the County Court the necessary details so that a summons can be served. The person bringing the action is called the plaintiff, while the person against whom the action is brought is the defendant. To serve the summons the plaintiff will have to pay the appropriate fee to the Court. This is worked out on a sliding scale, depending on the amount claimed. If a plaintiff is totally successful in his claim he will ultimately recover his fee.

Once the defendant receives the summons he may accept that he owes the money involved and pay up in full. It is more likely that he will wish to dispute the claim in whole or in part, and then he must send in his defence and any counter-claim he may have. The forms sent to him provide him with places to fill in these details. If the defendant does nothing at all in response to a summons, then the plaintiff will obtain judgement, and may then want to use the various procedures available through the County Court to enforce the judgement.

Once the defendant sends in his defence and/or his counter-claim, a date will be fixed for a pre-trial review in front of the District Judge of the County Court. Very often a settlement between the parties can be reached at this stage. Even if no settlement is reached, the value of the pre-trial review is that it is possible for the District Judge to see on which points the parties agree, and on which they remain in dispute.

He can decide what evidence it will be necessary for the parties to produce, and he can assess how long must be set aside for the trial of the case. Where necessary a date will be fixed for the trial. That may take place before the District Judge, where the amount claimed is small, or before a Circuit Judge.

Where the amount claimed is less than £500 the parties are encouraged to appear without professional representation and the arbitration (by the District Judge) will be conducted extremely informally. The rules of evidence will not be strictly adhered to. Arbitration in this context is quite different from commercial arbitrations which will be considered separately (see page 29).

Where there is to be a formal trial, this will be a proper hearing in open court, with 'wigs and gowns', and subject to the operation of the rules of evidence, such as giving evidence on oath. This is in contrast with the less formal atmosphere of the pre-trial review, and those cases which are set down for arbitration. If the plaintiff succeeds in his case, and a judgement is given in his favour, then he must hope that the defendant will comply with the terms of that judgement. Very often the judgement directs the payment of money, sometimes in a lump sum, or sometimes by stated instalments. If the defendant defaults, the plaintiff will need to use the procedures provided through the County Court to enforce his judgement. He may consider using execution. This consists of sending the court bailiff to seize sufficient goods of the defendant to satisfy the judgment against him. When the bailiff arrives, the defendant is given a further chance to pay, and many defendants do so at this stage. If it does become necessary for the bailiff to seize goods, they will be removed and sold by auction. All the costs involved in doing this will be added to what the defendant owes.

Where the defendant is in employment, a plaintiff may consider an attachment of earnings order as a method of enforcing his judgement. In essence this consists of the court informing the employer that he must deduct a specified weekly or monthly sum from the earnings of the defendant and pay that sum directly to the court. There is a protected earnings amount fixed by the court so that, in any week or month, the defendant must always be permitted to retain that amount of his wages or salary.

Where a defendant is beset by multiple debts and is being harassed by a number of creditors, he may consider asking the court to make an administration order. Effectively the result of this order is to consolidate all the debts, and the court will the decide the amount which is to be distributed pro rata amongst the creditors. The value of an administration order is that it relieves the debtor of the burden of dealing with all his separate creditors and ensures some fairness and uniformity of treatment between those creditors. It is a step short of bankruptcy, so of course it is essential that the debtor must be able to pay something regularly, as the order can only run for three years.

Where the defendant is hopelessly in debt, with no means to pay off the debts, the law provides the bankruptcy procedure to allow him to rid himself of those debts. Inevitably there is a price to be paid by the debtor, as there is still considerable social stigma attached to bankruptcy and an undischarged bankrupt is under a number of penalties. For example, it is a criminal offence for him to obtain credit of any kind, such as a bank loan or hire purchase, without revealing that he is an undischarged bankrupt.

Where the defendant owns property, for example his own house, the plaintiff may consider enforcing a judgment by means of a charging order on the property. If the defendant then sells the property, the plaintiff will have a claim against the proceeds of the sale. The drawback of this method of enforcement is that the plaintiff may have a long wait for his money.

In certain types of case coming before the County Court, for example bad neighbour disputes, the court may make an order called an injunction ordering the defendant to do, or stop doing, a particular thing. If the defendant ignores the injunction, his behaviour is then said to be in contempt of court, and he could be sent to prison. This is the ultimate sanction which ensures the injunctions are usually obeyed.

Much of the work of the County Court relates in one way or another to problems of debt. Of the 2.6 million cases commenced in the County Court in 1989, just over 90 per cent related to claims for money. Possession of land and personal injuries were the next largest categories. The Court also has extensive family and domestic jurisdiction covering divorce, maintenance, distribution of property of the parties to a divorce, access to children, wardship and adoption. The County Court also has the power to grant injunctions in domestic violence situations, the effect of which is, where necessary, to exclude one party from the matrimonial home.

The High Court

Where a civil case is outside the jurisdiction of the County Court, proceedings must be commenced in the appropriate division of the High Court. The High Court sits mainly in London but, since the passing of the Courts Act 1971, a number of centres have been designated throughout the country for High Court hearings. There are three divisions of the court. The Family Division hears cases involving divorce and children; Chancery hears cases involving trusts and wills; Queen's Bench hears cases involving breach of contract or negligence.

One particular aspect of the work of the Queen's Bench Division of the High Court is its supervisory jurisdiction over inferior courts and tribunals. The Queen's Bench Division has the power to grant orders of mandamus, for example, to compel the performance of some public duty imposed by the law on a particular person or body. Where an inferior court or tribunal has acted unlawfully, or in some way exceeded its power, the Queen's Bench Division may quash the decision of the inferior court or tribunal by making an order of certiorari. This procedure could be used when the inferior court or tribunal has acted in ignorance of the principles of natural justice.

The Court of Appeal and the House of Lords

Appeals from the County Court and the High Court in civil cases are heard by the Court of Appeal, which is presided over by the Master of the Rolls, and which normally sits with a quorum of three Lords Justices of Appeal. Hearings take place in London. If cases reach this level of appeal, it is likely that they involve some important point of law or a new application of existing principles, and the case may well be important as a precedent for the future. As a last resort, there is a final appeal, with leave, to the House of Lords. Appeals are usually heard by five Lords of Appeal in Ordinary. Exceptionally, some appeals go direct to the House of Lords from the High Court, using a 'leap-frog' procedure.

Criminal cases

The Magistrates Court

The scope of the criminal law is much wider than merely dealing with cases like murder and theft. Today no business, industrial or commercial organization can ignore the criminal law as there is a wide range of statutory offences e.g. trade descriptions or offences under the Health and Safety at Work Act 1974.

All criminal cases begin in the Magistrates Court. The process used there will depend upon whether the offence is less serious (a summary offence) or more serious (an indictable offence) or an offence triable either way (either summarily or on indictment depending on a number of factors). With summary offences the trial takes place in the Magistrates Court, usually before a bench of three magistrates. With indictable offences, the role of the Magistrates Court is to hold a preliminary hearing to establish if there is a sufficient case made out for it to be committed to the Crown Court for trial. These are committal proceedings. If the offence is an 'either way' offence, then it could be tried in the Magistrates Court in appropriate cases, or otherwise committal proceedings will be held to send that case to the Crown Court.

The work in the Magistrates Court is undertaken by a bench of magistrates or justices of the peace. Historically their office is a very ancient one, and can be traced back to the thirteenth century. In those early days, much of their work was administrative rather than judicial. They were selected for their local knowledge and that still continues to be a feature of their appointment today. Magistrates are appointed by the Lord Chancellor in the name of the Queen. The only qualification for office is that a magistrate must live within fifteen miles of the commission area for which he is appointed. There is an explanatory booklet published by the Lord Chancellor: *The Appointment and Duties of Justices of the Peace in England and Wales*. This booklet makes clear that certain persons will not be appointed, for example, those over the age of sixty, persons convicted of certain offences, undischarged bankrupts, persons whose sight or hearing is impaired, persons who are serving members of the armed forces or members of the police forces. Magistrates must be British subjects, both men and women are eligible, and there are no property qualifications. Names of potential magistrates are put forward to the Lord Chancellor by advisory committees whose constitution is kept secret. This is to prevent the committees being pressured or lobbied. Candidates can have their names put forward by various groups or organizations, but it is also possible for a candidate to put himself forward. In making appointments to a particular bench, the Lord Chancellor must aim to achieve a balance in terms of sex and politics, as well as seeking to reflect different occupations and backgrounds. This balance is important for maintaining general public confidence in Magistrates Courts.

Before appointment, every person selected to be a magistrate must undertake to complete the required training, as well as agreeing to undertake a fair share of the duties of a magistrate. Preliminary training has been obligatory since 1966. This is designed to ensure that the magistrate learns to act judicially; obtains a sufficient knowledge of the law to follow normal cases; obtains a working knowledge of the law of evidence; understands the nature and purpose of the sentences a magistrate imposes; and understands the relationship which should exist between magistrates and court officials. Once the preliminary training has been completed a magistrate may then sit in court, initially as an observer. Training will also include instruction from the clerk of the court, and there will be visits to institutions like prisons. Further refresher training is available throughout the period of service as a magistrate which may include training for work in the juvenile court or for sitting in the Crown Court.

A new magistrate will sit with at least one and usually two other more experienced magistrates, and although he has an equal voice in the decision making, it is likely that he will learn initially from his more experienced colleagues. None of the training is designed particularly to turn magistrates into legal experts. It has always been regarded as a particular strength of the magistracy that people are judged by their fellow men who bring sound judgment and common sense to the task. On questions of law the magistrates will be guided by the clerk to the justices.

The clerk is in charge of the administration of the Magistrates Court, as well as being its chief legal adviser. In large urban courts the clerk will usually have a sizeable staff including deputy clerks, clerical staff, finance and accounting staff and court ushers. The range of the clerk's functions will be extensive, covering the organization of courts, the sitting of magistrates and their training. When advising the magistrates, the clerk is restricted to advising on law and procedure and should not participate in their decision on the facts.

Where an accused person pleads guilty before the magistrates the hearing will consist largely of any plea in mitigation, together with enough information about the offence and the circumstances in which it was committed to enable the magistrates to impose an appropriate sentence. Where an accused pleads not guilty, a full trial takes place. The accused may be represented by a solicitor. It is for the prosecution to prove its case beyond all reasonable doubt. A person is presumed to be innocent until proved guilty. Each side may call witnesses to give evidence who can then be cross-examined by the other side. Other evidence may also be available, for example clothing, weapons, photographs. The press may be present to report the case and the court has a public gallery where any member of the public may come to hear the proceedings. If the magistrate finds the accused not guilty, he is acquitted. If he is found guilty he must then be sentenced to an appropriate punishment. The magistrates may order an absolute discharge at one end of the scale or may commit the guilty person to prison at the other. Between these extremes they may fine the offender or put him on probation or sentence him to a community service order. In deciding the appropriate sentence magistrates will have regard to the needs of society as well as the needs of the offender himself. It should be borne in mind that as well as ordering a suitable punishment, courts will be anxious to seek to rehabilitate offenders.

Where the penalty imposed is a fine, the court maintains systems whereby such moneys can be collected. An offender may ask for time to pay. If a fine remains unpaid, one of the ways to remedy that situation is for the court to employ a bailiff. He will then be empowered to seize goods from the debtor ('levying distress') sufficient to cover the amount of the unpaid fine, together with the costs involved. This can be a very effective procedure where the debtor is a company or business with substantial assets, but it tends to be less effective when used against private individuals who may be unemployed and without any worthwhile assets. There are limits on the penalties which magistrates can impose. Usually they may not sentence a person to longer than six months in prison, or impose a fine greater than £1,000. In some cases, the offence in question may carry a maximum penalty fixed by Parliament. Inevitably, that maximum will become out of date, because of the effects of inflation. To counter this problem, the Criminal Justice Act 1982 fixes standard scales of fines, from scale 1 to scale 5, and the maximum represented by these scales can be adjusted from time to time by order of the Secretary of State.

Some of the main criticisms levelled against Magistrates Courts relate to the magistrates themselves. They are sometimes perceived as middle aged, middle class, professional people. There has been a recent trend to try to appoint younger magistrates, but inevitably as they can serve until they are seventy, some will be elderly. It is generally desirable that a bench should be well balanced, and no doubt the Lord Chancellor would like to appoint more wage earners, but many feel that taking the necessary time off work to fulfil their magisterial obligations (probably a minimum of one half day per fortnight) could interfere with their position at work.

The strength of the system of lay magistrates undoubtedly lies in the appointment of local people with local knowledge who give their services free. An alternative would be to appoint the necessary number of stipendiary magistrates (legally qualified, full-time paid magistrates) but this would be costly, and would deprive the system of a feature, the lay element, in which the public appears to have faith. However, in large conurbations it is common to appoint a number of stipendiaries.

The Crown Court

The Crown Court was established in 1971, replacing the former Assizes and Quarter Sessions. The Crown Court was created as a direct result of the recommendations made in a Royal Commission Report under the chairmanship of Lord Beeching, to attempt to deal more conveniently, efficiently and economically with the workload of cases. The new court was designed to simplify the previous structure of courts; to use judges as flexibly as possible; and to position the courts in places where they were most needed and where the public had best access to them. In order to create maximum flexibility within the Crown Court it was decided to create centres operating at three different levels. First-tier centres can undertake all types of criminal work, and additionally can be used by High Court judges to hear civil cases. Second-tier centres can hear the full range of criminal cases, but undertake no civil work. Third-tier centres are visited only by circuit judges and District Judges, which inevitably curtails the range of criminal work that they can undertake.

Cases in the Crown Court can be heard by a number of different types of judge. These are either the High Court judges who are not permanently present in the Crown Court, but visit at intervals and then hear the most serious cases; the circuit judges, a new rank created by the Courts Act 1971 whose task is to staff the County Courts and to undertake a significant part of the relatively serious crime workload of the Crown Courts; or the recorders, who are part-time judges appointed from the ranks of practising barristers or solicitors, who generally undertake to sit for a minimum of four weeks each year.

The Crown Court has considerable flexibility in the range of judicial manpower available to it, so cases can be listed according to their degree of seriousness for hearing by the most appropriate type of judge. Cases are classified in four categories. Class 1 offences are of the most serious type, for example murder or offences under the Official Secrets Act 1911. These cases are tried by a High Court judge. Class 2 offences, for example manslaughter or rape, are usually tried by a High Court judge, but may be released to a circuit judge. Class 3 offences, which are all crimes not falling into any of the other categories, can be tried by a High Court judge, circuit judge or recorder, but would usually be heard by a circuit judge. Class 4 offences include all offences triable either way where the defendant has elected to be tried at the Crown Court. Class 4 offences will usually be heard by a recorder.

The role of the court listing officer is vital in ensuring a smooth flow of cases through the court. He will be aiming to have courts sitting in all of his available court rooms and will need to gauge the approximate length of the cases. He will be guided by his knowledge of the number of witnesses to be called and his experience of past cases. The administrators in the courts are well aware that judicial time is an expensive commodity, and that sittings need to be organized to maximize the use of the judges available. An effective system of justice should aim to bring cases to trial as early as possible, bearing in mind the constraints of preparing a case and getting together for the hearing all the advocates and witnesses involved.

In cases in the Crown Court where the accused pleads not guilty, the court will sit with a jury to try the case. The jurors will have been summoned at random. Those eligible must be registered as electors, aged between eighteen and sixty-five, and ordinarily resident in the UK. Some people are ineligible for jury service, for example police officers. Some are disqualified from jury service, for example certain people with criminal records. Some people may seek to be excused from jury service, for example MPs or doctors. There are no property qualifications nowadays. Jurors are paid travelling and subsistence allowances and compensation for loss of earnings.

The use of the jury is another example of the use of laymen in the English legal system. The rules used to demand that a jury of twelve recorded a unanimous verdict but now a judge can accept a ten to two majority verdict. If the jury cannot reach a majority verdict it must be discharged, a fresh jury sworn in and the case reheard.

The practice of using juries is often criticized, on the grounds that it is an expensive system to operate; that jurors may not have the necessary intellectual skills, particularly in long and complex fraud cases; that juries may be swayed by professional advocates and make their decisions for the wrong reasons; that jurors are pressed into service and some are very reluctant; and that jurors could more easily be approached and bribed than judges. Apart from small changes in the rules about eligibility and some changes regarding the number of jurors who may be challenged without cause and required to step down, there are no plans to radically alter or dispense with the system of jury trial.

If an accused is found guilty in the Crown Court he will be sentenced by the judge on the basis of guidelines suggested by the Court of Appeal, which include taking into account any previous convictions. The judge will be aware of the maximum penalties which can be imposed for various offences. A sentence will be imposed in respect of each offence for which the accused is convicted but where there are several sentences these are frequently made to run concurrently. Where the sentence is one of imprisonment the court has the power to make it suspended, so that the person convicted will only serve the sentence if he re-offends during the period of suspension.

Appeals from the Crown Court lie to the Court of Appeal and may be against conviction and/or sentence. Where the appeal is against conviction, it may be allowed if the Court of Appeal considers that the verdict of the jury was unsafe; or that there has been a wrong decision on a question of law; or that there has been some material irregularity in the trial. Further appeal lies to the House of Lords.

Tribunals

A significant feature of dispute-solving since 1945 has been the rise in the number of tribunals created by Act of Parliament to deal with specific questions. Common examples of tribunals are the Industrial Tribunals, Rent Tribunals, Social Security Appeal Tribunals and Medical Appeal Tribunals. The reasons for this trend are:

- The volume of work could not be given to the ordinary courts as the system would have become overloaded.
- The questions to be resolved by tribunals are frequently specialized, and the expertise of specialists can be used in the decision making.
- Tribunals can dispose of cases quickly, cheaply and informally.

Each type of tribunal has its constitution fixed by the statute creating it. For example, under the Social Security Act 1975 a Medical Appeal Tribunal (which determines questions of disablement arising from industrial injuries) consists of a legally qualified chairman and two medical specialists. The tribunal may have its own appeal structure created by the statute. For example, appeals from the Medical Appeal Tribunal lie to a Social Security Commissioner.

The outcome of the type of case being heard by tribunals can have important financial consequences for a claimant, e.g. if he is refused a pension. Many of the rules of law applied are complex, yet there is no legal aid available to pay for a claimant to be legally represented at the hearing. Despite the intention that the proceedings should be informal, lack of proper representation may put a claimant at a considerable disadvantage. If he considers that the tribunal has given the wrong decision he may be able to appeal. However, if he considers that the proceedings have been improperly conducted, he may apply to the High Court, asking it to exercise its supervisory powers over the tribunal. The High Court can interfere if it can be shown that the tribunal has failed to abide by the principles of natural justice, which require that each party is given the opportunity to put his case forward, and that the tribunal is not biased in favour of one side.

Arbitration

Going to court can be an expensive, public and time-consuming activity for the parties to a dispute. It may be better to agree to arbitrate, when the parties themselves can exercise some control over the choice of arbitrator. This process is particularly useful where a dispute involves points of a technical nature. In some types of contract (e.g. building contracts) it is common for the parties to agree not to refer disputes arising from those contracts to the court until they have submitted to arbitration. Then, if a dispute does arise, it will be a breach of contract if one of the parties tries to take the case to court instead of using the arbitration agreement. Although the parties must finance the arbitration themselves, the process has obvious appeal because of its speed and privacy. Once the arbitrator gives his decision (award), it can be enforced like a court judgment.

The law governing arbitrations is to be found in the Arbitration Acts 1950–1979 together with the general principles of the law of contract. For the Act to apply there must be a 'written agreement to submit present or future differences to arbitration'. The written agreement need not name the arbitrator, and if necessary the court can appoint a suitable person. The most usual course is for the parties to agree that the arbitrator will be nominated by some outside body or organization e.g. Association of British Travel Agents, or the local Chamber of Trade or the President of the RIBA. The arbitration can be undertaken by one person but sometimes, as a variation, each side may be required by the terms of the agreement to appoint an arbitrator. The two arbitrators may then appoint an umpire who would decide the issue if the two arbitrators should be unable to agree. The JCT standard form building contract provides for the appointment of a single arbitrator.

On normal contractual principles, the two parties to an arbitration agreement are free to fix the terms of their own agreement. They are precluded from ousting the jurisdiction of the court, as this is regarded as contrary to public policy. In effect, this means that they cannot insert a clause stating that the arbitration is final and that neither party may have any recourse to the courts. The courts have power to supervise arbitrations, and may remove an arbitrator who has misconducted himself.

A number of terms are implied into an arbitration agreement by the Arbitration Act 1950 unless the parties have agreed otherwise. These include that the parties to the agreement must be prepared to be examined on oath by the arbitrator; that they must produce all documents required by the arbitrator; that the arbitration will be final and binding on the parties; and that the arbitrator can award costs.

Once the arbitrator makes his decision, 'the award', it can be enforced just like a court order or judgment. The parties are more likely to find the decision of an arbitrator acceptable but they pay a high price for this alternative to court proceedings as they are responsible for financing the arbitration proceedings.

The distinction between arbitration and valuation has always been regarded as problematic. In arbitration the aim is to settle an existing dispute. A valuation seeks to prevent a dispute arising, by allowing a third party to fix the value or price. The distinction is not always clear and the third party may be anxious to be sure of his status, as a valuer can be sued for negligence but an arbitrator cannot. This was an important point in issue in the case of *Sutcliffe v. Thackrah* in 1974, where an architect issued an interim certificate on the basis of which his employer paid the contractor. The employer subsequently sacked the contractor and wanted to recover damages from him for proven shoddy work. The contractor went into liquidation, so the employer then sued his architect for his negligence in certifying the poor work. In issuing the certificate, does the architect act as a valuer or an aribitrator? Once the architect issues a certificate, the employer is then obliged to pay. But the architect is *not* at that point determining a dispute between the employer and the contractor, although his duty when certifying is to act impartially between them. In consequence the architect in this case could be held liable for his negligent certification.

Administrative control

Where a dispute involves allegations of maladministration by a local or central government department or agency it may be possible to refer the dispute to the appropriate Commissioner for Administration (often referred to as the Ombudsman), who can investigate the complaint and make recommendations for putting the matter right. Unfortunately, the Commissioners have no power to order anyone to do anything, but the publicity attached to their reports may be sufficient to make a defaulting person or body act differently.

Affording the law

Where the ordinary man in the street is a party to a dispute, many of the procedures outlined above may seem inhibiting to him, either because he fears what it may cost to be involved with 'the law', or because he doubts his ability to cope with complex rules and procedures. If he wants to engage a lawyer to advise him, what will that cost him? To what extent can he be helped financially to afford the services of a lawyer? The answer lies in the legal aid and advice scheme. The scheme provides:

1   *For the provision of advice and assistance* – under the rules of the Legal Advice scheme, a solicitor may do anything which is normally regarded as part of his work, short of actually starting legal proceedings. He can write letters, negotiate, draw up documents, take statements, or prepare a written case for a client to use himself

at a tribunal. There is, however, a twofold financial restriction:

(a) The client requiring advice must be financially eligible. The solicitor will make his calculation as to this on a special form (the Green Form). He can determine whether the client is within the scope of the legal advice scheme, and if so, what contribution if any he must make towards the cost of the solicitor's service. The client's 'disposable income' and 'disposable capital' are calculated by reference to fixed criteria.

(b) The solicitor who wishes to aid a client by using the scheme may not undertake more than £50 worth of work unless he obtains prior permission from the Legal Aid Area Office to increase that figure.

2 *For the provision of actual representation in court proceedings* – the court case may be a criminal prosecution or a civil action. Legal aid in these two areas has always been administered separately.

Civil legal aid is based on the system of financial eligibility rather similar to that for the legal advice scheme. As before, the client may be assessed as liable to pay a contribution. A person seeking civil legal aid must also show to the satisfaction of a local committee that he has reasonable grounds for taking, defending or otherwise being a party to the proceedings. An important point to remember is that costs incurred in granting legal aid may be recovered out of any money received following a successful action. The administration of the legal aid scheme has now been transferred to a newly constituted Legal Aid Board, under the Legal Aid Act 1988. Major changes in the provision of legal services are now possible as s.4 confers a power to enter into contracts with persons and bodies other than solicitors (e.g. CABs) for the provision of advice and assistance.

Criminal legal aid is somewhat different in that applications are made direct to the court and there are no strict financial limits.

The legal profession

Even if a person is financially eligible to be legally aided, he may be uncertain how to find a lawyer to look after his case. The term 'lawyer' is a general word embracing all those who are learned in the law. Practising lawyers are divided into solicitors and barristers. The two professions are entirely separate, with their own entrance requirements and examinations. Solicitors are usually compared to general medical practitioners with barristers being seen as the equivalent of consultants. This can be rather misleading, however, as a solicitor, more usually in a large firm, may have an extremely specialized practice, while a young barrister seeking to make his name as an advocate may have to be prepared to be a 'jack of all trades'. No one may consult a barrister except through a solicitor. If no solicitor is known, public libraries or Citizen's Advice Bureaux keep referral lists of solicitors practising in their localities.

The legal profession was subjected to an intensive scrutiny in a Royal Commission chaired by Lord Benson in 1979, but little has happened as a result of its recommendations. It was basically in favour of the present division of the legal profession. However, in January 1989, the Lord Chancellor published three Green Papers (consultative documents) containing far-reaching proposals for changes in the legal profession, including:

- Ending the monopoly of the bar in the higher courts.
- Alternative ways of funding litigation, with contingency fees as a possibility.
- Mixed practices of different professionals.
- Allowing banks and building societies to undertake conveyancing work.
- The appointment of solicitors to the High Court bench.

The Green Papers were unfavourably received by many practitioners, both solicitors and barristers, and even senior judges spoke out against the proposals. Many of their proposals have now been implemented by the Courts and Legal Services Act 1990. Additionally, the Act has appointed a new Legal Services Ombudsman, who took up office in 1991, and created a new Advisory Committee on Legal Education and Conduct. The new Ombudsman is able to order payment of compensation to complainants.

3

Central and local government

The structure of central government

When society develops to the point where the activities of its members need to be directed and controlled, it will require a government. The tasks of government are: to formulate and carry out policies, which is its executive function; to frame laws, which is its legislative function; and to enforce those laws, which is its judicial function. At the same time as it grants power to a government to fulfil these functions, society wants to see control exercised over the government so that it does not become too powerful or dictatorial. Such control is exercised through the rules of the constitution, rather as a club or association is controlled by means of its rules. A striking feature of the British Constitution is that it is unwritten. Unlike countries such as France or the USA, we cannot point to one document embodying our guaranteed rights. Nevertheless, important constitutional laws are contained in a number of historic Acts of Parliament. These Acts are not invested with any special protection and could be revoked or altered by the same processes as any other Act of Parliament. By contrast, in certain foreign constitutions there are entrenched provisions which can only be changed by special procedures.

The leader of the political party which commands a majority in the House of Commons will be invited by the monarch to form a government. The House of Commons is one part of Parliament which consists of the monarch, the House of Lords and the House of Commons. The Queen is a constitutional monarch who exercises her powers only on the advice of her ministers. The House of Lords, which is the upper chamber of Parliament, is a non-elective assembly. Its members include hereditary peers, life peers, Lords of Appeal in

Ordinary (a maximum of eleven judges who are specifically a
to the House of Lords to hear appeal cases from the civil and u.
courts but who are also entitled to take part in all business of the
House of Lords) and the Lords Spiritual. The Lords Spiritual are not
peers. They comprise the Archbishops of Canterbury and York, the
Bishops of London, Durham and Winchester and the next twenty-one
most senior bishops of the Church of England. Inevitably the major
criticism of this element of representation in the Lords is that it is
exclusive to the Church of England. Indeed, over the years, the make-
up of the House of Lords has been subjected to regular criticism. This
mainly centres on the fact that the House is largely aristocratic and
non-elective, with an inevitable inbuilt permanent Conservative
majority. It is often thought that the House of Lords has little power
today since the Parliament Acts of 1911 and 1949 restricted its role to
the delaying of legislation rather than its out and out rejection. In
answer to the criticisms of the House of Lords, however, it is worth
remembering that the quality of membership of the Lords overall is
high, reflecting a wide range of backgrounds and experience, with life
peers being selected from trade unions, commerce and industry,
public life and the armed forces. Standards of debate are generally
accepted to be high. The part which the House of Lords can play in
improving and refining legislation sent from the Commons is
regarded as an important and significant part of its functions.

The House of Commons is the elected chamber of Parliament with
650 Members of Parliament. Each MP represents a constituency and
elections must be held at least once every five years, at a time chosen
by the Prime Minister when he or she believes it will be politically
opportune.

Once the result of the general election is known, the leader of the
political party which commands a majority of the House of Commons
will be invited to form a government. Many of the MPs will be hoping
to hold office in the government. The new Prime Minister will then
select the Cabinet team and ministers for the various government
departments. The Cabinet represents the most important departments
but is of no fixed size and the selection of ministers to be in the Cabinet
may reflect the government's policies and priorities. Traditionally the
Cabinet will always include the Chancellor of the Exchequer, the
Home Secretary, the Foreign Secretary and the Lord Chancellor. To be
of a reasonable working size, the Cabinet is likely to consist of about
twenty-four ministers. Outside the Cabinet, however, there are other
ministers and junior ministers and in total the government is likely to
have over 100 members. Some ministers will be members of the House
of Lords but it would be an unpopular move to appoint too many from

the Lords because they cannot be questioned in the House of Commons, a corrective and control feature much prized by MPs.

The government, once formed, is Her Majesty's Government, and the ministers are Her Majesty's Ministers. The new session of Parliament will be formally opened by the Queen, reading the Queen's Speech from the Throne in the House of Lords. Originally all executive power was vested in the monarch, but a series of historical events reduced the power and produced the modern figurehead monarchy of today. All acts of government are done in the name of the monarch but not necessarily with the monarch's personal participation. The Queen does, however, preside at meetings of the Privy Council. All bills going through the two Houses of Parliament require the Royal Assent to become Acts of Parliament. In theory the Queen could refuse her Assent but in this, as in most of her activities, she is bound by constitutional conventions. The principal convention is that the Queen exercises her formal legal powers only on the advice of her ministers. It is said that the Queen has 'the right to be consulted, the right to encourage and the right to warn.'

There is very little formal law governing our constitution and, therefore, many of the 'rules' under which central government and the Crown operate are simply conventions. A constitutional convention is a rule of political conduct, not a strict law in the sense that there is no sanction to enforce such a convention. Conventions can change imperceptibly over a period of time and it can therefore be argued that they keep the constitution flexible. Conventions have been described as 'the flesh which clothes the dry bones of the law, they make the legal constitution work, they keep in touch with the growth of ideas.'

It has been seen that the government of the day will emerge largely from members of the House of Commons. The House of Commons itself has three main functions; to make laws; to control national expenditure and taxation; and to criticize policy. Its law-making function has already been considered. In order to carry on its business the first task of the newly elected members of the Commons is to elect their Speaker who is an impartial chairman of the proceedings in the House. Usually this will mean the re-election of the previous Speaker if he is prepared to stand. Proceedings in the House of Commons take place in the Chamber with the government side sitting to the right of the Speaker's chair and the opposition to the left. The Chamber is not large enough to accommodate all the members at once, but usually they only want to be present in force for a limited number of great debates, or when there is going to be a division (i.e. a vote). MPs are paid salaries and have an allowance for secretarial expenses. They enjoy free travel within the UK on parliamentary business, and telephone calls and postage from the Commons are also free.

There is no formally recognized career path towards becoming an MP. The 650 MPs in the House of Commons represent a wide range of backgrounds and many have worked previously in the fields of journalism, the law, teaching, social work, finance and accountancy. There are comparatively few MPs now with shop floor experience from factories, mines or steel works. Many will have prepared themselves for their careers at Westminster by service with local authorities or trade unions.

Procedure of the House of Commons

There is a 'bible' of procedure in the House of Commons, a book called *Parliamentary Practice* by Erskine May. It started off as a small handbook, but as the procedure of the House of Commons has become more complex, the book has grown and grown. The procedure is complex because of the range of activites and interests with which the House must deal. Inevitably rules are important where the Speaker needs to control the activities of 650 volatile and articulate MPs of strong conviction, many of whom hold violently opposing views. If there are disputed points of procedure, the final word lies with the Speaker.

After numerous assorted items of business including question time, private notice questions, ministerial statements, introductions of new members and requests for emergency debates, the House eventually gets down to the main business of the day which might be a major debate or the second reading of an important bill. When an issue is put to the vote in the House of Commons, the Speaker puts the question and he must then weigh up whether the 'ayes' or the 'nos' have succeeded. If his assessment is challenged, he orders the lobbies to be cleared and the division bells will be rung, tellers are appointed and members must file through the appropriate lobby to record their votes. The tellers give the results to the Speaker who announces the outcome to the House.

Parliamentary questions

Question time takes place in the House of Commons on Mondays to Thursdays and lasts about forty-five minutes. On Tuesdays and

Thursdays fifteen minutes are devoted to Prime Minister's questions. Other ministers take it in turn to be questioned on a rota basis. Questions in Parliament have been a feature of the House of Commons for about 200 years but the present format and style of question time can be traced to the turn of this century, when it was decided to fix a definite time each day at which questions would end and the public business of the House would begin.

There are a number of reasons why an MP may wish to ask a question. He may wish to elicit factual information. He may well be asked by a minister to table a question to give the minister an opportunity to make a public statement in the House. The question may seek redress of a grievance for a constituent. Very often in such a case the question will only be asked if initial approaches to the minister or department concerned have drawn a blank. Questions in Parliament are not the only option open to an MP acting for a constituent. He can also refer the matter to the Parliamentary Commissioner for Administration. The question may be designed to embarrass a minister. This can be achieved particularly successfully in the follow-up to the oral question in what are called supplementaries. Although the minister will have notice of the question tabled, a cunning supplementary might find him unprepared. It is likely, however, that he will be well briefed by his civil servants with information to anticipate any supplementaries. Again, the question may be designed to enhance the reputation of the MP concerned, as opportunities to speak in the House are extremely limited.

The value of the parliamentary question can be considerable, especially if it ensures that a minister gives his personal attention and consideration to issues or problems which would otherwise be handled by officials in his department. Often decisions will have been taken at quite a low level within the department. On a closer look at the file, the minister may have occasion to reconsider his decision or redefine the policy within his department.

Question time can be regarded as an important time for the ordinary member of Parliament, the backbencher, particularly when it is remembered that this is part of the day when the parliamentary whips are not in control. Moreover, starred questions for oral reply are not usually asked by leading frontbenchers (members of the Government or Shadow Cabinet) although supplementaries may be put by them. The publicity potential is very great as question time takes place at a fixed time each day at the start of the day's business when the chamber is likely to be at its fullest and the press are in attendance, as there is always the prospect that a minister may be caught out or shown up in some way. A leading writer on constitutional law, De Smith, has said of question time:

Parliamentary reputations have been made and ruined in the rapid cut and thrust of question time. For a few minutes the House comes to life audibly and visibly; wit, feigned or genuine outrage, cheers and jeers intrude upon the solemnity of the proceedings; government and opposition are briefly locked in verbal combat; the Prime Minister and the Leader of the Opposition may gain or lose a point or two in the public opinion polls; a backbencher shows his ministerial potential, and the House wonders how much longer the Minister of Cosmology can last.

Private member's bills

If the opportunities to ask questions are restricted, then the opportunities to introduce a private member's bill are even more limited. The number of private member's bills passed in each session is always small, often not running into double figures. As a general rule private members will seek to introduce bills which do not require public expenditure, because if this were necessary the bill would face further hurdles. The government would then need to be persuaded to put forward a financial resolution. If a member wishes to introduce a private member's bill there are three possible ways of doing it: by winning a high place in the annual ballot; under the ten minute rule; or under Standing Order No. 37. The safest of these three courses is winning a high place in the ballot for promoting a private member's bill. This takes place annually. Successful MPs may have some personal preference for the measure which they wish to introduce, or an MP may be solicited by various pressure groups anxious to promote some particular measure. Occasionally the government itself has small measures that it wishes to promote. Where it has no time in the government programme, it may approach an MP who has been successful in the ballot asking him to take on a particular bill. Once a member knows what the subject matter of his bill is to be, he must then see to its drafting. This can be a costly process, especially if the bill is lengthy. The first ten placeholders in the ballot do, however, receive a small allowance towards drafting costs.

The committee system of the House of Commons

Whenever there is a very large organization with significant amounts of business to transact, it is common to find delegation of some of that business to specialized committees. In the House of Commons, delegation can be to a Committee of the Whole House, when the committee consists of all of the MPs. But, usually, two main types of committee are used – the standing committee and the select committee. It has been suggested that the names of these two types of committees are misleading. Standing committees are those specifically set up to consider the committee stage of a particular bill, after which the committee will be suspended, i.e. it does not 'stand'. Select committees on the other hand will usually operate for the duration of a Parliament.

Standing committees

These consist of sixteen to fifty members who are chosen to reflect the political strength of each party in the House. A government with a large majority will, therefore, enjoy a large majority in standing committees. The actual members for each committee are chosen by the Committee on Selection, which is itself a select committee. The chairman of the standing committee will be chosen by the Speaker from a panel of members which he selects at the start of the parliamentary session. The main task of the standing committee is to consider amendments to individual clauses of the bill before them. This is the first time that the specific terms of the bill will be given detailed clause by clause consideration. Standing committees sit in the mornings. Because of the number of votes on amendments, many of them of critical importance to the government if the substance of its policy is to be actively carried through, the whip system operates fully over the activities of these committees.

Select committees

Some of the select committees are permanent features of the life of the House of Commons but with extremely varying functions. At one end of the scale is the Services Committee (previously the Kitchen Committee) which controls the staff and services of the House of Commons and is responsible for catering there. At the other end is the prestigious Committee on Privileges which considers any breaches of privilege referred to it. The most significant recent development in the field of select committees occurred in the early 1980s, following recommendations made by the Select Committee on Procedure. That committee reviewed the procedures of the House of Commons and made proposals for changes. It was thought necessary to establish a new system of departmental select committees, fourteen in all, to scrutinize the work of the major government departments. These have been in operation since 1980 and are established with a permanent membership for the duration of a Parliament. The committees are small, seven to eleven members and the chairmanships are divided between the political parties, although the government would tend to retain the chairmanship of the more important committees like Home Affairs. They are free to determine for themselves which areas they will investigate.

Once a committee decides upon an area of investigation it will usually appoint its own expert advisers. It can call before it witnesses from industry and commerce, from the government and the civil service. It publishes its findings in a report to the House, to which the government must respond. Because of lack of parliamentary time, only a very small proportion of these reports is ever debated in the House, but there is, nonetheless, considerable value in the work of these committees. Their work is a means by which scrutiny and control of the executive is provided. They produce a considerable amount of information with which MPs may arm themselves for debate and questions. That information can be useful to add to the armoury of material used by pressure groups. Because issues are considered in some detail, MPs can develop considerable expertise. Membership of these committees is highly prized amongst MPs and they foster a co-operative sense of cross-party unity.

Financial procedures of the House of Commons

The Treasury, under the Chancellor of the Exchequer, is the government department with responsibility for the management of the economy. Inevitably, as Treasury approval is required for all large-scale expenditure, it is a significant department, but its influence may wax and wane depending on the forcefulness of individual Chancellors.

In order to run the essential services of the country, money must be raised and collected, and some priorities have to be established about how it should be paid out. There must also be mechanisms for controlling how that money is used. The government has substantial revenues from trading and commercial activities, but significant amounts have to be raised by taxes, which may be annual taxes like income tax, or longer term taxes like stamp duty.

The major financial statement of the year in the House of Commons is the Budget Speech delivered by the Chancellor of the Exchequer, usually in March. The proposals contained in the Chancellor's speech will ultimately be implemented in the Finance Act, but it may be several months before the Act receives Royal Assent. In the meantime, authority to collect annual taxes like income tax needs to be renewed, and the gap between the Budget and the Finance Act will be bridged using the authority contained in an annual Provisional Collection of

Taxes Act. The appropriate resolutions will be passed as soon as the Chancellor has finished delivering his Budget speech.

In former times, it was common to raise taxes specifically for particular items, but now all moneys raised are lumped together into one fund, the Consolidated Fund, which is effectively just an account at the Bank of England.

There is a Treasury and Civil Service Committee, one of the new breed of select committees established in 1980, with eleven members. Its terms of reference are to examine the expenditure, administration and policy of the Treasury, Board of Inland Revenue, and Boards of Custom and Excise. There is also a Public Accounts Committee which has the task of ensuring that parliamentary grants have been applied to the objects which Parliament has laid down. That committee considers financial irregularities, wasteful and extravagant expenditure and imprudent contractual transactions. Its reports are debated annually and command great respect in Whitehall.

There are many ancient conventions with regard to financial matters in Parliament. Most significant amongst these are that the granting of public money and the imposing of taxes is the function of Parliament, not the government; that the granting of public money and imposing of taxes must begin in the House of Commons and be finally determined by the Commons; and that the redress of grievances must precede any grant of public money. There must be no taxation without representation.

The Civil Service

Initially, when a minister takes over a new department or ministry, it might seem a daunting task to have to quickly learn all that is necessary for him to be able to make appropriate decisions. However, the role played by the Civil Service should not be forgotten. Civil servants are the permanent officials employed in the ministries. Unlike the American system where all officials change when the President changes, our Civil Service is permanent. The civil servants work for the government of the day whatever its political complexion. Civil servants cannot stand for election as MPs, and may only play a limited role in local politics. The civil servants in most senior positions are in close touch with their ministers, and play a part in the formation of policy, watching over bills on their way through Parliament and keeping their ministers supplied with information to enable them to answer questions in Parliament. They will frequently make decisions by applying rules and policy to individual cases, and when this happens, such a decision is regarded as having been made on behalf of the minister, who must accept responsibility for what has been done.

The structure of local government

There has been a long tradition of local administration in England, dating back to 1066. With poor networks of roads and the dangers of travel, the advantages of control and decision making resting with local organizations were obvious. But as those justifications have gradually disappeared, it may be questioned whether it is necessary in the twentieth century to divide responsibilities between central and local government. Two of the main advantages are:

1 The variations necessary for different local conditions can be introduced.
2 Local people will be involved, and those living in the area will see some benefit from the effort which they contribute.

Local authorities were reorganized in 1972. Basically, the structure is a division of the country into counties which in turn are divided into districts. In large conurbations, the counties are called metropolitan counties; the districts within them are metropolitan districts. Below district level are the parishes. Counties, districts and parishes all have councils. The type of council will determine the range of functions, although some functions may be shared. County councils have responsibility for matters such as highways, fire, police and social services. District councils have responsibility for housing, public health, rates and refuse collection. Parish councils have responsibility for footpaths, allotments, burial grounds and bus shelters. Planning is an example of a responsibility shared between county and district councils.

Local authorities are examples of bodies enjoying corporate personality, i.e. the local authority is a 'person' recognized by the law. It is run by a council of elected members within the powers granted to the local authority by the Act of Parliament which created it. The members of the council may change at each election, but the council has permanent officials, called its officers, who fulfil a role rather like that of the civil servants. Commonly a local authority has a Clerk or Chief Executive, a Medical Officer, an Education Officer and a Treasurer. The business of a local authority is transacted at council meetings, sometimes meetings of the whole council, but more often meetings of smaller committees set up for specific purposes, and with powers delegated to them, e.g. the planning committee. These committees must now reflect the political balance of the council as a whole.

Meetings are open to the public, unless the council resolves to meet in private, usually because publicity about a particular matter would be prejudicial to the public interest.

Council members may represent a particular political viewpoint and it is quite often the case at local government elections that the votes of the electorate will swing against the political party in power in central government. This can produce conflicts between local and central government, e.g. on issues such as the sale of council houses or the size of rate increases. This naturally raises the question, to what extent is a local authority truly independent? The answer to this lies in the amount of control which can be exercised over the local authority.

Control of local authorities

Every local authority must act within the scope of the powers granted to it. A local authority is a statutory corporation, which can only do such things as are authorized expressly or impliedly by the Act of Parliament which created it. If the local authority acts in excess of its powers, its actions are said to be '*ultra vires*' (beyond its powers) and void (of no legal effect). Obviously, it would require immensely detailed legislation to spell out everything a local authority could do. Consequently, by s.111 of the Local Government Act 1972, authorities are empowered to do anything which is reasonably incidental to their authorized activities and designed to facilitate the discharge of any of their functions.

Where a local authority has acted in a way which causes someone to be aggrieved, it will be necessary to check whether the authority acted under some express power, some implied power, or in some way reasonably incidental to an existing power. Not only must the local authority show that it had power to carry out a particular act, it must also be able to show that, procedurally, it carried out the act in accordance with the prescribed rules. A typical example of how things can go wrong occurred in 1967, in *Bradbury v. Enfield London Borough Council*. This case involved the reorganization of schools and the introduction of the comprehensive school system. Where the local authority intended to 'cease to maintain' a school, it was obliged to submit its proposals to the minister and give public notice of its intentions, to allow affected persons to make objections. The local authority took the view that what it was proposing to do in its reorganization plans did not amount to ceasing to maintain any of the schools involved. An aggrieved person applied to the court to stop the authority going ahead with its plans. An injunction was granted, because the behaviour of the local authority was *ultra vires* as it had failed to observe a mandatory procedural requirement.

When the help of the courts has to be sought, it is on the basis of judicial review of the local authority's decision or actions. The courts have a number of remedies available: including an order of certiorari, which is used to quash an *ultra vires* decision; prohibition, which is used to prevent an *ultra vires* action which is about to take place; mandamus, which is used to compel the performance of a public duty; and declaration, which simply makes clear what the court determines the legal position to be.

One possible way to give greater scope for action to a local authority, without rendering it constantly liable to claims of *ultra vires*, is to give the authority discretion as to whether, or how, it will act. Although this may appear at first sight to be a welcome prospect, the exercise of discretion is fraught with problems. Complaints may arise from the way in which the discretion has been exercised and in making its decisions the local authority will usually be obliged to exercise its discretion reasonably and to observe the rules of natural justice. These rules are usually stated to be *audi alterem partem* (hear both sides) and *nemo judex in causa sua* (no one should be a judge in his own case). In practice, these rules often require a local authority to give prior notice of their intentions to persons who may be affected by their decisions, so that such persons have an opportunity to put forward their own case; and a local authority should exclude from the decision-making process anyone who has some pecuniary interest in the decision, or who has some other bias.

Where it is suggested that an application to the High Court may be needed to control the activities of local authorities, many individuals would be deterred by the expense involved or by the formality of the procedures. There are, however, Commissions for Local Administration, which have created ombudsmen for local government. A local commissioner can investigate complaints of maladministration resulting in injustice. If a member of the public wants to take a case to the local commissioner, the procedure is to refer the case to a member of the authority concerned. The word 'maladministration' is not defined, but had been said to cover instances of bias, neglect, inattention, delay, incompetence, ineptitude, perversity and arbitrariness. If the commissioner finds that there has been maladministration, he will make a report, and the local authority concerned is then under a duty to consider the report, and notify the commissioner of the action it proposes to take. Its actions could include compensating persons who have suffered injustice, but the commissioner has no direct power to order or award compensation. Nor does the commissioner usually propose a remedy, but in those cases where he is dissatisfied with the response to his report by the authority, he may issue a second report with more positive proposals about remedies.

Control by central government

The main type of control which central government can exercise is financial. The control can consist of either withdrawing grants or refusing loans or capping expenditure. Without financial support from central government, and without the ability to raise loans, no local authority could function for long. Admittedly, there are other forms of income available to it, especially the rates levied on business property within the area. There are also less significiant amounts, such as rents from council houses, profits from undertakings run by the local authority (e.g. swimming pools, markets, buses) and fees from the granting of various licences. However, the inadequacy of their income is apparent when it is realized that their funds have to be supplemented annually by central government rate support. The domestic rating system has been withdrawn, and is superseded by a community charge, commonly called a poll tax. This tax has proved to be immensely unpopular, and it is presently intended to replace it.

When considering the role of central government in controlling local authorities, it is important to emphasize that much of the control is informal, exercised in the process of consultation which takes place with various government departments. Circulars, codes of practice and memoranda issued by central government departments form the basis of much decision making at local authority level. What is more, a local authority is often unable to proceed without some formal approval being given by a Secretary of State, e.g. approval of its structure plan under the Town and Country Planning Act 1990.

The range of services and amenities provided by local authorities is vast. Not surprisingly, there will be some people living in the area covered by a council who will be dissatisfied with the council's efforts. It should be remembered that ultimate control lies with the electorate, whether at the time of the elections, or by the strength of opinion they express to their councillors, or through the media. It is clear from the low level of votes cast at local elections that some of these controls are not fully used.

Bye-laws

Within its own area, a local authority will have power to regulate activities by means of bye-laws, either under general legislation or by virtue of private Acts of Parliament. When making bye-laws, a local authority is usually governed by the procedures of s.236 of the Local Government Act 1972. A bye-law must be made under the seal of the council and must be confirmed by the appropriate authority, which will usually be the relevant Secretary of State. Before confirmation, the local authority must publish notice of its intention to submit the bye-law. Once submitted, the confirming authority will usually check to ensure that the bye-law is *intra vires*, but this is not the only test which it must satisfy. Unlike laws made by statute, bye-laws are subject to the requirements that they must be reasonable; they must be certain; and they must be consistent with the general law. If valid and effective, a bye-law may impose penalties for breach. It is usually possible for anyone to institute proceedings for breach.

Public corporations

We have just considered the situation in which central government devolves some of its power to local authorities. It has become a trend of the twentieth century for central government to devolve other administrative tasks onto specially created bodies, which are known as public corporations. Among well-known examples are British Coal, the BBC, the Atomic Energy Authority, Health Authorities, the English Tourist Board, the Horse Race Betting Levy Board and the Advisory, Conciliation and Arbitration Service.

Many of these public corporations are established to manage commercial undertakings. As far as possible, they are expected to be self-sufficient and make a profit, although the statute creating the public corporation often expressly requires the undertaking to be run in the public interest, and that may not be compatible with making a profit!

All public corporations are created by Act of Parliament or Royal Charter, and the constitution of each is governed by its particular creating instrument. In general, however, such an Act will provide for an appropriate minister to appoint a chairman and members, usually after consulting appropriate bodies. Once established, the public corporation is a separate legal 'person', and may carry on those activities for which its creating instrument provides.

Control over public corporations is exercised either by use of the *ultra vires* rule, or, in some cases, by ministerial control. Although it is important that the activities of public corporations should be subject to control, they can only operate effectively if there is as little interference from central government as possible. Central government has created the public corporations in question and should trust them to carry out their specific tasks. Nonetheless, ultimate control does lie with Parliament, as it is always possible for a public corporation to be wound up by statute. The public also has some opportunity to play a part in controlling a public corporation, either by seeking publicity for adverse opinions about the corporation or by using one of the various consultative councils established to act as sounding boards for public opinion.

Over recent years, there has been a significant trend towards privatization of the public utilities. This move has resulted in water, gas, electricity, generation of power and telephone services becoming public companies, with their shares quoted on the Stock Exchange (see page 54).

4

Business organizations

Partnership

When a person wants to set himself up in business there is nothing to prevent him simply trading on his own account, with only his own money at risk. As such, the law would describe him as a sole trader. Trading in this way, however, may involve a number of drawbacks:

- He may lack adequate funds to develop the business.
- There is no one with whom he can share responsibility for running the business.
- If the business gets into financial difficulties, he will have unlimited liability for its debts. Creditors will not be restricted to seizing the assets connected with the business. Even his home may have to be sold.

The sole trader may be able to overcome the first two of these disadvantages by forming a partnership. This relationship is described by the Partnership Act 1890 as 'existing between persons who carry on business in common with a view to profit'. The arrangements for a partnership can be very informal, but it is advisable to have a properly drawn up agreement, in case disputes arise between the parties.

Partnership is a very suitable form of business association for professional people, e.g. accountants, architects, quantity surveyors and consulting engineers. Under the 1890 Act all partners are legally entitled to take part in the running of the business, but in practice the parties can make whatever arrangements they like. All partners are agents of each other for the purposes of partnership business (e.g. making contracts, paying money and engaging staff on behalf of the firm). For this reason, it may be sensible to limit the number of partners. By law, the maximum number is usually twenty. There is no limit on the number in partnerships of certain professional people like accountants and solicitors. A partnership is often referred to as a firm e.g. a firm of solicitors, but legally that term has no significance. The law is concerned to know, is this a partnership or a company? The word 'firm' might be equally appropriate to a firm of builder's merchants trading as a limited company, but the legal consequences of dealing with a partnership and a company can be entirely different.

The relationship among partners is a very special one, as potentially each could expose his fellow partners to unlimited liability. The law determines that it is a relationship of utmost good faith. This means that intending partners should make a full disclosure of any relevant facts or circumstances. The relationship is often described as being more difficult than marriage – after all in marriage there is only one spouse to contend with! Wherever possible, potential disputes should be avoided by a carefully drafted partnership agreement. Unless such an agreement is drawn up, the rules of the Partnership Act 1890 will apply. The Act provides that partners are entitled to share equally in the capital and profits of the business. That certainly may not accord with the wishes of partners who have contributed capital in differing proportions. A formal agreement allows for detailed rules about capital and profit sharing, and matters like the running of the firm, engaging in other business activities, retirement of partners and dissolution of the partnership.

Forming a partnership introduces others who will share liability for debts of the business, but that liability continues to be unlimited. All the partners are fully liable for all the debts, and again, creditors are not restricted to assets connected with the business. Even the advantages of a partnership (e.g. privacy with regard to the conduct of business affairs and accounting) may not outweigh the drawback of unlimited liability. An alternative which can avoid this is the formation of a company for the running of the business.

Company incorporation

The process of forming a company is referred to as incorporation. This is a very significant legal step, because the business then becomes known in law as a corporation. This is to distinguish it from groups or bodies which are not incorporated, and which are usually referred to as unincorporated associations. These latter groups have no separate legal existence or personality distinct from their members. So, the Mid-Tyne Angling Club is simply an identifying name for a group of people who have come together with a common interest. There is no legal person called Mid-Tyne Angling Club, i.e. it is not a separate legal entity or personality.

The phrase 'legal personality' means a person or organization which is recognized by the law as having legal rights and owing legal duties. All human beings in this country have a legal personality, although the law may impose restrictions on their capacity to act in certain ways, (e.g. any child under eighteen years of age has legal personality but lacks capacity to make a will, or own land). The law can also confer legal personality on an organization which has become incorporated.

Incorporation can take place by three methods:

1 *By Royal Charter* – this was the method used to create the original trading companies (East India Trading Company and Hudson Bay Trading Company) but it was more important as the means of creating many royal boroughs and institutes.
2 *By Act of Parliament* – many of the public corporations and local authorities have been established in this way, e.g. British Coal, British Airways.
3 *By virtue of the provisions of the Companies Act 1985 as amended* – under the rules of the Act, a number of different types of company can be created. For trading and general business purposes, a company limited by shares is by far the most common. The amount of shares owned by each of the members of the company then fixes the extent of his or her possible liability.

The fact that a company has a separate legal personality, quite distinct from its members (i.e. its shareholders) confers a number of advantages. These include a power to sue and be sued in its own name, the right to own and transfer property, the possibility of perpetual succession unless the company is wound up and the possibility to enjoy limited liability.

If a company gets into financial difficulties, creditors will be paid out of the assets of the company. If those assets are insufficient, the individual shareholders do not become personally liable. The extent of the liability of a shareholder is the amount he owes for his shares. Once he has paid for his shares he risks losing that amount if the company founders but no more. Limited liability is the most appealing feature of forming a company. However, a price must be paid for this advantage; limited liability companies are under statutory duties to publish certain financial details in the interests of both their creditors and the general public.

Creating a company

The actual creation or formation of a company is achieved by drawing up appropriate documents (including a Memorandum of Association and Articles of Association) which are submitted to the Registrar of Companies. The Memorandum is the company's most important document as it sets out the objects for which it is formed and thereby determines or limits the powers of the company. Although the Memorandum can subsequently be altered, this is by no means easy and it is preferable to make sure that it is correct from the outset. The Memorandum is a public document which may be inspected by persons interested in the company.

The Memorandum must set out:

1   *The name of the company* – the company will have a registered name but it may choose to trade under a different name, its business name. Business names are regulated by statute (Business Names Act 1985). The name chosen for the company must not be the same or too similar to that of an existing registered company, nor likely to give the public a false idea of the purpose for which the company is being formed. Any word such as bank, government or trust in a company name could be very misleading. In the case of a limited company, the word 'limited' must usually be the last word of the company's name. Where the company is a public company, it must include the words 'public limited company' or the abbreviation 'plc' in its name.

2   *The location of the registered office* – all that is required in the Memorandum is a statement as to which country the company is located in. This establishes the 'domicile' of the company, which may be important in choosing which system of law should apply. For example, Scots law applies to companies registered in Scotland. The company must also file a separate note of the address of its registered office.

3   *The objects clause* – this clause sets out exactly what business the company can engage in. Traditionally, these clauses have been very long, with the draftsman attempting to cover every possible activity which a company may wish to undertake. This was justified because of the *ultra vires* principle, whereby any activity undertaken by the company outside the scope of its objects clause was *ultra vires* (beyond its power) and void.

Two recent changes made by the Companies Act 1989 have greatly altered the position. Now, a company's memorandum may simply state that the object of the company is to carry on business as a general commercial company. If an objects clause of this new type is used, then the company can indeed carry on any trade or business whatsoever, and it would have power to do anything incidental or conducive to the carrying on of any trade or business by it. All existing companies could change their more limited objects clauses to incorporate this new wider provision. However, one cautionary note should be added. Although this simple new wide-ranging clause is now perfectly acceptable in theory, in practice companies may still opt for much more specific and detailed objects clauses, because institutions such as the banks, who may be considering loans to the company, will be keen to establish in which fields their money will be risked.

So far as the *ultra vires* rules are concerned, for any third party who deals with a company, the position set out in the 1989 Act is that the validity of acts done by the company shall not be called into question on grounds of lack of capacity by the company. Moreover, the third party is not bound to enquire as to whether the activity is permitted by the company's memorandum. Of course, the directors of the company which thus acted beyond the scope of its objects clause would be in breach of duty, and a shareholder could seek to bring proceedings to restrain any proposed activity which would be beyond the scope of the company's capacity.

4   *Member's liability* – where a company is limited by shares this clause simply states that liability is limited. In some more unusual cases, a company may be limited by guarantee, in which case the Memorandum must state the amount which each member has guaranteed to contribute if the company has to be wound up. Exceptionally it is still possible to create a company with unlimited liability but this is rare.

5   *Capital* – this clause states what the company's share capital is to be, and its division into shares of a fixed amount. This amount is the authorized capital of the company. For private companies there is no legal maximum or minimum fixed but a public company must have an authorized capital of at least £50,000. The figure chosen merely establishes the authorized amount which the company may issue as shares, although it may choose to issue only a portion of the authorized capital.

6   *The association clause* – by this clause the subscribers (of whom there must be at least two) declare that they agree to take the number of shares noted against their name.

By law, this forms the minimum contents of the Memorandum. The Articles of Association set out the internal rules and regulations for the running of the company, covering matters such as meetings, rights of shareholders, voting, appointment of directors, duties of directors and payment of dividends. There is a model set of Articles provided by the 1985 Act, called Table A, and it is very common for companies to adopt Table A with suitable amendments.

The articles are particularly significant for the members, as they are effectively the terms of the contract between the member and the company. Any violation of the rules contained in the Articles is a breach of contract. Members can sue to enforce their rights in ordinary breach of contract claims.

Public and private companies

It is common to think of private companies as small family firms, and public companies as the large business giants, and in practice this is often the case. A company which starts as a private company may expand its activities to such an extent that it decides to 'go public' and seek the change of status to a public company. There are a number of simple differences between public and private companies. For example:

1   A private company can be formed with two members and one director whereas a public company needs two members and at least two directors.
2   A private company need not obtain from the Registrar a certificate entitling it to do business whereas a public company must have such a certificate, and commits offences by trading without it.
3   A public company must satisfy the minimum capital requirement (i.e. its issued share capital must be at least £50,000). This rule does not apply to private companies.
4   A private company may exercise its borrowing powers immediately upon incorporation. A public company may not do so until it has alloted shares up to its authorized minimum capital of £50,000.
5   Private companies may still restrict the transferability of their shares, if they choose. They would usually choose to do so in cases where they want to preserve control of the company within a family. Restrictions normally operate by giving the directors the power to refuse to register transfers. Where such a discretion is given by the Articles, it places immense power in the hands of the directors, but they must act throughout in good faith. Public companies may not restrict the transferability of their shares if they want to be quoted on the Stock Exchange.
6   Private companies may be freed from some of the rigours of the rules about publication of accounts, depending on their size. For

these purposes size is determined by factors like turnover, assets and numbers of employees.

Management of a company

Companies are run by a board of directors, which is normally appointed at its annual general meeting. With private companies it is a common requirement that directors must have a certain holding of shares in the company. Where it is a small family business this is usually not difficult as directors may be members of the family. The company, being an artificial person, must act through human agents, and that normally means through the board of directors. The board will often delegate duties to paid employees, who may also be directors. Once appointed, a director is under duties to show good faith to the company and to take reasonable care. This means, for example, that a director is obliged to reveal any personal interest in a contract made by the company, particularly if he stands to profit by the contract.

The directors, or those acting under delegated powers, must act within the powers granted to them by the documents creating the company. In particular, the objects clause in the Memorandum of Association sets out the purposes for which the company was formed and the limits within which it can do business.

The first directors of the company will be those nominated to the Registrar of Companies on the formation of the company. Thereafter, the articles should provide for the appointment and retirement of directors. If shareholders are dissatisfied with one of the directors, they may choose not to re-elect him or, alternatively, they may seek his removal from office by passing an ordinary resolution. However, so dramatic a step is surrounded by numerous safeguards. The member proposing the resolution must give twenty-eight days' notice to the company before the relevant meeting; the company must then give other shareholders twenty-one clear days' notice of it; the company must notify the director concerned and he has the right to circulate a written statement setting out his point of view; the ordinary resolution must be passed by a simple majority of those voting. The director concerned may well have enhanced voting rights which allow him to beat off such a threat. If a resolution to remove a director is successful, it should be remembered that he may also have a contract of service with the company, and substantial compensation may need to be paid to him.

A board of directors is likely to have a Chairman, who will preside at directors' meetings. The board may also decide to appoint a Managing

Director, who will often have a contract of service with the company, and to whom much of the day to day management of the company is delegated. A company is legally obliged to have a company secretary, who may also be a director.

How a company divides its management between directors and shareholders is largely a question to be determined by the Articles. In practice, the rights of members to participate in management, particularly in large public companies, is extremely limited. A member does have some say by virtue of his voting power at meetings, but he may be one of a very large number of shareholders, holding very few shares, and his opinion may carry no weight. The wishes of the majority should normally take effect but not where the impact of that is to perpetrate a fraud on the minority.

The law has been alert to the problem of protecting minority shareholders and provides a number of means which can help to secure some protection. One example is shareholders' agreements, whereby the members enter into a separate contract with each other regulating how certain aspects of the company will be run. A statutory example of protection is the right of a minority shareholder to apply to the court if the company's affairs are being carried on in a way which is unfairly prejudicial to some of the members. Alternatively, a member could petition the court to wind up the company on the grounds that such a winding up would be just and equitable. These rules could be a particularly effective sanction in small private companies with, say, only half a dozen members, where the rights of one of them are being seriously prejudiced.

It may be that what concerns members most is the income that their shares will produce. A declaration of a dividend is usually made at the company's Annual General Meeting. Every company must hold such a meeting in each calendar year, not more than fifteen months apart, although a private company can dispense with the AGM, along with some other procedural requirements, if the company has passed an elective resolution. Any kind of business may be transacted at an AGM as long as appropriate notices have been served and appropriate resolutions are passed. If business needs to be transacted before another AGM is likely to be held, an Extraordinary General Meeting may be convened, either by the directors, or by members who together hold one-tenth of the company's paid-up share capital. Resolutions may be ordinary, special or extraordinary. The differences between them relate to the length of notice to be given, the size of the majority required and the need, in some cases, for subsequent registration of the resolution. The 1989 Act introduces a new type of resolution, an elective resolution, which may only be passed if everyone entitled to vote does so in favour of the resolution.

The Chairman of the board will usually chair company meetings. He must process the business in accordance with the rules contained in the Articles, and in accordance with the general rules of the common law. Voting on resolutions can be on a show of hands but sometimes the more formal procedure of a poll may be demanded. The Articles usually provide for situations when members can insist on a poll. The advantage of a poll is that proxies can vote too.

Company finance

In order to provide adequate resources to allow the company to develop and flourish it may be necessary for a company to borrow money or look at other methods of funding such as government grants, as well as taking account of the capital raised by the issue of shares. The advantages of share capital are that it does not have to be repaid (unless redeemable shares have been issued) and therefore has a permanence about it, and dividends are only payable if the company makes a profit.

The size of the company's share capital may well determine how much it can borrow, especially in the early stages of a newly formed and developing company. Lenders will be reluctant to advance more than the members of the business have themselves risked. Where a company needs sizeable amounts of money it may be possible to attract funds under government sponsored schemes like the Business Expansion Scheme or Investment Funds. A person who invests his money in a company under the Business Expansion Scheme enjoys tax concessions, especially if he pays tax at a higher rate.

A company can sometimes improve its financial position by siting itself where it may benefit from central and local government or EEC grants and loans. The schemes will vary from time to time, reflecting the political stance of the government of the day. Examples of schemes have included Enterprise Zones and Regional Development areas. Sometimes, the incentive to set up in a particular place will consist of very favourable rents and rate-free periods.

Where a company needs to borrow money it may turn first to its own shareholders, who can provide loans called debentures. Like all forms of borrowing the issue of debentures is only possible if the directors are empowered to borrow by the Memorandum and Articles. It is possible to give debenture holders greater security by creating a charge over the assets of the company.

All lenders of money worry about how they will be repaid if the company gets into difficulties. A lender may be prepared to make the loan only on condition that he is given some security in the event of the company being unable to pay. If that happens the lender can then realize his security i.e. sell it, to repay himself what he is owed.

One type of security is the fixed charge, which is a mortgage over a specific thing like a building. Inevitably the company cannot dispose of, or realize, the property which is subject to the charge without the consent of the lender. This could be particularly restricting in a developing business, so the company may prefer to borrow against the security of a floating charge. This is a mortgage of assets of the company, such as the stock in trade, which changes from time to time. It is in the contemplation of both lender and borrower that the company should be free to carry on its normal business, dealing as usual with those assets. The company continues to have the flexible use of whatever is comprised in the charge. However, once the borrower defaults the floating charge is said to crystallize. This means that it becomes a charge attached to the assets available at the moment of crystallization and the company is henceforth prevented from dealing with those assets. The parties may have specified a number of circumstances which will give rise to crystallization.

Floating charges are a device by which a company can raise money without affecting its ability to trade. However, they could have the effect of misleading persons who are thinking of dealing with the company, because the company might look in a more affluent and healthy financial position than is truly the case. The problem is overcome to some extent by requiring company charges to be registered with the Registrar of Companies within twenty-one days of being made. The company is legally obliged to effect the registration, but it would be sensible for the lender to do so too, because a charge which is not registered in time is void. Once the charge is registered it is part of the information which is available for public inspection. Any person about to deal with a company, and needing information about its financial viability, could make a search. That would reveal any charges registered, the date the charges were created, the person in whose favour the charge is made and the property over which the charge operates.

Raising money by the device of the floating charge is a procedure only available to companies. This gives a company an advantage over a trading partnership, which could borrow only against the security of fixed assets.

Winding up of companies

A company is an artificial body and theoretically it could continue forever with a constantly changing membership as shares are bought and sold. If a company is to be dissolved the process is referred to as 'winding up' or 'liquidation'. The directors may decide on this course, in which case the dissolution is voluntary, or it may occur by order of the court.

If the winding up is brought about because a company has financial problems the rules of liquidation are now contained in the Insolvency Act 1986. A government White Paper, published in 1984, stated that the role of insolvency legislation is:

1 To establish effective and straightforward procedures for dealing with and settling the affairs of insolvents in the interests of their creditors.
2 To provide a statutory framework to encourage companies to pay careful attention to their financial circumstances so as to recognize difficulties at an early stage and before the interests of the creditors are seriously prejudiced.
3 To deter and penalize irresponsible behaviour and malpractice on the part of those who manage a company's affairs.
4 To ensure that those who act in cases of insolvency are competent to do so and conduct themselves in a proper manner.
5 To facilitate the reorganization of companies in difficulties to minimize unnecessary loss to creditors and to the economy when insolvency occurs.

To achieve these aims a new breed of professionals, called insolvency practitioners, has been created. They are authorized to act in liquidations and must provide a bond or security of £250,000 for each appointment as a practitioner as security in respect of losses caused by fraud or dishonesty.

When a company is in financial difficulties a full liquidation process may be unnecessary. It may be possible to save the company by using voluntary arrangements. The proposal for such a voluntary arrangement can be made by a director. The proposal will be for a composition in satisfaction of the company's debts or a scheme of arrangement of the company's affairs. The insolvency practitioner will then be appointed to act as a supervisor, implementing the scheme. The value of such a voluntary arrangement is that it can be organized with the minimum of involvement of the High Court, as it will be approved at meetings of the creditors and the company.

Where a company is likely to be unable to pay its debts another alternative procedure is an Administration Order. The court will make such an order if it believes that by doing so it can secure the survival of the company or that it would give time for a voluntary arrangement to come into being. There will be a court hearing. If an order is made it directs that, for the time being, the affairs, business and property of the company are to be managed by an administrator. While the order is in force there can be no order for the liquidation of the company. The administrator has three months to draw up a statement of his proposals, which are put to meetings of the creditors and the company.

Where liquidation of the company is necessary, this may be a member's voluntary liquidation, which can occur where the company is solvent; a creditor's voluntary liquidation, which occurs where the company is insolvent and where the wishes and interests of the creditors will prevail; or a compulsory liquidation, which arises by order of the court, following the presentation of a petition seeking such an order.

For a compulsory liquidation, a winding-up petition may be based on a number of grounds, including the ground that the company is unable to pay its debts. This is deemed to be the case where a creditor who is owed more than £750 has demanded his money and has remained unsatisfied for three weeks. He is said to have made a statutory demand. Other evidence accepted by the court that the company is unable to pay its debts may be dishonouring a bill of exchange, or proof that the company's assets are less than its liabilities, or proof that a creditor entitled to execution has been unsuccessful. This means that a creditor was granted a warrant of execution to levy distress against the goods of the company, but his warrant has proved ineffective because there are insufficient goods to satisfy his demands.

Proceedings for compulsory liquidation are commenced in the County Court or the High Court, depending on the amount of the company's share capital. Once a petition has been presented any disposition of company property is void unless approved by the court. This discretion is important because it means that the company can continue to trade, but it allows control over activities which may be detrimental to the interests of some of the creditors.

If the court decides to make a winding-up order, certain immediate consequences follow:

- A liquidator is appointed.
- All actions against the company must be stayed.
- A first meeting of creditors may be convened.
- The director's duties and powers cease.

- The business of the company can carry on only to the extent that it is beneficial to the liquidation.

The liquidator must take control of all the company's property. He must call in all the assets, realize them, and distribute the proceeds to the appropriate creditors. Some property of the company may not be available to the liquidator, e.g. where the contract by which the company was acquiring the property provides that the company's interest in the property will end in the event of liquidation, or where a company is purchasing goods under a contract containing a valid retention of title clause. The liquidator will also be concerned to discover whether transactions immediately prior to the liquidation were undertaken to defeat the rights of creditors, or some groups of them. If so, the transaction may be void. Examples include cases where a company transfers property for no consideration, or for a consideration significantly less than the real value; or a transaction involves a preference, where a company puts one of its creditors into a more favourable position than the creditor would be under the liquidation.

Once the liquidator has realized all the assets he then pays the costs and expenses of the liquidation. He must next pay off the creditors, who must have submitted formal proof of their debt. Secured creditors will usually realize their security to settle what is owed to them but they may prove any outstanding balance not covered by the security. Fixed chargeholders take separately, but those holding floating charges rank after preferential creditors. This tends to emphasize the superior security provided by a fixed charge. The creditors rank in the following order:

1 *Preferential creditors* – this group rank equally among themselves after the expenses of the winding up. Examples of preferential creditors include:
   (a) PAYE.
   (b) VAT referable to the previous six months.
   (c) National insurance contributions due for the previous twelve months.
   (d) Employees' remuneration due for the previous four months, not exceeding £800 (this figure can be adjusted from time to time by the Secretary of State).

2 *Amounts secured by floating charges.*
3 *Unsecured creditors* – all other creditors rank equally amongst themselves.

If there are surplus funds left over after distributing to the creditors these are distributed to the members of the company according to their rights and interests.

Where a company has been wound up this may reflect seriously on the competence and integrity of the directors. In that case, the courts have extensive powers to disqualify directors for specific periods. In some cases the disqualification may be based on activities of the director which could involve criminal liability but there is no overall requirement that the behaviour must infringe specific criminal law rules. One example where a director could be disqualified is for 'unfitness' to be concerned with the management of a company .

Once the process of winding up has finished, the company is removed from the Register and is dissolved three months later.

5

The law of contract

The nature of a contract

In business and commercial life the law of contract underpins a huge range of activites as diverse as engaging staff, buying supplies, arranging insurance, leasing premises, raising loans and buying shares. These transactions all involve making a contract which must comply with the general principles governing all contracts. The modern law of contract has largely evolved from case law, although major pieces of legislation such as the Unfair Contract Terms Act 1977 have radically altered some of the rules. There is no complete code of rules governing the making of a contract. Where a dispute arises between the parties, litigation or arbitration may be necessary to determine the rights of the parties. The courts have generally taken a 'laissez faire' approach to the making of contracts, indicating that the parties are free to make the contract of their choice, with which the courts will rarely interfere.

However, the role of the courts ought not to be overemphasized. Of all the millions of contracts entered into daily only a very small proportion ever involve litigation before the courts. On the whole the parties carry out their obligations and by that means discharge their contract. Even where problems do arise some compromise or settlement may be reached between the parties without the need to take action in the courts.

Contracts are based on the idea of a bargain. Each side must put something into the bargain. A contract may be defined as 'an agreement which is binding on the parties'. Within that definition lies the first problem. The ultimate bargain arrived at between the parties may not have been 'agreed' in the commonly understood sense of that word. There are a number of reasons why this is so. First, English law adopts an objective approach to decide whether there is an agreement between the parties. It is pointless to ask an individual who is now in dispute whether he intended to make a contract. Rather, the courts ask the question; 'Would a reasonable man think that there was an agreement between the parties?' Second, 'agreement' may not seem to be present where one party has little or no choice in the terms he is obliged to accept. There are many contracting situations where, because of the superior bargaining strength of one of the parties, the other has little or no choice but to accept the terms. Third, there are many cases where little or no negotiation takes place between the parties (e.g. sales in a self-service store) but the 'agreement' between the parties is largely created by implied terms (e.g. terms implied into contracts for the sale of goods by virtue of the Sale of Goods Act 1979).

To return to our definition of a contract (an agreement which is binding on the parties) it is always possible for an injured party who is suffering from some breach of contract to sue to enforce it. Enforcing the contract means seeking an appropriate remedy from the court. In most cases that remedy will be an award of damages. It is only in very limited types of case that a court would order one party specifically to perform his obligations. If the court does grant such an order it is called specific performance.

Formation of the contract – agreement

It has become customary in English law to regard agreement as consisting of offer and acceptance. This is only a method of analysing the bargaining process. It is not necessary for the parties to use these words. An offer exists when one party effectively declares his readiness to be bound by a set of terms without any further negotiation. In other words, the offeror (the person making the offer) has reached a stage where he is content for the other party to say he accepts, and at that point a valid, binding contract will come into existence. If the parties are not at such an advanced stage in their negotiations, no offer may yet exist. Often, what appears to be an offer may only be some kind of enticement to bargain, which the law calls an invitation to treat.

The courts have had to consider numerous instances where the argument turned on whether a definite offer was made. In the case of goods on display in a shop window, or goods on supermarket shelves, the court would normally find that such a display was an invitation to treat – the shopper must come forward and make an offer to buy. Similarly in auction sales, when an auctioneer calls for bids, he is not 'offering' to sell the goods, but rather inviting potential buyers to put forward their offers.

The problem regarding offers can also arise in relation to price lists or catalogues which are sent to customers. These are usually construed to be a mere indication of the goods available and their likely selling price. Any other interpretation could give rise to serious practical difficulties. Consider a case where a firm sends out a price list of second-hand earthmoving plant which it has available for sale. The circular may go to dozens of companies who could be interested to buy. If there is only one model of a particular type on the list and several purchasers come forward saying that they wish to buy it the supplier could find himself in breach of contract over and over again as he is unable to supply them all with the equipment. It is better to construe the price list as a mere invitation to bargain, a 'display' of what the firm has to sell, and think of the approaches by potential buyers as the offers, which the seller can accept or reject as he chooses.

Where a case arises which causes doubt the court approaches the issue of whether any offer has been made by using an objective test of the intention of the person concerned. Would a reasonable man, knowing all the circumstances of the case, think that an offer has been made? The court takes into account the words used. In one case, where a letter said 'I may be prepared to sell . . .', the writer could not yet be said to be ready to be bound in contract without further negotiation. Even if the word 'offer' is used, that is not conclusive in law that an offer exists.

If it is clear that the intention is to make a firm offer it may be made orally or in writing. It comes as something of a surprise to many people to discover that English law has very few rules about formality or written evidence in contracts. Apart from exceptional cases such as contracts for the sale of land, transactions worth hundreds of thousands of pounds can be binding even when made orally. Of course there may be sound reasons for making a contract in a more formal way, as subsequent disputes may be capable of being resolved simply by reference to a written agreement.

An offer can be made to an individual, when only that person can accept. The offer may be made to a group and, in certain cases, it may be made to the world at large, for example, in cases offering a reward to a finder. The offer is only effective when it has been communicated to the other party, the offeree.

Counter offers

The offeree has a number of options open to him. He may wish to accept the offer, in which case he must exactly accept the precise offer which was made to him. If he seeks to bargain further or to introduce new terms he is not accepting, rather he is making a counter offer. The law provides that the effect of a counter offer is to terminate the original offer. So if the counter offer is not acceptable the person who made it cannot try to revive the original offer. He must make a fresh offer. This situation can be of vital importance where the person making the final offer may be fixing the terms of the deal. The offer – counter offer situation arises frequently in business where each side in the negotiations may be trying to make the contract on the basis of their own 'pro forma' standard documents. This gives rise to what is known as the battle of the forms. A classic example can be seen in *Butler v. Ex Cello Machine Tool Co.* where the seller offered to sell a machine tool for £75,000, which would be delivered in ten months' time. The seller's offer was made on a printed form containing various conditions, one of which was a price variation clause allowing for an increase in certain circumstances. The buyers placed an order, using their own standard printed order form. On the bottom of the buyers' form was a tear-off slip, which the seller was asked to return to the buyers. The seller duly returned the slip. It contained the words 'we accept your order on the terms and conditions thereon'. When the tool was ultimately delivered, the seller sent a bill for over £78,000. Its claim for the increased amount was unsuccessful. Its original quotation was an offer. The buyers had made a counter offer which did not contain a price variation clause. The seller had accepted the counter offer by returning the tear-off slip.

Of course, not every communication from an offeree will necessarily amount to a counter offer. Once an offer has been made, the offeree may simply wish to seek further explanation of its terms to satisfy himself that he is getting the best deal possible. So there may be a fine distinction between the cases. For example X offers to sell Y his car for £3,000. If Y replies 'Will you take £2,700?' he is still negotiating and making a counter offer. But if Y replies 'Is that cash or is there any possibility of HP?', he may simply be seeking to clarify the terms of the offer.

Acceptance

Not only must the offeree accept the exact and precise offer made to him; he must also communicate his acceptance to the other party.

Normally, the offeror must actually receive the acceptance. This tends not to create problems where the parties are face to face, or using some form of instantaneous communication such as the telephone or a telex machine. In all of these cases, the contract is made when the acceptance is received by the offeror.

The situation is somewhat different if the parties are negotiating at arm's length. This will usually be a case where they have been dealing with each other by post. The offeror can lay down rules about how the offeree has to accept but in most cases he will not have done so. Then it may be appropriate to use what is called the 'postal rule'. When this applies, an acceptance made by letter is effective, and the contract comes into existence, when the letter is posted. Inevitably this means that a legally binding contract exists for some time before the offeror actually learns that he is legally bound. That can sometimes be inconvenient, but an offeror could overcome the problem by stipulating as part of his offer that he will only be bound on *receipt* of the acceptance. In *Holwell Securities v. Hughes*, the offeree wanted to accept an offer under the terms of which he had to accept by a notice in writing by a fixed date. He posted a letter of acceptance but it did not arrive until after the fixed date. The court held that the phrase 'notice in writing' indicated that the offeror must actually receive the acceptance by that date. Merely posting a letter was no use in those circumstances. The 'postal rule' is merely a rule of convenience and the courts would not apply it in cases where it was manifestly absurd to use the post (e.g. a case where the offeror had indicated that he needed a very speedy acceptance). Nor will the rule be applied if the offeror has prescribed some other method of acceptance.

The offeror can lay down quite elaborate rules for acceptance. The courts may then be faced with the problem that an offeree has purported to accept but has not followed the precise method stipulated. Generally the courts will allow an acceptance by any method which is equally as effective as the one which was prescribed. It is a question of construing whether the offeror was making a suggestion, or whether that method and no other must be used. For instance, if the offeror says 'Drop me a line to tell me if you want to buy', does that mean he is insisting on acceptance only by letter?

The rule that acceptance must be communicated means that silence cannot usually amount to acceptance. This is important because otherwise an offeror could impose obligations on the offeree: 'I offer to sell you my car for £3,000. If I do not hear from you before 9 pm I will assume that you have accepted'. If this were permitted, it would force the offeree into a bargain.

Termination of offers

An offer can be said to be terminated by its acceptance because at that moment there is a legally binding contract. There are, however, a number of ways in which an offer may be brought to an end. The offer itself may have been made subject to a time limit. If there is no acceptance before that time, the offer will automatically lapse. Where there is no fixed time limit the offer will remain open for acceptance for a reasonable time. What is reasonable will vary with the circumstances and the nature of the subject matter.

Once he has made an offer, the offeror may change his mind and wish to withdraw it. Revocation is always possible before an offer has been accepted. To be effective, the fact of revocation must be communicated to the offeree; in postal cases this means the letter must actually be received and not merely posted. This can cause conflict where the parties are negotiating at arm's length using the post where the postal rule of acceptance is relevant. The letter revoking the offer may be posted first, but if it arrives *after* a letter of acceptance has been posted it will be too late to withdraw.

Where an offer has been made for a fixed time the question may arise whether it can be revoked during that time. In reliance on the offer remaining open, the offeree could be going to considerable trouble to put himself into a position where he can accept, e.g. by raising finance. If the offeror revokes before the fixed time is up the offeree may have no legal basis for complaint. Effectively this fixed offer situation is really two distinct offers: 'I offer to sell you my car for £3,000, and I offer to keep the offer open for seven days.' If the offeree wishes to enjoy the benefit of the seven days time limit he must accept the second offer and 'buy' it by giving some consideration for it. This is what happens when a person buys an option but in most everyday situations it would not occur to people to offer to 'buy' time in this way. The rules of consideration are considered on page 69.

Certainty of the agreement

Even though the parties think they have reached agreement the courts may find that there is no legally binding contract because of lack of certainty. Naturally the courts do not want to disappoint people's expectations so they approach any question of vagueness or uncertainty with the idea in mind that 'a thing is certain if it is capable of being made certain'. An agreement which appears vague at first sight may be capable of being given a sensible meaning, either because the parties have dealt together before or because there is some custom of the trade or business. In some cases the parties themselves may be aware that their agreement is vague or incomplete and they may provide for future resolution of these aspects by including an arbitration clause. Sometimes it is possible to fill in missing terms by reference to a statute. For example, if the parties have failed to agree on a price and goods have now been supplied under the contract, s.8 of the Sale of Goods Act 1979 provides that where no price has been fixed and no method has been agreed for determining the price, the buyer must pay a reasonable price.

The agreement

Once the processes of offer and acceptance have culminated in the formation of the agreement the terms have become fixed between the parties. That has been the object of their negotiations – to determine the extent of their obligations to each other. Once agreement is reached it cannot be altered by one of the parties without the consent of the other. If any alterations or variations to the agreement are to take place then the relevant rules of consideration should also be borne in mind.

There can be great difficulty in establishing what has become a term of contract. A distinction has to be drawn between statements made which go to the core and essence of the transaction and those statements which merely influence the decision to enter into the contract. The former are terms, where a breach gives rise to a right to claim for damages for breach of contract. The latter are representations, where rights may be available if the statement made was untrue and in some way induced the contract.

Consideration

English contract law is based on the idea of a bargain. There must be some exchange between the parties. One party must be doing something or giving something in consideration of what the other is doing or giving. Consideration can be defined simply as the 'price' each party pays for the right to enforce the other party's promise. It is important to remember that consideration will not always be money although it is quite usual for money to be the consideration provided by one of the parties. If I sell you my car for £3,000 my consideration is giving you the car and your consideration is giving me the £3,000. If we make that agreement and provide for the exchange to take place at the end of the month then our agreement is still a binding contract *now* because our exchange *now* is an exchange of promises. In consideration of you promising to pay me £3,000 at the end of the month I promise to hand over my car to you then.

This type of consideration, based on promises which are to be performed in the future, is called executory consideration. It is surprising how often people fail to realize that there is a legally binding obligation in such a case. Take the example of a shopper who orders a chair in a furniture store, delivery to be in six weeks' time, when the customer will be invoiced for the chair and will then send payment. Later the same day, having placed the order, the customer wants to back out. That would amount to breach of contract. The customer might say that the furniture store had not even had time to send the order off, but the store has lost the profit on the sale and no doubt has been put to some trouble and expense in dealing with the customer.

In order to provide a valid consideration, the law insists that it must not be past. *Re McArdle* illustrates the principle. Members of a family were all entitled to a share in a house on the death of their mother. While the mother was still alive one of the sons and his wife went to live with her. The son's wife made several improvements and alterations to the property for her own comfort and convenience. When the mother died the other members of the family promised to pay the son's wife for all the work that had been done. When they failed to pay she could not enforce their promise as she had given no valid consideration for it. The work she had done was in the past and had not been done in consideration of their promise to pay. The promise and the act were independent of each other. To be a valid consideration there has to be an inter-dependence of promise and act.

There are some situations which look like past consideration but which are not true instances. Take the case of a person requesting someone to perform services for him, in circumstances where he must be expecting that he will have to pay, for example where he asks an accountant to deal with his tax affairs. Once the service is performed any subsequent promise to pay in such a case is enforceable because by asking for the service there is an implied promise to pay a reasonable amount.

Although contracts are based on the idea of a bargain the law does not insist that the two sides of the bargain must be equal. This is often expressed as a rule that consideration need not be adequate. It is up to the parties to make the contract of their choice. One person, for good reasons of his own, may be prepared to pay far more for goods than they are really worth. Generally, contract law allows great freedom to the parties in making their bargain and each is supposed to look after his own interests and strike the keenest bargain possible. One of the maxims of the law is *caveat emptor* which means 'let the buyer beware'. Where the two sides of the bargain are seriously unequal that may be evidence of fraud, duress, mistake, or incapacity, in which case there may be some basis on which the court could set aside the contract. However, if the person complaining has simply made a bad bargain the law will not intervene.

While not insisting that the two sides of the bargain must be equal the courts will insist that each side of the bargain must have some value in the eyes of the law. This may be so even where the consideration consists of something intrinsically worthless. This point is illustrated in *Chappell & Co. v. Nestlé & Co.* where the chocolate company was running a promotional scheme. In return for three chocolate wrappers and a postal order for 1/6d (7½p) the chocolate company would send the customer a pop record. Chappell's were entitled to receive royalties on the selling price of all sales of the record. The question arose here whether the record was sold for 1/6d or whether the wrappers formed part of the consideration. Even though the chocolate company simply threw the wrappers away the House of Lords found that they did form part of the consideration.

Duties already owed

It seems obvious that you are not providing any consideration where you simply behave in a way in which you were legally obliged to act. This view is accepted by the courts in relation to both public and contractual duties owed. Take the case of *Collins v. Godefory* where a witness was under a public duty to attend and give evidence because he had been ordered to do so by the issue of a subpoena. The witness was promised money by the defendant in the case if he came and gave evidence. Once he had given his evidence was it possible to say he had done so in consideration of the defendant's promise to pay? The court held that the witness gave no consideration for the promise as he was already under a duty to give evidence. He was doing nothing more than his duty.

In those cases where it can be shown that a person does more than his public duty requires, then he may have provided consideration for a promise to pay. This can be seen to be the basis of the decision in *Glassbrook Bros v. Glamorgan CC*, where a mine owner requested police to provide a twenty-four hour guard over his property. Although the police were under a duty to prevent crime and protect property they were not required to mount a continuous guard. The mine owner promised to pay for the service and it was held that the local authority could recover the money from him as the police were doing more than their public duty. They had, therefore, given consideration for his promise to pay.

The same sort of situation can arise where a duty is owed under a contract. Suppose you have asked me to supply 100 sausage rolls for your village fair and you have paid me for them. Under the terms of our agreement I am due to deliver the sausage rolls at 12 noon on 1 June. I fail to arrive at 12 noon and when you contact me I sound reluctant to make a delivery. You then promise to pay an extra £10 and, in consequence, I make the delivery. What consideration do I give for your promise to pay £10? I was already contractually bound to deliver the goods so I am doing nothing more than performing an existing duty. In an example such as this, the courts have traditionally found that I could not enforce your promise to pay £10 as I had given no further consideration for it. An old case, *Stilk v. Myrick*, has long represented that view of the court. There, sailors were promised extra pay for sailing a ship back to port when some of the crew had deserted. Later, the shipowner refused to pay, as the sailors were already obliged by their contract to sail the ship back, and had therefore simply performed the duty they already owed under the contract.

Such a decision may be entirely correct as a pure application of the law, and no doubt it prevents situations of near blackmail arising where a person could apply pressure to the other contracting party to pay more, simply by threatening not to perform. But inevitably that 'pure' approach may fail to recognize the true pressures of business life and the market place. In a more modern shipping case, the *Atlantic Baron*, the court was able to enforce a promise of extra payment for the building of a ship by finding that the shipyard did more than they originally promised, and had therefore given consideration for the extra payment.

Some judges have gone so far as to say that *any* promise to perform a pre-existing duty should be good consideration, because it is a benefit to the person receiving performance. When the argument is carried to these lengths, in our sausage roll example, I could recover the extra £10. The benefit to you would be that you receive performance with none of the aggravation of needing to sue for breach. The detriment to me is that I give up the possibility of being in breach of contract – and there is no doubt that this can be a very valuable right. Having agreed to sell sausage rolls to you for a fixed price, I may now find that I can sell the same goods so advantageously elsewhere that it actually pays me to be in breach with you and suffer the consequences.

Much of this thinking has been further developed by the Court of Appeal decision in *Williams v. Roffey*. The facts there were that building contractors had subcontracted the carpentry work on a block of 127 flats to the plaintiff, for a price of £20,000. The plaintiff was entitled to interim payments under the contract. After he had completed nine of the flats, and done preliminary work on the others, he had already received over £16,000. He then realized that his price for the work was far too low. The building contractors began to get anxious, as they would become liable under penalty clauses in their main contract if the work was not completed on time. They knew that the plaintiff was having difficulty because he had underpriced the job. They suggested a meeting with him, at which they agreed to pay him £10,000 more, on condition that the work was completed on time. In view of the extra payment, the plaintiff went on with the work. He completed eight further flats but then stopped work. When he tried to recover what he alleged was due to him under the contract, the building contractors refused to pay any part of the extra £10,000, on the grounds that the carpenter had given no extra consideration for it. In the Court of Appeal, the carpenter was held to be entitled to the extra money, because the building contractor had obtained a benefit, in that they were avoiding the penalty under another contract.

Of course, an important feature of the case was that there was no suggestion of 'blackmail' by the carpenter. Indeed, he had been approached in the first instance by the builder who had made the suggestion to pay extra. Moreover, if the court had been determined to look for something in the carpenter's behaviour which could amount to performing more than his mere contractual duty, no doubt they could have 'found' it. For example, it could be said that the carpenter's agreement to undertake the work in a different sequence could be a detriment to him and a benefit to the builders.

It is difficult to make a judgement yet as to the ultimate effect of the Williams case on the development of this area of law, but it is clear that the courts have found it easier to discover a valid consideration where performance of a duty owed to a third party is involved. Consider the following example. A is contractually bound to supply the engines for a ship being built by B. The engines are due to be delivered by 1 January. C has a contract with B to charter the ship from 1 June, immediately on its completion. It begins to look as if A is going to be late in making delivery of the engines. C is extremely anxious that the ship should be finished on time as he stands to lose an enormous sum of money if his charter of the ship is delayed. C approaches A and promises him £10,000 if he will get the engines to B by 1 January. If A does deliver the engines to B on time, can he then claim the £10,000 from C? The courts have been inclined to take a more relaxed view in this type of three-party situation, and in a number of cases (e.g. *New Zealand Shipping Co. v. A. M. Satterthwaite & Co.*) they have allowed A to sue for the £10,000. The reasoning seems to be that there is a detriment or burden to A because, by binding himself in a contract to C as well as to B, he lays himself open to two actions for breach of contract if he fails to deliver the engines. Moreover, it might have been more to A's liking to be in breach of contract with B and face whatever consequences that might have brought. Now he foregoes that possibility because of his agreement with C.

In such cases it would be important to check that there was nothing in the transaction which was contrary to public policy. Latterly the courts have shown themselves willing to control these situations by developing rules of economic duress (see page 99).

Part payment of a debt

Problems can arise in finding valid consideration where one party seeks to perform his contract by doing something less than he is contractually obliged to do. Take the example of A who owes £100 under a contract to B which is due for payment now. A may be in financial difficulties, so much so that B agrees to accept £75 in full settlement. What consideration has A given for B's promise to forego £25? The courts would say that the £25 was still due and B could sue to recover it despite his promise. It would be quite different if, at B's request, A had paid £75 at an earlier date. That would be a detriment to A and a benefit to B and A would then be providing consideration for B's forebearance.

The difficulty with the proposition advanced above is that, in practice, people dealing together do frequently make concessions to each other within the framework of their legally binding agreement. These concessions or variations are usually informal and may work perfectly well so long as the parties remain on good terms. If their relationship becomes strained one of them may wish to revert to the strict terms of their original agreement. The other will want to know if the variation can be regarded as binding. Traditionally, in order to enforce the variation, it has to be 'paid for' by some extra consideration. There is sometimes a way round this problem, however, by the application of the equitable principle of promissory estoppel.

Equitable principles operate to abate the rigours of the operation of the common law. Undoubtedly, there can be grave hardship where one contracting party has relied on some concession by the other, only to see it abruptly withdrawn. That was the state of affairs in *Central London Property Trust v. High Trees House*. The contract in that case related to a lease of a block of flats in London where the rent was to be £2,500 per annum. Because of the war it became extremely difficult to find tenants for the flats, so the landlord agreed to reduce the rent by half. When the war ended the landlord wanted to revert to the original rent and was also keen to know whether he could recover the arrears of rent. Effectively, what the landlord had done was to make a promise, within the framework of an existing contract, where the tenant gave no consideration for the promise, but where obviously the tenant had relied on it. On the authority of earlier cases the High Court found a principle of equity whereby if A leads B to suppose that A will not enforce his strict rights under the contract, then A cannot go back on his promise where it would be inequitable. Applying this principle in the High Trees case, the court would not allow the landlord to recover the arrears of rent. But the court also found that the end of the war acted as notice that the promise (made only because of the war) was no longer operative.

At first sight this case may seem to strike at the very core of the doctrine of consideration. Further examination shows that not to be the case. A number of points must be borne in mind. It was made clear in cases subsequent to the High Trees case that this equitable principle of promissory estoppel can only be pleaded by way of defence. In the colourful language of judges it is a shield and not a sword. There must be circumstances which show it would be inequitable for the promisor to go back on his word, at least without giving notice of his intention to revert to the original terms of the contract. Of course there may be cases where once a concession has been made it is impossible to revert to the original terms e.g. if the concession related to an extension of time for delivery. This raises important questions about the scope of promissory estoppel, as it seems that the effect of the promise or concession should be intended only to suspend legal rights and not to extinguish them completely. This fits well with the idea that the promisor can revert to the original terms by giving reasonable notice. Certainly if the scope of the rule is seen to be thus limited it gives rise to fewer legal difficulties.

It must be stressed that the development of promissory estoppel is based on equity. 'He who seeks equity must do equity' and 'he who comes to equity must come with clean hands'. It follows from these maxims that a person seeking to take advantage of promissory estoppel must himself have behaved properly. This aspect was critical to the decision in *D & C Builders v. Rees*, where two jobbing builders were owed money by Mr and Mrs Rees. Mrs Rees knew they were in a grievous financial state and she persuaded them to accept less than they were owed in full settlement. So desperate was their plight that they accepted the smaller sum but determined to see what they could do later to recover the rest. Mrs Rees claimed that they had promised to accept the smaller sum, that she had acted in reliance on their promise and that it would be inequitable to allow them to go back on their word. The court had no hesitation in finding that her own behaviour was inequitable as it verged on intimidation so they refused to allow her to take advantage of the equitable principle.

Although promissory estoppel can be seen as an important safe-guard against some of the harsher aspects of the common law rules it must be remembered that consideration is still essential for the creation of a valid contract, although there are limited circumstances where it may not be necessary to support some modification within the contract.

Only parties to a contract may sue to enforce it

It is a general rule of contract that in order to enforce a contract you must have given consideration, i.e. you must be a party to the contract. You have no right to sue merely because you were the intended beneficiary of a contract. In *Tweddle v. Atkinson*, where a young couple were about to be married, their respective fathers promised *each other* that each would pay a sum of money to the son. One father did not pay. The son attempted to sue him but failed as he was not a party to the contract. The defaulting father would have to be sued by the other father.

The importance of this rule is that it creates the notion of *privity of contract*. Although the rule can be inconvenient at times, it remains a fundamental part of contract law. It can have significant repercussions in the law relating to exclusion clauses (see page 85).

Intention

If both parties to a contract provide valid consideration that may be taken to indicate that they intend to make a legally binding arrange-ment. However, in English contract law, the courts look for a separate element of intention. Traditionally the courts have viewed the cases as falling into two categories: commercial arrangements where the parties are presumed to have intended to create a contract; and family, domestic and social arrangements where the parties are presumed not to intend to create a contract. The presumptions are sensible in most cases. Take the example of a parent who gives pocket money to a child or two friends who arrange to meet for supper. In either case, one party would never expect to be sued for breach of contract if such arrangements collapsed.

The problem facing the courts arises where one party to an

arrangement is seeking to rebut the normal presumption. In family arrangements he may want to prove that a legally binding agreement was indeed intended. He must then satisfy the court that this was so. Many of these cases turn on problems between husband and wife on the breakdown of marriage. In one case, *Merrit v. Merritt*, relations between the parties were so strained that they met in the neutral territory of a car park to discuss the disposal of their matrimonial home. Once they had arrived at a decision the wife insisted that the husband should jot down the main points on a piece of paper. The court found here that the parties did intend to create a legally binding contract, influenced no doubt by the rather formal steps that the wife had insisted on, and also by the fact that the relationship between the parties was breaking down, so that they were no longer closely bound in a family or domestic situation.

Where one party seeks to rebut the presumption, the court may also be influenced by the degree of certainty and detail with which the parties made their arrangements. In *Jones v. Padavatton*, the details of the arrangements with regard to a house were so sketchy that it was impossible to believe that the parties could have intended to make a legally binding agreement. In other cases it seems that as the family relationships become less close, so the strength of the presumption diminishes. In *Parker v. Clark*, where the parties were uncle and nephew, there was found to be an intention to create a legally binding agreement, but no doubt the amount at stake, together with the fact that the terms of the agreement obliged the nephew to give up his own home to come to look after the uncle, also influenced the court. There seemed to be little difficulty in establishing the appropriate intention in *Simpkins v. Pays*, where three people living together regularly participated in a competition. When one of them was ultimately the winner, she was obliged to share her winnings with the other two.

In a commercial situation it is considerably more difficult to rebut the presumption that a contract was intended. The courts will require convincing evidence that the parties intended otherwise. In *Rose and Frank Co. v. Compton Bros* the parties indicated in a written document that their arrangement was a 'gentleman's agreement, binding in honour only'. In the face of such convincing evidence the court was obliged to find that there was no contract.

Sometimes the parties want to lift their transaction outside the framework of contract law because they do not want the trouble and expense of litigation. This can frequently be seen as a condition in competitions and is one explanation of the football pools cases, where a punter who believes he has a winning line cannot sue to enforce his win. Provided the parties have made their intentions sufficiently clear, the court will accept their decision.

Form of the contract

As a general rule, English contract law does not require contracts to be made in any particular form. In practice many contracts are oral, which often leads people to assume that it would be difficult to sue to enforce such a contract. Certainly there may be problems of proof but in the end it may be a matter of judging which party the court can more reliably believe. Where a contract is put into writing to provide the necessary proof, the writing can in turn prove to be problematical. There may be a dispute about its precise meaning, or it may fail to spell out the entire contract between the parties.

Exceptionally the law sometimes requires contracts to be made in writing (e.g. hire purchase contracts). In these cases it is usually necessary to look at the appropriate statute to see the precise form the writing must take and also to determine what will happen if the parties have not complied with the rules. Rules about the precise form of the contract can be a useful device for protecting consumers. In the Hire Purchase Acts certain information contained in HP agreements needs to be displayed in prominent boxes, by which means it is hoped to draw those aspects more particularly to the attention of the consumer.

Despite the freedom about the form of the contract there has long been special treatment for contracts for the sale of land. As early as 1677, rules were laid down that contracts for the sale of land must be evidenced by a note or memorandum in writing, otherwise the contract would be unenforceable. These rules were re-enacted in more or less the same form by s.40 of the Law of Property Act 1925. Evidence in writing was meant as a safeguard against fraud but ironically the need for such evidence has sometimes been the very means by which people could perpetrate a fraud. The rules were regarded as un-satisfactory and, when the Law Commission took a detailed look at the workings of s.40, it reported: 'As a result of judicial attempts to prevent the statute being used as an instrument of fraud, it is virtually impossible to discover with acceptable certainty, prior to proceedings, whether a contract will be found to be enforceable . . . s.40 would appear ripe for reform'.

That reform has now taken place with the repeal of s.40 by the Law of Property (Miscellaneous Provisions) Act 1989. Section 2 of the new Act provides that contracts for the sale or other disposition of interests in land can only be made in writing, and must incorporate all the terms expressly agreed between the parties. The contract must be signed by both parties, or their agents. Incorporation of the express terms may be by reference to another document, and the rules also make provision for the methods employed by solicitors engaged on behalf of the parties, where it is common to 'exchange contracts'. Sales of land by public auction are excluded from these rules, as are short leases (see page 277).

Although these new rules seem designed to promote greater certainty, in that it should be easier to determine when a legally enforceable contract for the sale of land exists, one major problem remains to be tackled. It is still the case that people who are unaware of these rules may 'shake hands' on an oral agreement for the sale of land, and the purchaser may then incur expenditure on the land concerned, only to find that the vendor refuses to complete the transaction. Take the example of an oral agreement for the sale of a house, where the parties agree that the prospective purchaser can have a key for the property, and may undertake work on the property in advance of the legal transfer to him. If the purchaser were to install central heating and undertake extensive decorating work, it would be disastrous for him if the vendor then refused to transfer the house to him. In such a case, the vendor would seem to receive improper protection from the new rules. The aggrieved purchaser would be unable to sue for breach of contract because the s.2 rules state that a contract for the sale of land *can only be made in writing*. Lack of writing, therefore, means that there is no contract.

Problems of the sort outlined above were previously solved by the use of discretionary equitable relief, in the form of the equitable doctrine of part performance. In the absence of the necessary note or memorandum in writing, this equitable principle used to permit specific performance of the contract if the behaviour of the parties was in itself sufficient to indicate the existence of a contract. Unfortunately, there is no scope now for the application of this discretion, as it depends for its efficacy on the fact that lack of writing under the old s.40 rules merely rendered a valid contract unenforceable. It did not deny the very existence of a contract, which is the result achieved under the s.2 provisions of the new Act. Clearly, the equitable doctrine of part performance has been repealed along with s.40.

The Law Commission did consider the difficulties that the new rules would create, and in particular they examined the plight of a would-be purchaser who had expended money and effort on the property. They considered that the present law contained a sufficient armoury of weapons by which to assist such a person, such as an action for restitution, or suing on a *quantum meruit* if work had been undertaken on a property. It will take time for cases to come before the courts to show whether the Law Commission's faith in these solutions is justified.

One interesting application of the new rules had already come before the courts in *Spiro v. Glencrown Properties Ltd.* This case involved an option to purchase land, where the vendor and prospective purchaser had both signed an agreement creating the option, which conformed in all respects with s.2. Later, when the would-be purchaser served a signed notice to exercise the option, the vendor attempted to argue that the documents already signed merely amounted to an irrevocable offer and that it was the notice exercising the option which brought about a contract for the sale of an interest in land. As this notice was signed only by the purchaser, it did not satisfy the rules of s.2. The court dismissed that argument, preferring instead to construe the original agreement as the contract, conditional upon the exercise of the option. When the purchaser served the signed notice, he was thereby fulfilling the condition. It was the original agreement which needed to satisfy the s.2 rules, and as it clearly did, the vendor was bound.

Subject to contract

It is common in dealings relating to land for the parties to be anxious to take expert advice before finally committing themselves to a binding contract. Negotiations are often carried on 'subject to contract'. Those words will usually be interpreted by the courts to mean that the parties have not yet concluded a contract. The very words deny the existence of a present contract. Of course, much depends on the precise words used, as the role of the court is to seek to construe what the parties must have intended. In one case the parties declared their agreement to be a 'provisional agreement', but the effect of that phrase was quite different and the court held that their agreement was binding from the start (*Branca v. Cobarro*). It seems to follow from the cases that where the parties use the phrase 'subject to contract' in a written document, that document is not a contract, even if it complies in all other respects with s.2.

Capacity to contract

One protective feature of the rules of contract is found in the situation where a person cannot effectively look after his own interests when bargaining. Protection is principally afforded to minors but some rules also exist to protect drunkards and the mentally disordered. Minors are persons below the age of eighteen. The age limit was reduced by the Family Law Reform Act 1969, before which it was twenty-one. The rules regarding the capacity of minors to contract stem from the twin objectives of protecting the young person against his own immaturity and inexperience, while at the same time seeking not to unduly burden the adult who deals with a minor.

Even minors have to be supplied with the necessities of life. The law has recognized this by providing that minors must pay a reasonable price for necessaries which are sold and delivered. In this context, necessaries are defined as goods suitable to the minor's station in life and to his actual requirements at the time of sale and delivery (Sale of Goods Act 1979 s.3). This definition concentrates on goods but similar rules could operate where a minor was provided with necessary services. The wording of the Act makes it clear that there is no problem in cases where a minor pays cash. Difficulties start to occur where goods have already been delivered and the supplier now wants to recover his money. To succeed, he must satisfy the court that the goods were suitable to that minor's station in life and to his actual requirements. It can readily be appreciated how difficult it can be to apply such a rule in practice, as a trader is unlikely to know in detail about a minor's station in life, or the extent to which he is already supplied with the goods in question.

It must be emphasized that these rules about minors' contracts do not have the significance they once did. Many of the worst problems disappeared when the age for protection was lowered to eighteen. Set against that, young people now live in a society with many expensive goods available to them. A trader can always protect himself, if he is in doubt about a person's age or their ability or willingness to pay, by insisting on cash. Where he has not done so he enjoys some minimum protection in that he can sue to recover a reasonable price for those goods or services deemed to be necessaries.

Where goods supplied are not necessaries, new rules operate under the Minors' Contracts Act 1987. Generally it provides that minors' contracts do not bind the minor, but are binding on the adult. The most important situation likely to be covered by this rule is the case of the minor who buys non-necessary goods which he has failed to pay for. If he has paid he cannot get his money back, except in those circumstances where an adult could also recover his money. Although the Act provides that these contracts are not binding on the minor, certain legal consequences do occur when such a contract is made. Ownership in the goods concerned does pass to the minor. Section 3(1) refers to 'property acquired' by the minor. As ownership has passed to the minor it follows that he can transfer ownership if he sells the goods to a third party. This is an important rule for the protection of innocent third parties.

These rules may come into operation in cases where a minor has persuaded a tradesman to supply him with goods on credit by telling lies about his age. Such behaviour amounts to the tort of deceit, but the trader could not, in the alternative, sue for damages for deceit because the law has long taken the view that enforcement of a contract against a minor must not be permitted by such a back-door route.

If the trader can neither force the the infant to pay, nor recover damages for deceit, he will be anxious to know if he can take the goods back. Equity has always frowned on deceitful behaviour by minors and would, in appropriate cases, grant an order for restitution whereby the goods would be restored to the trader provided the minor still had them in his possession. Now, under s. 3 of the new Act, some effort has been made to improve on that situation. The court is given a discretion to order a minor to restore property acquired under a contract, or property representing it. It is not clear how widely this last phrase will be interpreted. It obviously seems to cover the situation, say, where a minor obtains stereo equipment for which he has not paid, and then swaps it with a friend for a motor scooter. The motor scooter would be property representing the stereo equipment acquired under the contract. The real problem still seems to be where a minor sells the stereo and only has the money he has received. It is unclear in such a case whether the minor must hand over the money.

Despite the protections they enjoy, minors are bound by beneficial contracts of service, education, training or apprenticeship. The courts have shown themselves ready to give a broad interpretation when deciding exactly which contracts fall into these categories. Surprisingly, the courts have long held that where the minor is a trader, contracts are not binding on him even though he would benefit by making a profit. Where the contract is of a type which confers an interest of a continuing nature on a minor (e.g. a contract to buy land or shares in a company) the rule is that the minor may avoid liability for the future on such contracts by repudiating during his infancy.

Despite the recent changes in law, most traders are probably placing their faith in the fact that young people will seldom learn about these rules while still young enough to be able to abuse them!

The contents of the contract

Once it is clear that a contract has been agreed, it may then be necessary to establish precisely the obligations which each party has undertaken. Of course, this analysis will not be necessary if everything goes well between the parties and each performs the contract to the entire satisfaction of the other. However, the rules are important not only in problem or dispute solving, but also in contract planning, particularly in a business situation. The more the parties understand the rules, the better they are able to use them to ensure that subsequent problems do not occur, or where they do, that they can be solved with a minimum of expense, delay and irritation.

Where a contract consists of buying a cup of coffee from a machine, or paying the fare on a bus, it may be difficult to imagine what the contents of such a contract are. But all contracts have terms. These may be express or implied. The express terms will be those specifically negotiated between the parties, either orally or in writing. Remember that the parties are largely free to fix their own terms. Contract law still adheres generally to the principle of freedom of contract. The parties must strike their own bargain. In effect, this imposes a serious restriction on the extent to which terms can be implied in a contract.

Implied terms may be incorporated from an Act of Parliament. One of the commonest examples is the set of implied terms incorporated into sale of goods transactions. Without any need for specific negotiation by the parties, terms are implied relating to fitness for purpose of the goods, and their merchantable quality. The courts have a limited role to play in judicially implying terms, but great care is needed to ensure that judges are not seen to be making the agreement for the parties. It is usually said that terms can only be implied by the judges if it is necessary to give 'business efficacy' to the arrangements made by the parties. This may occur where the parties have already undertaken a substantial part of the contract and they come up against some problem or difficulty which they did not provide for. In such cases a judge can imply a term where it is clear that, had the parties put their minds to the problem at the appropriate time, both would have agreed to the term proposed.

Terms are the obligations under a contract but inevitably they will not be of equal importance. Take, for example, a term about the time of a delivery of goods. This may be of paramount importance where goods are perishable or where it is clear that they will be of little commercial use unless delivered on time. In other cases the time for delivery may be far less significant. The law has to find some way to grade or classify terms, because it must seek to offer remedies appropriate to the significance of the term which has been broken. Traditionally, the law classified terms as major terms, which it called conditions, and minor terms, which it called warranties. The terminology is unfortunate, as both of those words have sundry other meanings and uses in the law of contract. Conditions are said to be those obligations which are of the essence, which go to the very core and heart of the contract. Breach of a condition always gives the injured party the right to sue for damages. Over and above that, the injured party may also have the right to repudiate the contract. This means that he is entitled to regard himself as no longer bound by the contract. A warranty is of more peripheral importance, often said to be merely collateral to the main purpose of the contract. An injured party can sue for damages for breach of warranty but has no right to repudiate the contract.

The problem with this traditional approach to classifying terms is that it requires a decision to be made about the status of the term at the time when the contract was made. In effect this emphasizes the importance of the intention of the parties, as it should be clear from what was said and written, and from all the surrounding circumstances, whether they intended a particular term to be a condition or warranty. This approach creates business certainty, as it would be possible to say at the outset what remedies would be available for particular breaches. But it takes little account of the realities of business life, where the term breached may be only a warranty, but the consequences could turn out to be very serious. This would leave the victim of the breach in a situation where he would be forced to go on with performance of the contract and be limited to a claim for damages.

Consider as an example the problem which arose in *Hong Kong Fir Shipping Co. Ltd v. Kawasaki Kisen Kaisha Ltd*. One of the terms in a contract to charter a ship for two years provided that the ship should be in every way fitted for ordinary cargo service. When the ship was delivered at the beginning of the two-year charter period it was unseaworthy and when it made its first voyage, repairs were needed which took four months to complete. Did the breach amount to a breach of condition? If it did, the charterer could repudiate liability under the contract and thus rid himself of the burden of this unsatisfactory vessel over the remainder of the two-year period *and* sue for damages. If it was only a breach of warranty his claim would be limited to damages and he would be left with the vessel for the remainder of the charter period.

In the Hong Kong Fir case, the Court of Appeal chose a novel solution, preferring instead to say that some terms are 'intermediate' or 'innominate'. Such terms defy initial classification as conditions or warranties and the parties must wait until the scale of the resulting breach is known, at which point the term can be suitably classified. Obviously this produces a much less certain situation between the parties during the currency of the contract.

This development in judicial thinking did not in fact assist the charterer in the Hong Kong Fir case. The term in issue was held to be only a warranty, so the charterer had no right to repudiate the contract. As he had wrongfully repudiated, he was obliged to pay damages to the shipowner.

The same problem of classifying a term was before the Court of Appeal in another charter party case, *The Mihalis Angelos*, where the term related to the date when the ship would be ready to load. In the event, it was nearly a month after that date before the ship was ready. The term was held to be a condition. The court made the point that it was influenced by earlier cases holding similar clauses to be conditions and it was vital to remember that 'one of the important elements of the law is predictability'. One important point emerging from this case is that it may already be established, either by statute or an earlier precedent, that a particular type of clause falls into the category of a condition. Then there is no scope for attempting to classify it as an innominate term. But where a term could be either a condition or a warranty, and it is not clear which the parties intended, and where the range of possible breaches and the scale of the resulting harm is very wide, then the court may classify it as innominate. This classification is theoretically made at the time when the contract is made, but the remedy available for breach of the term will only be established once the scale of that breach is known.

The appropriateness of this 'wait and see' approach is well demonstrated by the facts in the Hong Kong Fir case. There, the clause in question required that the ship was to be 'in every way fitted for cargo service'. These words were so wide in potential interpretation that there could be breaches ranging from failure to supply the vessel with a proper number of anchors, or to put on board medical supplies, to totally defective engines at the other end of the scale.

It is clear that the courts remain anxious about creating business uncertainty. The House of Lords has confirmed that the traditional division into conditions and warranties is still acceptable in many cases (*Bunge Corporation v. Tradex Export SA*). They have, however, left the way open to use the more flexible Hong Kong Fir approach in a limited number of cases where this may be justified. Clearly the problem can be largely overcome by the parties being sufficiently specific at the outset about the result of each type of breach. This is a classic example of how rules of contract law can have a planning function.

Exclusion and limitation clauses

Although many terms in contracts will be concerned with creating obligations, it has become increasingly common for the parties to seek to limit or exclude liability which would otherwise arise under the contract. Exclusion and limitation clauses are frequently encountered in contracts involving car parks, dry cleaners, film processing, package holiday deals, furniture removal and insurance. They may take forms such as 'No liability accepted for any damage caused by flooding' or 'In the event of a breach, our liability is restricted to ten times the contract price'.

Exclusion clauses fall into two main categories: those negotiated between parties of equal bargaining strength, where such clauses can be seen to facilitate business activity and to allow the parties to allocate risks between themselves and organize which of them should insure; and those imposed on a weaker party by a stronger party who may enjoy a monopolistic position, where the weaker party has no option but to accept. Clauses falling into the latter category are, not unnaturally, unpopular with the courts. In the past the judges strove to protect victims of harsh exclusion clauses, but some of the techniques developed by them to afford protection produced unfortunate results in business cases, sometimes upsetting the very carefully negotiated arrangements between the parties. The courts have never had a power at common law simply to strike out exclusion or limitation clauses on the grounds that they are unfair or unreasonable because contract law proceeds on the assumption that the parties are free to fix the terms of their bargain for themselves.

Judicial dislike of exclusion clauses has always meant that courts will only allow reliance on such a clause if it has effectively become part of the contract. The incorporation of the clause into the contract can occur:

1   By one party signing a document containing the clause, of which he would then be deemed to have notice whether he had read it or not.
2   By one party giving reasonable notice of the clause to the other. Reasonable notice may be given in a contractual document but not every piece of paper passing between the parties can be so classified. Generally, contractual documents are those pieces of paper on which a reasonable man would expect to find conditions printed. This would usually include documents such as airline tickets or standard company order forms. It would not include things such as mere receipts for the payment of money. In any case, such a receipt would often be handed over too late, as it is vital that reasonable notice be given before, or at the time when, the contract is made. Once the parties have finished negotiating and finalized their deal it is too late for one of them to try to change it or add to it unilaterally. Where no contractual document passes between the parties the exclusion clause can be incorporated by the reasonable display of a notice at an appropriate place, so that its contents could have been read before the contract was made.
3   By virtue of a 'course of dealings' between the parties. Where two

people have dealt with each other regularly, always using the same terms, the court may be prepared to say that adequate notice has been given of any exclusion clause. This principle is only likely to be applied between business parties who have regular commercial dealings.

In cases where the court accepts that the exclusion clause is properly incorporated and forms part of the contract, the judge will next consider what the words of the clause mean, and whether the wording covers the actual facts which have arisen. In the construction or interpretation of the clause the standard policy of the courts is to construe any ambiguity strictly against the interest of the party seeking to rely on the clause. In one case involving motor insurance, a clause in the contract provided that the insurers need not pay out on a claim under the contract if the vehicle was carrying 'an excessive load'. In fact, it was a five seater car carrying six persons, but the judge held that the word 'load' did not include people.

Prior to 1977, when the Unfair Contract Terms Act was passed, the judges had to use these construction and interpretation techniques boldly in order to protect victims of harsh clauses. In consequence, there was a very distorted result in many of the cases. Such striving on the part of the judges is much less necessary now since the 1977 Act was passed, and they have been urged by the House of Lords to give the relevant words in an exclusion clause their plain and natural meaning. Nevertheless, the two common law rules relating to incorporation and construction are still relevant, though the provisions of the 1977 Act now govern the majority of problem cases in this area.

Unfair Contract Terms Act 1977

The scope of this Act is wider than its name would suggest as it deals with notices limiting liability in the law of tort as well as exclusion clauses in the law of contract. One advantage of introducing statutory control of exclusion clauses is that a flexible approach can be taken, making a distinction between the type of clause negotiated between businessmen on an equal footing, and other clauses 'imposed' by businessmen on consumers. The Act does not apply to all contracts – insurance contracts for example are outside its scope. Although the Act is fairly general in its coverage there are other specific Acts of Parliament which also prohibit particular types of exclusion clause.

The main sections of the Act only apply in 'business liability' situations. This phrase is defined as meaning liability for breach of duties arising from things done in the course of business (s.1(3)). So, except in sale of goods transactions which are considered separately, (see page 125) the Act does not extend to what may be regarded as private transactions. Once the Act is shown to apply, it has two different techniques for dealing with offending exclusion clauses. Some are rendered totally ineffective however they are drafted. Others can survive and take effect if they satisfy the requirement of reasonableness set out in the Act.

Sections 2 and 3 are the most important general sections of the Act. Section 2 deals with liability for negligence, which is defined by s.1 of the Act as:

1 Breach of a contractual obligation to take reasonable care or exercise reasonable skill in the performance of the contract; or
2 breach of common law duty to take reasonable care or exercise reasonable skill; or
3 breach of the common duty of care imposed by the Occupiers' Liability Act 1957.

If negligence results in death or personal injury, then it is not possible to exclude or limit liability either by an exclusion clause in a contract or by a notice displayed generally. So, where a contract contains a term that 'no liability is accepted for death or injury howsoever caused', then if death or injury is caused by negligence, the relevant clause will be rendered totally ineffective.

Section 2 also provides that where loss or damage (other than death or personal injury) is caused by negligence, an exclusion clause *can* take effect *if* it satisfies the requirement of reasonableness. This requirement will be analysed in conjunction with s.3.

Section 3 covers two different situations. First, where one party deals as a consumer, and second where one party deals on the other's written standard terms of business. Both of these situations require further explanation. Dealing as a consumer means that one party is not making the contract in the course of a business but the other party is. A classic example would be taking your car to be serviced. You deal as a consumer, while the garage deals in the course of a business. Or it could be having your house rewired. You deal as a consumer and the electrician deals in the course of a business. What constitutes 'written standard terms of business' is not entirely clear as the phrase is not defined by the Act.

In either of these two situations s.3 provides that the other party, having committed a breach, cannot exclude or restrict his liability for that breach unless the exclusion clause satisfies the requirement of reasonableness. An example will help to illustrate the working of the section. Imagine that you take a film to be processed by a high street photographic shop. On the counter is displayed a clear notice to customers that in the event of the film being lost or spoilt, liability is limited to a replacement film. When you go to collect your photographs, they cannot be found and the shop tries to rely on the exclusion clause. It will only be able to do so if it can prove to the court that the clause satisfies the requirement of reasonableness. This means that, in relation to contract terms, it must be a fair and reasonable term to include, given what the parties knew or ought to have known at the time when they made the contract. The burden of showing that it was fair and reasonable is on the person now seeking to rely on the clause. The answer will obviously depend very much on the circumstances of each case, but a judge approaching the problem is given some limited help by the Act itself. It is clear from s.11 that there are cases where the judge must consider whether it was possible for the parties to have protected themselves by insurance. For instance, there are situations where a businessman may be prepared to quote two prices for a job. A high price will reflect the fact that he is prepared to accept all liability. A low price may be conditional upon him excluding some liability. Naturally, when I consider his prices I may well choose the low price if I can easily and cheaply insure against the risks myself or if I already have insurance which covers those risks.

The Act itself provides guidelines which will sometimes be relevant when determining reasonableness. The court may take into account:

1   The relative bargaining strength of the parties. One factor which might be important here is whether the goods or services could have been obtained easily elsewhere.
2   Did the customer receive some inducement to agree to the term? The example quoted above where a customer chooses the low price is an instance of an inducement. The court will also keep in mind whether a similar contract made with someone else would have been likely to contain an identical term.
3   Did the customer know, or ought he reasonably to have known, of the existence and extent of the term? Bearing in mind the importance of showing that the term has been properly incorporated into the contract this guideline seems to suggest that there is one standard for deciding on incorporation but a different one for deciding reasonableness.
4   Where the term excludes liability only if a party fails to comply with some condition, was it reasonable to assume when the contract was made that it would be practicable to fulfil the condition? An example might arise where a clause states: 'No liability for any breakages in transit which are not reported to us within five minutes of delivery.' Even when the contract was made it would be clear that such a condition was not practicable.

5   Where the contract relates to a sale of goods which have been specially manufactured, processed or adapted to the buyer's requirements, that may give the seller wider scope to limit his liability.

There are relatively few decided cases to clarify the requirement of reasonableness. That may be a good thing, as it is important to remember that these cases turn on their own individual facts. *George Mitchell v. Finney Lock Seeds Ltd* makes a useful illustration of the rules. The farmer wanted to plant Dutch winter cabbage in a field of some sixty acres. He was sure that he could make a handsome profit on the vegetable as it would be ready to harvest when home-grown vegetables were in short supply. He obtained the seed from Finney's at a cost of £192. The terms of the contract provided that liability was limited. In the event of the seed being defective, the sellers would refund only the price of the seed. They also excluded 'all liability for any loss or damage arising from the use of any seeds supplied by us and for any consequential loss or damage arising out of such use, or for any other loss or damage whatsoever.'

Whatever the seeds supplied might have been, they were not Dutch winter cabbage. The crop failed and the farmer sued for £63,000. The company was prepared to refund £192. The case turned on whether Finney's could rely on the clause. They could only do so if the clause was a fair and reasonable one. In the House of Lords the judges were conscious that this was the first interpretation of the 'fair and reasonable' provision. They made clear that arriving at a decision as to what is fair and reasonable is not like the exercise of discretion, but the court must put a number of factors on the scales and see on which side the balance comes down. 'There will sometimes be room for a legitimate difference of judicial opinion . . . and the appellate court should treat the original decision with the utmost respect.' When looking at the facts of the present case, the judges took into account that the farmer had been a regular customer of the seed firm for many years and had had plenty of opportunities to read the exclusion clause. It was not a difficult clause to understand. Similar clauses would be found in every seed firm's contracts, and had never caused farmers as a body to protest through the National Farmers Union. So far as the question of insurance was concerned, the seed firm could have insured against the risk of crop failure without needing to significantly raise the price of seed. The court was also influenced by the fact that the seed firm usually sought to negotiate settlements in cases like this, rather than rely on the strict terms of the exclusion clause. This latter fact was regarded by the court as particularly significant as they thought it pointed to the seed firm themselves recognizing that their own clause was unreasonable. Taking all of these factors into account, the House of Lords held that the clause was not fair and reasonable.

The 1977 Act has been of great importance and value in that the flood of complex, and often irreconcilable, decisions on exclusion clauses has virtually stopped. It is clear that it will be easier to justify a clause which merely limits liability, as opposed to one which seeks to exclude liability completely. Other relevant aspects of the Act are considered separately in relation to misrepresentation, sale of goods and occupier's liability.

Misrepresentation and mistake

The basic idea of misrepresentation is a very simple one to grasp. One party makes a false statement which has induced the other to enter the contract. This area of law is regarded as complex, largely due to the number of overlaps with other areas of law, so that it is seldom possible to view a misrepresentation in isolation. The overlaps occur either when misrepresentation induces a mistake; or when the statement made, depending on its relative importance, may be classed as a representation or a term; or because the law of contract and the law of tort have separately developed ideas about negligent statements.

In complex contractual negotiations, both parties will make many statements to each other about the subject matter. We have already considered the problem of classifying terms of a contract. Terms may result from statements made which now form part of the contractual obligations. Alternatively, the statement may be of less importance and may not become part of the contract. Nevertheless, that statement may weigh with one party in influencing him to make the contract. He is induced by the representation. Some statements may simply have been designed to create a good bargaining atmosphere and these may give rise to no liability at all. These examples are sometimes referred to as 'tradesmen's puffs'. In one case, where a seller described a car as 'a great little goer', no liability could arise from such a claim.

The court must determine into which category a statement falls. When deciding between terms and representations they are influenced by factors such as:

- How early in negotiations was the statement made?
- Was an oral statement subsequently included in a later written contract?
- Did the person making the statement have special knowledge on the subject matter of the contract?

The answers to these questions will not necessarily produce a definite solution. Each case will turn on its own facts.

Where a false statement is classed as a representation it is possible for it to be made innocently, negligently or fraudulently, depending on the maker's state of mind. The classification is important because each type of misrepresentation gives rise to different remedies. It is also important to distinguish terms from representations because of the different remedies available. Non-compliance with a term results in breach of the contract. Misrepresentation is a false statement standing outside the contract and not forming part of the obligations and does not, therefore, involve a breach of contract. The difference in the remedies available used to be so great that the distinction between a term and a representation assumed immense importance. Since the changes in the law introduced by the Misrepresentation Act 1967, it is now far less significant.

Figure 2 shows how any particular statement can be graded. Take an example like 'The car has only done 20,000 miles', or 'This lorry can carry thirty tons'.

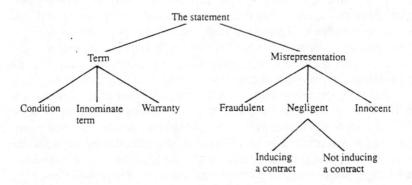

Figure 2   *The grading of terms and misrepresentations*

Misrepresentation is defined as a false statement of fact, made by one party to the other, before or at the time of contracting, which is one of the causes which induces the contract. Within the definition, a number of points of difficulty occur.

1   There must be a statement, but the courts have been prepared to imply a statement from behaviour. 'A nod or a wink, or a shake of the head or a smile' from the purchaser, intended to induce the vendor to believe the existence of a non-existing fact, would be sufficient.

2 The statement must be of fact. This excludes statements of intention, statements of opinion and statements of law. Statements of opinion give rise to particular problems, as they can be made by someone who has more knowledge and information in the particular bargaining situation. This makes the statement seem especially authoritative. It seems as if the maker of the statement knows facts which justify him in holding that opinion. In one case a vendor, trying to sell property which was let, described the tenant as 'a most desirable tenant'. The vendor knew that the tenant was in arrears with his rent and earlier rent had only been extracted with considerable difficulty. In these circumstances, knowing the facts as he did, the court held that the vendor could not reasonably hold such an opinion. They regarded his statement as actionable misrepresentation (*Smith v. Land and House Property Corporation*). In that case, the vendor had superior knowledge. He alone knew the problems about the tenant. Compare the situation in *Bisset v. Wilkinson*, where a vendor was selling land in New Zealand. In response to an enquiry from the purchaser, the vendor said that the land could carry 2000 sheep. The vendor had never kept sheep nor had the land ever been used for that purpose, so he had no facts on which to base this opinion. It was only an opinion and not actionable as misrepresentation.

3 Since there must usually be a false statement, it follows that keeping silent cannot usually constitute misrepresentation. If I want to sell my second-hand car, and I say nothing at all about its condition or performance, it will be up to a prospective purchaser to enquire specifically about anything that concerns or worries him. This is part of a general principle in contract of 'let the buyer beware' (*caveat emptor*). I would be under no duty to point out faults and defects. Of course, if I am asked specific questions then I should answer honestly, otherwise my statements could amount to misrepresentation. There are some situations, however, where the law imposes a positive duty to speak. In these cases silence can constitute misrepresentation. These situations are:

(a) Where one party tells a half truth but remains silent about some fact which distorts the positive statement made. An example is where a prospective purchaser asked about the farms on an estate, enquiring whether all the farms were let. The vendor replied that they were (a positive statement) but failed to go on to say that all the tenant farmers had given notice to quit, (silence distorting the positive representation) (*Dimmock v. Hallett*).

(b) Where the relationship between the parties is fiduciary (a relationship of trust) e.g. solicitor and client, or banker and customer. If one then makes a contract with the other, there is a positive duty to disclose known material facts. This rule is significant when considering undue influence.

(c) Where the contract is one involving utmost good faith. The commonest example of such a contract is insurance. Here the facts are all within the knowledge of one party. On the strength of what he tells the other, that other must decide whether or not to accept the risk and how much to charge as a premium. The law imposes a positive duty in these cases to reveal all material facts. Insurance contracts are discussed in greater detail on page 134.

4   The false statement must actually help to induce the contract. There will be many occasions when false statements are made, but they do not act as an inducement. This may be because the other party does not hear the statement, or does not believe it, or is not in any way influenced by it, but makes his decision to enter the contract for quite separate reasons.

Where all the relevant features of misrepresentation can be proved, the injured party will want to know if he can escape from the contract, and also whether he has any claim for damages. The answer depends largely on the type of misrepresentation involved. Was it a statement made fraudulently, negligently, or innocently? Once the maker's frame of mind is established, the remedies can be considered

Fraudulent misrepresentation

This is defined as a false statement made knowingly, without belief in its truth, or recklessly, careless whether it is true or false. In the very limited number of cases where this can be proved, the behaviour of the person making the false statement would amount to the tort of deceit. Unfortunately, it is very difficult to convince a court that a statement falls into this category. As one judge commented: 'A charge of fraud is such a terrible thing to bring against a man that it cannot be maintained unless it is shown that he has a wicked mind'.

Negligent misrepresentation

This category of misrepresentation was introduced by the Misrepresentation Act 1967, and is one of the factors which has effected a significant improvement in this area of the law. A statement is negligent if it was made in circumstances where the maker had no reasonable grounds for believing it to be true. He may have thought that he was making a true statement but the court will evaluate whether the basis for him so believing was reasonable. This may be a difficult question to resolve, and much may be at stake. An important commercial case, *Howard Marine and Dredging Co. Ltd v. Ogden & Sons Ltd* will illustrate the problem.

In order to tender for a large excavation contract with a water authority, Ogdens needed to hire or buy barges to move spoil out to sea. They approched Howard Marine and had extensive discussions and negotiations with Howard's manager. He thought that two particular barges would be suitable for Ogden's needs, and he told Ogdens that each barge could carry 1600 tonnes. He was basing his statement on his recollection of information contained in *Lloyds Register*. In the company's files about the barges, the manager could have discovered that the *Lloyds Register* figure was wrong. The actual carrying capacity of each barge was nearer 1000 tonnes. Ogdens were successful in getting the excavation contract, and they immediately hired the two barges from Howards. As soon as they began using them they realized the vast discrepancy between the manager's statement and the true carrying capacity. Ogden's refused to pay any further hire charges for the barges and wanted to claim damages from Howards. Obviously the court had to classify the statement made. First, they had to consider whether it was of such importance that it could be regarded as a term of the contract. Given the fact that the statement was made quite early in the negotiations, and not subsequently included in the charterparty (the written hire contract), the court found that it was not a term. What kind of misrepresentation was it? By a majority verdict only, the Court of Appeal found that this was a negligent misrepresentation. One of the judges thought that it was reasonable for the manager to rely on *Lloyds Register*, which was normally famous for its detail and accuracy; but the other two judges thought that the manager should have referred to, and checked in, the authoritative file on each barge.

Liability for negligent misrepresentation under s.2 of the 1967 Act can only arise if the statement causes the other party to enter into a contract. There is considerable overlap in this area with the law of tort, and negligent statements are a problem area. Just before the 1967 Act was passed the courts had an opportunity to consider what liability, if any, should arise from negligent statements. In the case of *Hedley Byrne v. Heller* the facts involved a company who wanted assurances about the financial stability of a prospective customer. They asked the customer if it was in order to approach the customer's bank for a credit reference. The bank negligently informed the company that the customer was financially sound. Subsequently, the customer went into liquidation, and the company suffered losses in excess of £15,000. As they were unlikely to get their money from the customer, the company was anxious to sue the bank. On these facts, it is clear that the bank's statement had not induced any contract between the bank and the company, so s.2 of the 1967 Act could not cover such a case. That section requires that a person must have entered a contract. Could the company recover the damages against the bank in the tort of negligence? The law on negligence had not developed at that stage to cover such mis-statements causing pure financial loss, but the House of Lords in the Hedley Byrne case showed themselves ready, in appropriate circumstances, to develop the law and award damages.

In the mid-1960s, this created a sudden new wealth of possibilities where a person was a victim of a negligent statement. It has become common to refer to negligent statements which result in a contract as negligent misrepresentations, and those which do not result in a contract as negligent mis-statements. While it may be to a plaintiff's advantage to have more possible causes of action, these twin developments in respect of negligent statements make the law more complex than it need be. See page 216 for further treatment of negligent misstatements in the law of tort.

Innocent misrepresentation

Since the 1967 Act, this is limited to those cases where the maker of the statement honestly believed that his statement was true *and* he had reasonable grounds for believing it to be true.

Remedies for misrepresentation

Once it is clear which type of misrepresentation is involved, the next problem is to establish the appropriate remedy. All types of misrepresentation have the same effect on the contract, which is to make the contract voidable at the option of the party misled. This means that the injured party can seek to rescind the contract, to have it set aside as if it had never existed. The parties would then be restored to their original positions. This is known as the remedy of rescission, and in some circumstances it can be achieved on a self-help basis without any court assistance or intervention. Inevitably such help will often be required, especially where the party at fault will not cooperate. There will be times when a court is unable to order rescission. The remedy is discretionary and will not be available in the following circumstances:

1   Where the court is unable to restore the parties to their original

position. This could be the case where goods sold have been consumed, or inextricably mixed with other goods.

2   Where the injured party has affirmed the contract. This means that the injured party is fully aware of the false statement but has shown himself prepared to go on with the contract.
3   Where the injured party has delayed too long in seeking rescission. There is no precisely defined time limit, but a long delay once all the facts are known may in itself be an affirmation of the contract.
4   Where third party rights have intervened.
5   Where the court decides to exercise its discretion under the 1967 Act to award damages in lieu of rescission.

Damages

When considering the availability of damages for misrepresentation, it must be remembered that the false statement in question may have induced the contract, but it does not form part of the contract obligations. If the statement was regarded as sufficiently important by the parties to form part of the contractual obligations, it will be classified as a term. If it then turns out to be false the appropriate remedies for breach of contract will be available.

As misrepresentations stand outside the contract, it follows that there can be no damages available in the law of contract. Where the statement is fraudulent, damages have always been available in the tort of deceit. Prior to the recognition of negligent misrepresentation, a misrepresentation made without fraud was innocent, for which no damages were available. Now, if a plaintiff can prove negligent misrepresentation under s.2, the court has power to award damages. It seems clear that these damages will be assessed on a tort basis rather than a contract basis. Where the claim is for negligent mis-statement within the Hedley Byrne principle, damages for the tort of negligence are available. The difference between tort damages and contract damages is significant, as it could result in quite different calculations. Tort damages are designed to put the plaintiff into the position he would have been in but for the tort; contract damages are designed to put the plaintiff into the position he would have been in if the contract had been properly performed.

Damages in lieu of rescission

Even if a false statement has been made, the remedy of rescission is sometimes far too extreme to produce a fair result. If I sell you my car, and tell you that it has done 30,000 miles, and you subsequently discover it has done 31,000 miles, it can often be quite satisfactory to award damages in recognition of the false statement. It may seem to give undue protection to the purchaser to allow him to back out altogether, although this will often be a question of degree. Under s.2(2) of the 1967 Act, the court has a discretion to award damages in lieu of rescission for negligent and innocent misrepresentation.

Limiting or excluding liability for misrepresentation

In the same way as it is possible to limit or exclude liability for obligations which would otherwise arise under a contract (see page 85) it is also possible to limit or exclude liability for misrepresentations which induce a contract. The relevant rules are contained in s.3 of the Misrepresentation Act 1967 which has been substantially amended by the Unfair Contract Terms Act 1977. Section 3 permits exclusion of liability for false statements (negligent or innocent, but not fraudulent), provided that the clause satisfies the requirement of reasonableness (see page 88).

Mistake

As a broad rule, English law admits few mistakes as affecting the validity of a contract. Often, when one party says: 'I made a mistake', what he really means is: 'I failed to watch out to make sure I was making a good bargain'. In such cases, the maxim 'caveat emptor' will apply – let the buyer beware.

In some instances where the parties are mistaken, no contract ever comes into existence between them. The extent of their misunderstanding is so great that it prevents them reaching true agreement. In one case the parties believed they had an agreement relating to a cargo of cotton coming to this country on a ship called *The Peerless* which was sailing from Bombay. By coincidence there were two ships, both called *The Peerless*, both carrying cotton and sailing from Bombay. As it was impossible to say which ship the parties had in mind, it was held that they had never reached a true agreement (*Raffles v. Wichelhaus*).

Sometimes, the state of confusion is caused by one person seeking deliberately to lead the other into making a mistake. This can occur where one person misrepresents his identity. Such fraudulent behaviour would be likely to give rise to remedies for misrepresentation. But in cases where it can be shown that the identity of the person was crucial, the mistake about identity may be so important that there is no real agreement. The contract would be void.

Other factors affecting validity and enforceability

A party seeking to enforce a contract may be unable to do so in cases where it was induced by duress or undue influence, or in cases where there is some illegality. These issues will be considered separately.

Duress

It is hard to imagine that any contracts are made nowadays as a result of threats of physical violence. The old rules about duress would only permit relief if the contract came about because of threatened or actual violence. Originally the result of such behaviour was that the contract was void i.e. there was no contract at all. Subsequently, the rule was modified. Now, if such facts occur, the injured party could seek to have the contract set aside. The modern effect of duress is thus to render the contract voidable.

These rules are of such limited significance that they would not be worth mentioning if it were not for the more recent trend in the cases towards establishing principles relating to economic duress. The cases which have developed this theme tend to be complex, but the usual scenario is that one party threatens the other with breach in order to gain some new concessions from the other. For example, one party sees that he has not negotiated a particularly good price for building a ship, so he threatens to abandon the contract unless the price is renegotiated. This will put the other party into an impossible position if he has already contracted to charter the new ship. Unless he agrees to the higher price he will find himself in turn in breach with his charterer. He could resort to litigation against the shipbuilder, but that is costly, uncertain and very time-consuming. The potential loss of business and goodwill may be so great that he reluctantly agrees to pay the higher price. At a later date, would a court allow him to recover the extra sum paid?

The courts have not yet developed a particularly coherent set of principles to solve such a problem. There must be more than mere commercial pressure. To establish economic duress, it is necessary to show that there has been such 'coercion of will' that there is no true consent to the new deal. Factors which the court will take into account were set out in a case, *Pao On v. Lau Yiu Long*, 1979:

1   Did the victim protest?
2   Did the victim have any other course of action open to him, e.g. could he have sued?
3   Did the victim receive independent advice?
4   Did the victim take immediate steps to try to avoid the new deal?

This developing area is one which is likely to cause considerable difficulty for the courts, as these situations may arise between businessmen who are of apparently equal bargaining strength, where the courts have a traditional reluctance to interfere with the contract as agreed between the parties. However, the argument has succeeded in a recent case, *Atlas Express Ltd v. Kafco Ltd*, 1989.

Undue influence

Rules of undue influence were developed in equity because of the narrowness and harshness of the old common law rules about duress. Where there is behaviour falling short of such open violence or threats of harm, equity may grant relief if a contract has been brought about by undue influence. There is no precise definition of this phrase, but it usually occurs where there is a dominant/subservient relationship between two people and the dominant party seeks to take advantage of, or exploit, the other.

Undue influence is automatically presumed to exist in some relationships, e.g. solicitor and client, or parent and child. In other instances it is not presumed but may be proved to exist. Where a contract is highly favourable to the dominant party it may be avoidable on grounds of undue influence. The courts will look to see whether the dominant party took advantage of the weaker party, or abused his own position. If so, the contract may be set aside where the transaction is to the manifest disadvantage of the weaker party.

Some of the cases in this area involve the big banks, where they have obtained signatures on guarantees and mortgages from relatives or debtors, often visiting them in their homes and giving them no chance to receive independent advice. The court must weigh very carefully whether such a transaction was only agreed to because of the bank bringing undue influence to bear. *National Westminster Bank Ltd v. Morgan* and *Midland Bank Ltd v. Shepherd* are recent useful illustrations of these rules in practice.

Illegal contracts

The phrase 'illegal contracts' is used here to cover those situations where contracts are either void or illegal at common law or by statute. A wide range of situations is thus encompassed, for which the law offers numerous solutions. Sometimes the illegality involves an immoral contract, such as a contract to commit a crime, or to pervert the course of justice. On some occasions Acts of Parliament designate particular types of contract as unlawful, for example gaming and wagering contracts. In these cases the results of making such a contract will frequently be governed by the Act.

There is a general power available to the courts to interfere with contracts where it can be seen that such contracts are contrary to public policy. Such a potentially wide-ranging doctrine must be applied with caution, because the judges must not forget that the parties are largely free to fix their own bargain. Inevitably the definition of 'public policy' must remain somewhat flexible as it will need to shift and change to reflect the changing needs of society. One judge remarked that public policy was 'a very unruly horse and once you get astride it, you can never know where it will carry you'.

Where contracts involve some considerable element of moral wrong-doing, it has been usual to describe them as illegal at common law. Examples would be contracts promoting sexual immorality. In these cases, neither party will be able to enforce the contract. But if one party is the 'less guilty' of the two, he may be able to recover money he has paid or property he has transferred. This will particularly be the case where one party can be seen to have clearly 'repented'.

Where less moral wrongdoing is involved, for example in contracts in restraint of trade, the approach of the courts is to declare void either the contract as a whole or its offending parts. A contract in restraint of trade is one whereby one party promises or agrees to restrict his individual freedom to contract. These clauses are frequently found in employer–employee contracts or in contracts for the sale of a business. They are regarded as important because so many disputes in this area are litigated in the courts.

It is useful first of all to establish why such clauses are regarded as contrary to public policy. Surely, one might argue, if the two parties agree, that should be the end of the matter. That would be to take a pure freedom of contract approach. However, viewed from the point of view of the public interest, it is seen as wrong and contrary to public policy that a person's skill and experience should be rendered effectively useless and sterile by a contract. The courts have, therefore, been active in controlling those contracts in restraint of trade which they regard as being unreasonable. The modern rule is that such an agreement will only be enforced if it is reasonable in the interests of the public and reasonable in the interests of the parties.

When judging what is reasonable, each case will tend to turn on its own individual facts, so precedents are of little value other than as examples. The courts have always made clear that it is not appropriate to incorporate a restraint of trade in every contract of employment. The employer cannot include such a clause merely to prevent competition. He may only restrain an employee when he has some legitimate business interest to protect. That interest is usually his trade secrets or his business connections i.e. his customers. Take the case of an employee who is engaged as a travelling salesman within a twenty-five mile radius of London. It may be permissible to include a clause in his contract that when he leaves his present employment he will not solicit any of the employer's customers within that twenty-five mile radius for a period of one year. It would clearly not be reasonable to restrict the salesman throughout the UK, as he only poses a threat to the employer within a very small area.

When evaluating the reasonableness of a restraint clause the courts will pay close attention to factors such as the area of the restraint and the time limit involved. The restraint should be no wider and no longer than is strictly necessary to protect the employer's business interests.

It will be clear that there is no precise science about clauses in restraint of trade. An employer who wishes to put such a clause into an employee's contract will have to tread carefully in his drafting to make sure that it goes no further in the restrictions it imposes than will be found acceptable by the courts. If the employer 'gets it wrong' in his drafting, he will pay a high price as the clause will be held to be void and will be struck from the contract. The only help the courts will give is to construe a restraint of trade clause in the light of the circumstances existing when the parties made their contract, in order to determine what they must have intended. By interpretation of the clause, it may be possible to limit in scope what otherwise appears to be too far-reaching. An example of this approach can be seen in *Home Counties Dairies Ltd v. Skilton*, where a milk roundsman, once he left his present employers, was to be restrained from selling milk or dairy produce for a period of six months. The phrase 'dairy produce' was so wide that, on a literal interpretation, the man could not even go to work in a supermarket selling yoghurt. The court held that the phrase had to be construed in the light of what the parties must have intended, and should therefore be more confined in its meaning.

The courts tend to concentrate on the issue of reasonableness as between the parties, but it should be borne in mind that rules of public policy are in issue, and public interest is always a factor which could sway a court's decision. This can clearly be seen in the case, *Pharmaceutical Society of Great Britain v. Dickson*. The society intended to change the rules for its members, many of whom were owners of small chemists' shops. As a result they would be severely restricted by their professional rules from dealing in non-traditional lines. For example, their shops would have to stop selling goods like paperback books or cassettes. For many small chemists these were high profit lines which effectively kept the business going. One chemist sought a declaration that such a change in the rules would be an unreasonable restraint of trade. The House of Lords clearly thought so and considered public interest to be a paramount consideration. Such a change in the rules could well have caused many small chemists' shops to close and thus deprived large sections of the public of an important amenity and public service.

Over the years the courts have been vigilant in finding restraint of trade clauses hidden in some unusual situations. In one case, the rules of a pension fund were held to operate as an unreasonable restraint (*Bull v. Pitney Bowes*). The principles have also been applied in cases involving licences for racehorse trainers (*Nagle v. Fielden*) and the transfer system for footballers (*Eastham v. Newcastle United*). These cases clearly demonstrate that the courts will not allow the parties to achieve through a back door what they could not do by a direct method.

Where the courts are prepared to interfere and find a restraint unreasonable it is void and struck from the contract. Where it is only one clause of a much larger contract, the remainder of the contract may be perfectly valid and enforceable. In some cases, especially borderline situations, the inevitable effect of declaring a restraint to be void is that the employer is left with no protection for his legitimate business interests. An example of this can be seen in *Commercial Plastics Ltd v. Vincent*, where a research chemist had been working on PVC but only on a limited aspect of its application. The restraint in his contract was drafted to cover too general a field of work on PVC and so the whole restraint was held to be void. The judges felt sure that the employer had genuine interests to protect, and with a properly drafted clause would have secured such protection.

This rigorous approach of the courts stems from the principle that the parties must make their own terms and cannot expect the judges to do this for them. In one limited circumstance the judges may be able to give some assistance. Where the restraint is couched as a series of alternatives, some of which are valid but some of which are too wide and thus unreasonable, the court may be able to sever parts which are excessive. Consider a restraint for 'twelve months within a ten mile radius of our shops at Newcastle or York'. If the employee has never worked in the York shop he probably poses no threat to the employer there and that aspect of the restraint could therefore be too wide and unreasonable. Using an approach known as 'the blue pencil test' the courts will simply cross out the words 'or York' and leave a valid restraint behind. Of course, this will be no help in a great many cases where the restraint consists of one overwide restriction e.g. a restraint for 'twelve months within 100 miles of our shop in York'. The judges have no power here to cut this down in scope if it should turn out to be too wide to be reasonable.

It is obvious that the rules about restraint are not clear or precise. The main value of putting a restraint clause into a contract is its deterrent effect. It acts as an early warning to an employee that he will not get away with interfering with his employer's interest. But even if no restraint is imposed, or a restraint has been struck out as unreasonable, it should be remembered that employees owe duties to their employers at common law under their contracts of service (see page 163).

Discharge of the contract

Discharge by performance

In the normal course of events, both parties to a contract expect that the contract will be properly carried out. Where both parties perform their obligations under the contract exactly and precisely as promised, then the contract is discharged by its complete performance. It follows that if either party does not exactly and precisely perform, there is a breach of contract. Contractual obligations arise by agreement, and it is right that both parties should carry out their obligations in full. A necessary result of this rule is that a person who only partly performs his obligations cannot be paid. This is clearly demonstrated in a case involving the installation of central heating. The job was done and the customer had not paid. But the heating failed to give the promised temperatures in the house and the boiler emitted vile fumes. As the installer had not exactly and precisely performed, it was held that he was not entitled to be paid (*Bolton v. Mahadeva*).

That case does demonstrate how harshly the rule of exact and precise performance can operate. Not surprisingly it is subject to a number of exceptions.

1   A party may be paid for partial performance where he has substantially performed the contract. So, if one party has performed exept for some trivial details, he will be entitled to be paid, less the value of the other party's counter-claim in respect of those trivial breaches.

2   A party may be paid where the other party is prepared to accept part performance. In these cases, however, the other party must have a genuine choice whether to accept part performance or not. So where I am due to deliver ten tons of coal and I arrive with only eight tons, you may agree to accept eight tons. But in the central heating case, the plaintiff had no such choice. The work was only partly done but it could not be undone. Of course, in those cases

where the other party does agree to accept part performance, his obligation to pay will be correspondingly adjusted.

3   A party who has partially performed may be paid as much as the work or performance is worth in cases where the other party will not permit him to complete his performance. In this case, of course, the person who will not permit performance is in breach, and the party who has partly performed may either sue for damages in respect of that breach, or claim a reasonable sum for the value of the work he has already done.

4   Where a contract is divisible, a party who had performed some parts may be paid for them. So, in a contract of employment with salary paid monthly, each complete month could be regarded as a divisible contract. In building contracts, any agreement about progress payments will make it a divisible contract.

Although the rules about precise performance are quite strict, there are, nevertheless, some defences which are regarded as acceptable excuses for non-performance or partial performance. For instance, the parties may have agreed to some lesser performance. The validity of their agreement will be the subject of rules about discharge by agreement (see page 106).

Or again, the parties may be unable to perform their contract as originally contemplated because of some external factor or event outside their control. The validity of such an excuse is considered under discharge by frustration (see page 107).

The parties themselves may have taken account of the need to change the rules about performance e.g. in a building contract more time may be needed if a contractor unearths antiquities, and their contract may make provision for altered performance.

The time for performance of the contract

It is often said that 'time is of the essence' in a contract, meaning that the time stipulated for performance is a major term, and any breach of that term would entitle the other to repudiate the contract. This will often be true, but each case will turn on its own facts. Have the parties expressly provided for a time for performance? If not, then the contract must be performed in a reasonable time. If a precise time has been fixed, the surrounding circumstances may make it clear that it must be adhered to. If I order a wedding dress to be completed in time for my wedding, time is clearly of the essence. But if I order a new armchair and you undertake to deliver it next week, it may not be so disastrous if you do not make delivery on time. Inevitably, in that situation, the time may come where the patience of the customer starts to wear thin. Then, although time was not originally of the essence in the contract, the customer can make it so by serving notice on the seller. The customer may indicate that, unless he has the chair by the end of the week, he regards the contract as at an end.

Tender of performance

Sometimes it is only possible to perform the obligations under a contract with the cooperation of the other party. Take the example of a sale of goods where the seller agrees to deliver. He needs the other party to be there to receive the goods. If he offers to perform, i.e. tenders performance, by taking the right amount of goods of the correct description and quality, and the other party will not accept them, then the seller can argue that he has done all he can, and he can then consider himself discharged from his obligations. In *Startup v. McDonald*, a delivery of oil was due to be made before 31 March. The seller arrived with the oil on 31 March, which happened to be a Saturday. It was very late in the evening, and the buyer refused to accept the delivery. This was held to be a valid tender of performance so the seller could recover damages for the non-acceptance of the goods.

Where the obligation under the contract is to pay money, there is only a valid tender if money of the exact amount is offered, made up in such a way as to constitute 'legal tender'. Of course it is quite common for the parties to have agreed expressly to payment in some other way e.g. by cheque. If no such agreement exists, the other party is entitled to expect money.

Discharge by agreement

What is created by agreement can be discharged by agreement. Although this statement is largely true, discharging a contract by agreement depends on the operation of the rules of consideration. Effectively, if the parties agree to discharge a contract they are making a new contract. That new contract will be supported by valid consideration if each party is giving up something of value by discharging the first contract. If I agree to sell you goods for £10, and I have not yet delivered and you have not yet paid, then we can discharge that contract by a new agreement. My consideration for the new agreement will be giving up the right to receive £10 and your consideration will be giving up the right to receive the goods.

Obviously, it is not so straightforward to achieve a discharge by agreement if one party has already performed. If I have already delivered the goods, my part of the bargain is complete. It would be possible to discharge our agreement by drawing up a deed, but this would be absurd to contemplate except in commercial cases involving very large sums of money. In these cases, the rules about waiver play an important part. In the example already given, I may agree to forego payment of the £10 due. What would prevent me from changing my mind at a later stage and suing for the money? It could be argued that I am prevented from going back on my earlier promise because of the defence of promissory estoppel (see page 74). As this is an entirely discretionary principle, the other party may feel less than secure in relying on it. I would also be prevented from suing for my £10 if we have made a valid variation of our original contract.

Discharge by frustration

When two parties make a contract their natural expectation is that both of them will perform it. However, in some cases, one party may find it impossible to perform his part of the bargain due to events quite beyond his control. The law of contract basically adopts a harsh principle that if contractual obligations are undertaken, then any non-performance for whatever reason amounts to breach.

However, since the nineteenth century, the courts have developed rules relating to 'frustration' or subsequent impossibility, in an attempt to achieve justice between the parties when things go wrong in an unforeseen way. If one party chooses not to perform because he now regards the contract as a bad deal he will be in breach. If the parties themselves have provided an express term to cover some particular event, then the terms of their agreement will take effect. The rules developed by the courts provide that if there has been a frustrating event it will have the effect of terminating the contract and discharging the parties. The resulting financial arrangements between the parties will then be dealt with, when appropriate, by the Law Reform (Frustrated Contracts) Act 1943.

The first problem is the difficulty of establishing which events should be regarded as frustrating events. Take as an example the closure of the Suez Canal. If my ship is locked in the canal as a result of the closure, then any contract I have made to hire the ship to you would surely be frustrated. But if I had a contract to transport your goods, and the closure of the canal simply means that I must use a longer and more costly route, then this is by no means certain to be found to frustrate the contract. In such a case my major complaint would be that I am not going to make a profit on our contract. This factor alone will not influence the court. Contracts inevitably involve risk, and the parties must look out for their own interests. *Davis Contractors Ltd v. Fareham UDC* is a good example of this point. In July 1946 the contractors had agreed to build seventy-eight houses for £92,000, the work to be completed within eight months. Owing to quite unexpected circumstances, and through no fault of either the contractor or the council, there was a serious labour shortage and necessary building materials were extremely difficult to obtain. As a result the job took almost two years to complete, and the contractor incurred extra expense of £17,500. He wanted to argue that the very long delay had frustrated the original contract, and as that would avoid the original contract, he could then claim payment for a reasonable sum. The House of Lords rejected the contractor's argument. One of the judges in the case said: 'The possibility of enough labour and materials not being available was before their eyes and could have been made the subject of special contractual stipulation. Frustration is not to be lightly invoked as the dissolvent of a contract.'

Examples of situations in which the court is prepared to find frustration include:

1　*A forecast event fails to take place.* A classic example was the cancellation of the coronation of Edward VII. Many people had made contracts to hire rooms to view the coronation procession. In one such case, *Krell v. Henry*, the contract for the hire of a room overlooking Pall Mall was held to be frustrated by the cancellation of the coronation. It is evident in a case like this that although the hirer could still use the room on the day in question, it is impossible for the parties to achieve the substantial object of their contract. There is an interesting contrast to be made with the case of *Herne Bay Steamship Co. v. Hutton*, where the contract indirectly arose out of the coronation activities. The Royal Naval Review was to take place at Spithead, and the plaintiff chartered a boat to cruise around the assembled foreign fleets in the harbour and to see the naval review. Because of the King's illness the review had to be cancelled. But the contract for the charter of the boat was held not to be frustrated, because it was still possible to enjoy a day's sailing, and see all the foreign fleets. In other words, the substantial object of the contract had not been destroyed.

2　*The subject matter of the contract is physically destroyed.* In *Taylor v. Caldwell* the contract provided for the hire of a music hall which burned down before the date for performance of the contract. The fire was accidental and the contract was held to be frustrated. A similar rule for goods which perish after the contract is made but before the date for delivery is contained in s.7 of the Sale of Goods

Act 1979. The contract would be frustrated provided neither party
was at fault. The same principle also applies where the person who
was to perform the contract dies, or becomes too ill to perform. This
rule is only appropriate where the contract calls for the services of
one particular person. So, if I hire a famous concert pianist to give a
recital, then death or illness of the pianist could frustrate the
contract. Where there is an ordinary on-going contract of employment, short-term illnesses would not usually frustrate the contract.
There will inevitably be borderline cases, where a long-term illness
rendering the employee unfit to perform his former duties may
amount to frustration. This sort of example should not give rise to
too many difficulties when it is remembered that such an
employee's contract could be terminated by giving appropriate
notice (see page 170).

3 *Subsequent intervention makes performance of the contract illegal.* This
situation can occur when parties have made a perfectly valid
contract, but before they perform it some change in the law makes
that type of contract unlawful. So, in *Metropolitan Water Board v.
Dick Kerr & Co.*, the defendants had undertaken to build a reservoir
for the Water Board. They were already at work when they were
ordered to stop by the government, which directed them to build a
factory instead. The court held that the contract with the Water
Board was frustrated. It is true that the defendants could have
resumed work on the reservoir very much later, but because of
changing costs of materials and labour this would have then been a
substantially different task from the one originally undertaken.
Obviously the reservoir example can be compared with the council
house case (Davis) discussed earlier. In the one case the rules of
frustration operated and the defendant was released from what
had become a bad bargain. In the other case, Davis Contractors
were held to their original contract. How can such a distinction be
justified? It seems that in most cases the courts will abide by the
traditional view that you must perform as you agreed, but there will
be exceptional situations where the increased cost of performance
is so great that it can be said to make the contract into something
radically different from what was contemplated by the parties. No
doubt this allows the courts to find frustration in extreme cases, but
it does demonstrate how difficult it is to pin down the scope of the
doctrine with any precision.

4 *Frustration affecting contracts concerning land.* It used to be thought
that the rules of frustration would not operate in the case of leases
or contracts for the sale of land. Two important cases emphasize
how significant the rules could be in such instances. In *National*

Carriers v. Panalpina Ltd a warehouse was let on a ten year lease. With five years of the lease still to run, the street giving access to the warehouse was lawfully closed off by the local authority because there was a listed building in a dangerous condition. It could only be demolished with the consent of the appropriate minister, which took almost two years to obtain. During all that time the tenant was unable to use the premises for warehousing as no lorries could gain access. He stopped paying the rent and claimed frustration of the lease. The House of Lords rejected his claim. One judge said: 'Under the bargain the land has passed from the lessor to the lessee with all its advantages and disadvantages. Why should justice require that a useless site be returned to the lessor rather than remain the property of the lessee?' In *Amalgamated Investment Co. Ltd v. John Walker & Sons Ltd* the facts involved the purchase of a piece of land which the purchaser intended to redevelop. He contracted to pay £1.7 million for the land. On the day after he signed the contract, officials at the Department of the Environment listed a building which was presently on the site as a building of special interest. This made it extremely difficult to go ahead with development plans, and the site without development potential was worth only £250,000. Despite the scale of the financial disaster the purchaser was held to be bound by the contract. Although it was now apparent that he had made a bad bargain, the contract was not frustrated.

From the cases and examples we have looked at, it is possible to state only a very broad principle. Frustration occurs when performance of the contract is impossible or when the parties can no longer achieve the substantial object they had in mind. It is essential that the supervening event should be outside the control of either of the parties. It it comes about through some act or election of one party, or as a result of negligence, then it cannot be frustration. Both of these points are well illustrated in *Lauritzen A. S. v. Wijsmuller B. V.* (the *Super Servant Two*), where the defendants had contracted to transport a drilling rig from the Japanese shipyard where it was being built to Rotterdam. The contract provided that the carriage would be undertaken between June 20 and August 20, and would be effected using either *Super Servant One* or *Super Servant Two*, both of which were large transportation units. In fact, it was always the intention of the defendants to use *Super Servant Two* to fulfil the contract but, unfortunately, it sank in January. In the meantime, the defendant had made other contracts to use *Super Servant One*, so that vessel was not available to be substituted. The defendants argued that the sinking of the *Super Servant Two* had frustrated the contract. The Court of Appeal held that this was not a supervening event such as to frustrate the contract, because the defendants could have performed without breach by using *Super Servant One*, and it was by their own election that they chose not to do so.

Inevitably, frustration often occurs after the parties have embarked on performance. Their valid contract becomes void at the moment of the frustrating event, and the parties are therefore discharged from further obligations under it. This can produce a very untidy and unfair situation, as it means that obligations which fell due before the frustrating event are still owed. Take the example of a contract to import and sell £10,000 worth of a particular type of toy, delivery to take place in November, with £2,000 payable on the making of the contract, and the remaining £8,000 to be paid within one month of delivery. The contract is made in June and £2,000 is duly paid. In October the government bans the import of the toy in question. At that point the contract is frustrated. But the buyer has paid £2,000 for which he has received nothing. The early approach of the courts to sorting out these problems was to decide that the loss lay where it fell. In an attempt to solve the financial plight of the two parties to a frustrated contract, the Law Reform (Frustrated Contracts) Act 1943 was passed.

The Act makes no attempt to define what frustration is. It simply deals with the consequences. Its two main objectives are to allow for the recovery of money paid and for compensation for partial performance. These will be considered separately.

1 *Recovery of money paid* – the Act provides that all sums paid shall be recoverable and all sums due cease to be due. Applying this to the sale of toys example, the £2,000 deposit could be recovered and the £8,000 would cease to be due. Of course, this may not be particularly fair to the seller, who may have incurred considerable expense in going about the performance of the contract. The Act recognizes this by providing that where expenses have been incurred before the frustrating event, and those expenses were 'in, or for, the purpose of performing the contract', the court may allow a party to recover in respect of those expenses, to the extent that the court thinks is just and equitable. In the toy example, the seller may have made phone calls and sent telexes and may have had transport expenses and insurance costs. The judge may say that he can keep £500 of the £2,000 deposit. Now the buyer is £500 out of pocket. That is an inevitable price which has to be paid when a transaction has gone wrong. The rules of frustration only operate where neither party is at fault, so inevitably, the courts are trying to make the best

of a bad situation and no solution will ever be perfect. They can only aim to achieve as fair a compromise as possible.

2   *Recovery of compensation for partial performance* – we have already seen that a frustrated contract will have commenced life as a valid contract, under which the parties may have started to perform their obligations. Suppose I have contracted to build you a house for £60,000 payable on completion. If I have completed three-quarters of the work when the government interferes and puts a ban on private building work, can I recover the value of the work I have done? The Act provides that if one party obtains a valuable benefit, by reason of work done in the performance of the contract by the other, the court may allow the party who has performed to recover a sum which does not exceed the value of the benefit conferred, and which is just in all the circumstances of the case.

The scale of disaster when such frustrating events occur can be seen in *BP Exploration Co. Ltd v. Hunt*. Hunt owned an oil concession in Libya. He did not know if oil would be found there or, if so, how much. He wanted, somehow, to finance the exploration of the oil field but to hold on to a share of any profits if large quantities of oil were found. He contracted with BP to share the field. BP would bear all the exploration costs and, if oil was found, Hunt would repay them from his share of the oil revenues. The exploration work cost a staggering $87 million. A large amount of oil was found and extraction had only just begun when the Libyan government confiscated the land and nationalized the concession. BP had done work in performance. Had that work conferred a valuable benefit on Hunt? Merely exploring for oil gave Hunt no valuable benefit, but its discovery greatly increased the value of his concession before it was nationalized. The judge calculated Hunt's valuable benefit to be the value of the oil already removed and the compensation he would receive from the Libyan government. This formed the upper limit of what he could have awarded to BP. He then had to consider what figure, up to that upper limit, he thought was just in all the circumstances. Although the judge thought that the 'valuable benefit' to Hunt was over $80 million, he awarded $35 million to BP, as it had been an agreed basis of the contract that it would bear the exploration costs. The exploration might have found no oil at all, and in that case it would have had to bear those costs in total with no claim at all against Hunt.

The 1943 Act may not apply if the parties themselves have included a term to cover the results of a frustrating event. It will be a question of construing or interpreting their term, to discover if they intended it to operate in such extreme cases. The rules of the Act have no application to contracts of insurance, so if I insure against sickness, pay a year's premium and then die after the first month, there can be no recovery of part of the premium. In some sale of goods situations the appropriate rules are found in s.7 of the Sale of Goods Act 1979, rather than the 1943 Act.

Discharge by breach

A breach of contract may occur because one party does not perform his obligations at all, or performs then late, or performs them in an unsatisfactory way. One of the major difficulties when looking at discharge by breach of contract is trying to establish exactly which breaches have the effect of discharging. Where such a major breach can be identified, the injured party may nonetheless want to go ahead with the contract, and simply ignore the breach, or more likely, seek compensation for it.

All breaches of contract, however large or small, give the injured party the right to sue for damages. In some cases it may be possible to exercise that right through set-off. Where a painter contracts to decorate the outside of your house for £500, to be paid on completion of the work, he may commit breaches by not burning off where specified, or by applying only one undercoat instead of two. In such a case, the injured party could solve the problem by deducting something from the £500 due. In some cases a contract may even provide a schedule of damages for specified breaches, thereby anticipating those which are likely to occur and providing a solution. Such an example is the case where a builder undertakes to complete a job by 30 June, and if he fails to do so, to pay £100 per day (agreed or liquidated damages) in respect of each day's delay thereafter.

A much more difficult question still remains – when does a breach put an end to the contract itself, or permit the innocent party to choose to treat the contract as at an end? And what exactly is meant when we say the contract is 'at an end'? As a general rule, where the party at fault is in breach of a major term (a condition) or in breach of an innominate term where the effects are serious, the innocent party can treat that behaviour as repudiatory, and regard himself as discharged from further performance. Where the breach is of a minor term (a warranty) the injured party is restricted to an action for damages and must continued with performance of the contract.

The various categories of terms have already been examined (see page 83). Let us assume that when the breach occurs it is clear which type of term has been broken. Take the case where you want to ship goods under refrigeration. You enquire whether the ship has refrigeration plant and are assured that it has. On that basis you contract to ship ten tons of soft fruit under refrigerated conditions. When you arrive to load the fruit, you discover that the ship had no refrigeration equipment. This is likely to be a breach of a major term, a condition. You now have a choice. You can treat it as a repudiatory breach and regard yourself as discharged from further performance, i.e. the obligation to pay the shipping charges. You can also sue for damages in such a case. No doubt you would take this course of action if you were able to find alternative shipping facilities immediately, or if you could sell the fruit in a local market. Where that is not possible, you may decide that you have no option but to ship your fruit in the unrefrigerated ship, thereby choosing to affirm the contract, but of course, you can still sue for damages for the breach. As you have affirmed, you have to pay the shipping charges, but if your fruit deteriorates as a result of the breach you can be compensated by the damages.

This example assumes that, even though the breach was major, you were left with a choice of courses of action, either to affirm and go on, or consider the contract at an end. Sometimes that will not be the case, as the very nature of the breach itself may put an end to the contract. Take the case where you engage a central heating contractor to install a system for you for £2,000, the work to commence on 1 June. If the contractor informs you in May that he has found more lucrative contracts and does not intend to come to do your job, he is effectively repudiating the contract in advance. You could now wait until June to see if he comes. If he fails to turn up then, this is a case of breach by non-performance. Or you could sue immediately, making clear that you are choosing to treat the contract as at an end. Where these situations occur in practice, the difficulty may be that the injured party needs to respond quickly to minimize the harm and inconvenience, and he may therefore act precipitately without the benefit of proper advice. Yet, once it is clear that the other party does not intend to perform it might be dangerous to wait and see if he will change his mind, because in the meantime the injured party could lose his rights through some supervening frustration.

Enforcing the contract – remedies for breach

The law provides remedies for breach of contract, but the extent to which purely legal remedies can be truly effective is limited. A remedy is necessary because things have gone wrong. An ideal solution would be for the parties themselves to plan in advance for situations which may arise. They can then impose solutions which are satisfactory to both of them. This contract planning role is very significant in the business and commercial world. The standard form building contract is an example where many contingencies are provided for, without the need to go to court. One advantage of such a system is that it creates a climate within which the parties can stay on reasonably good terms, which is vital if they need to do business with each other frequently. Sometimes the contract planning role can also avoid those situations where court action would probably be useless. There are business situations where the customer is asked to pay a deposit. Not only does this create a situation where the customer is more likely to perform but it also provides a ready small sum of compensation against his non-performance. An example would be 'same-day' photographic processing, where deposits are common.

One problem of seeking to enforce a contract through the courts is that the usual remedy for breach is damages. The courts are prepared to order the other party to carry out his obligations, but only in a very limited number of cases. If they will grant a remedy, it is called specific performance. Such an order is not readily available because the court may then need to keep the defendant under constant supervision, and it has neither the desire nor the means to do so. Moreover, in many cases, money will be adequate to compensate the plaintiff. The types of contract where an order of specific performance may be granted usually relate to sales of land and leases. No two pieces of land are identical, and it is thought that money cannot adequately compensate. That is quite a difficult idea to accept when the 'land' in question may be a semi-detached house on an estate surrounded by dozens of properties which are seemingly identical! The argument about the unique quality of the property can also be used, although less frequently, in relation to sale of goods. If the goods are in some way unique, or not readily obtainable, a court may be prepared to grant an order for specific performance. Indeed they have a discretion to do so under s.52 of the Sale of Goods Act 1979.

As the power to award specific performance is equitable and discretionary, a number of points will be borne in mind by the courts. They will not grant an order if it would operate very harshly on the defendant. Nor will they grant it where a plaintiff has delayed too long in seeking relief – delay defeats equity. This rule is not precise, and what counts as excessive delay will depend on the facts of each case. The order will not be granted if constant supervision would be required, nor in cases involving personal service, as it is thought that this would be tantamount to slavery. So if I contract with a famous painter to paint my portrait and he backs out of the contract I will not get an order of specific performance. It used to be suggested that an order of specific performance would not be granted in cases involving breach of contract to pay money, as damages would surely be an adequate remedy. This may not be so, and the problem was high-lighted in the case of *Beswick v. Beswick*, where a coalman sold his business to his nephew, who was to pay for it by paying the uncle £5 per week for his life and thereafter the money was to be paid to the coalman's widow. After the death of the coalman the payments to the widow were not made. She sued as the personal representative of her late husband and was awarded specific performance of the contract. This was the only way to achieve justice in this case.

There is another form of equitable relief, the injunction, which can be useful in a limited number of contract situations. This is particularly the case where a party to a contract has promised *not* to do a particular thing. A common example is a clause in restraint of trade, where an employee or a seller of a business promises not to compete. Where a breach of such a clause is proved the court may grant an injunction, but it should be remembered that the relief is entirely discretionary.

Awarding damages

In theory, an award of damages can be made in respect of every breach of contract, however large or small. The aim of the court when awarding damages is to put the injured party into the position he would have been in if the contract had been properly performed. This compensates him for loss of expectation. Somehow, the court has to arrive at an appropriate figure for the damages. This is described as the measure of damages. The figure can only be worked out once it is established for which harm the plaintiff can recover. He can only recover in respect of losses which 'arise naturally, according to the usual course of things; and losses which must have been in the contemplation of the parties when they made the contract'. This is the rule of remoteness of damage which was laid down in the case of *Hadley v. Baxendale*. The plaintiff's losses must also have been caused by the breach of contract. The two aspects of the remoteness rule can be seen at work in the case of *H. Parsons Ltd v. Uttley Ingham & Co. Ltd*, where the defendants manufactured and installed an animal feed dispensing hopper for Parsons, who was a pig breeder with a class 1 pedigree herd. The installation was carried out after the hopper had been transported by road. During the journey the driver had jammed the hopper ventilator with a rag to stop it rattling and he did not remember to remove it before the hopper was erected. Pig food was poured into the hopper and at first all seemed well. Inevitably, because the ventilator was jammed shut, the pig food eventually turned mouldy. Of course, there was a breach of contract here, and Parsons could undoubtedly claim damages in respect of the mouldy pig food. Unfortunately, the pigs had eaten the food and developed a disease which killed off a large proportion of the herd. In consequence, not only had Parsons lost more than 250 pigs, but he had also sustained the loss of a breeding season. Should he be allowed to recover in respect of the loss of the pigs? The scale of the problem can be clearly seen in this case where the defendants accepted liability with regard to the pig food and were prepared to pay damages of £1,802, but Parsons was trying to claim about £30,000. Parsons' claim was successful. The defendants must have contemplated that if they installed a defective hopper which made the food mouldy, the pigs could become ill. It was matterless that the degree of harm (the death of the pigs) was greater, as long as the type of harm (illness) could have been contemplated.

It is clear that the remoteness rules operate very flexibly, but the more the defendant knows about the plaintiff and his requirements, the more he is likely to be able to contemplate by way of potential harm.

Once the courts are clear about the harm or loss which falls within the remoteness rule they must then assess an appropriate measure of damages. Sometimes this will be quite straightforward, as in cases for the sale of goods where the seller has failed to supply. The buyer must now look elsewhere for the same goods and may only be able to buy at a higher price. The measure of damages is the difference between the two prices. Or a buyer may refuse to accept delivery of goods properly tendered under a contract. There, the measure may well be the loss of profit on the deal. Or a holidaymaker may cancel a booking for a country cottage late in the day, and the damages will be the loss of profit on the booking.

Where there has been a breach the injured party cannot just sit back and wallow in his misery. The law imposes on him a duty to take reasonable steps to mitigate his losses. A plaintiff cannot recover for any harm which could have been prevented by taking reasonable steps in mitigation. If a buyer refuses to take delivery of goods under a contract, the seller must take reasonable steps to find another buyer. In the holiday cottage example above, he must take reasonable steps to relet the property. An ironic result of taking reasonable steps to mitigate may be that the plaintiff actually increases his losses. In the holiday cottage example, he may place advertisements in newspapers and still not manage to relet the property. He can then include the cost of the advertisements in his claim for damages.

Of course, the plaintiff is the person who has been wronged so there is a limit to what he can be expected to do under the duty to mitigate.

As the defendant has committed the breach, he is hardly in a strong position to 'call the tune'. This is well illustrated in *Pilkington v. Wood*, where a solicitor gave incorrect advice to a client, in consequence of which the client found that his house had a defective legal title and was virtually unsaleable. When the solicitor was sued for damages he argued that the plaintiff had failed in his duty to mitigate as he could have solved the problem of the defective title by suing the person who had originally sold him the house. This was hardly asking the plaintiff to take a reasonable step, as such litigation would have been expensive and the outcome by no means predictable. The plaintiff was right not to have embarked on such a costly and uncertain procedure.

It used to be a feature of damages for breach of contract that nothing would be awarded for distress, injury to feelings, or disappointment. One justification for this rule may have been that it is very difficult to quantify such losses. The rule has been subject to an exception over recent years in cases where the plaintiff was contractually entitled to expect pleasure and enjoyment, not pain and distress! However, the sums awarded for distress and disappointment have not tended to be large. *Jarvis v. Swans Tours Ltd* shows the sort of case where an award for disappointment may be appropriate. The plaintiff had booked a holiday for himself and his family on the strength of a brochure which claimed that he would be joining a house party and special resident host. He would enjoy a welcome party and special yodelling evening, plenty of gemutlichkeit (good atmosphere) and, generally, he would be 'in for a great time'. In fact, by the second week of his holiday there were no other guests at all and in every other respect the holiday failed to live up to the brochure claims. Even the yodeller was a local man singing in his working clothes. When awarding him damages for disappointment the judge said: 'Mr Jarvis has only a fortnight's holiday each year. He books it far ahead and looks forward to it all that time. He ought to be compensated for the loss of it.' The court awarded him £125.

It has already been emphasized that by effective contract planning, the parties can provide in their contract for the sums to be paid in the event of specified breaches, a common example being late performance. Such contractually determined damages are called liquidated damages. The advantages of such a clause are clear. Problems can be resolved quickly and privately, without resort to the courts and, hopefully, in a manner which will preserve good relations between the parties. The parties also know in advance the risk and cost involved in particular breaches. On the other hand, such clauses can cause problems, particularly where the party agreeing to the clause lacks bargaining strength. In that case the result of the clause might be unfavourable to him. Either part may miscalculate the real effects of a specified breach and thus be unhappy to be regulated by what turns out to be an unfair clause. Against that, of course, must be set the fact that such clauses are freely negotiated, at least in theory!

The courts themselves are alert to the possibility that such a liquidated damages clause could operate harshly. If there is a dispute about the clause it is open to the court to consider whether it represents a genuine attempt by the parties to estimate their losses, in which case the clause will be enforced even if the estimate is wrong; or a clause inserted by one party to frighten or terrorize the other into performance. In the latter case the clause is classed as a penalty clause and is unenforceable. It is matterless what name the parties give to their clause. The court will determine which category it falls into, using a number of fairly flexible tests:

1 Does the clause provide for the same amount to be paid in respect of different breaches, some of which may be serious while others are trivial? If so, it will be hard to show that the clause was inserted as a genuine pre-estimate.
2 Does the clause provide for damage for breaches involving nonpayment of money at a level far higher than the sum unpaid? If you are due to pay £25 per week and I insert a clause saying that for every late payment you must pay me £100 that looks like a penalty.
3 Does the sum provided for by the clause appear to be harsh and unconscionable, given the breaches which are likely to occur?

Suing on a quantum meruit

Quantum meruit means 'as much as it is worth'. Generally, the rules about *quantum meruit* have no particular significance in the law of contract, because the contract itself should fix the amount of any payment due or the method of calculating it. In some cases, however, even the law of contract provides for the payment of a reasonable price. This could happen where minors have been supplied with necessaries. Another example is where goods have been sold and delivered, and accepted, but no price has been fixed. (s.8, Sale of Goods Act 1979).

There are times when the parties may think that they have a valid contract. They may have acted in reliance on that belief in performing obligations, only to find that the contract has not taken effect. In such cases if one party confers a benefit on the other, in circumstances where both believe that the benefit will be paid for, then the courts will allow the performer to recover a reasonable sum under the *quantum meruit* rules. This turned out to be a useful solution in *British Steel*

Corporation v. Cleveland Bridge and Engineering Co. Ltd, where the parties planned to enter into a contract but it had not been finalized between them. In ancipation of that contract one party began to perform. When a contract failed to materialize the performer was able to be compensated for the work done on a *quantum meruit* basis.

Limitation periods

The remedy of damages, as the principal relief for breach of contract, must be sought in time, otherwise any claim is statute barred by the Limitation Act 1980. The imposition of time limits is sensible because evidence eventually becomes stale and unreliable and a party at fault must ultimately have some certainty about whether he will be sued or not. In claims for breach of contract the time limit is basically fixed at six years from the date when the cause of action accrued. That usually means six years from the date of the breach of contract. The six year rule is extended to twelve years where the contract was made by deed under seal.

These rules are fairly rigid except where a plaintiff fails to discover that he has a cause of action because of the defendant's fraud. In these cases time only begins to run when the plaintiff discovers the fraud, or when he could with reasonable diligence have discovered it. 'Fraud' for these purposes could include cases where a defendant has deliberately concealed relevant facts from the plaintiff. This is what happened in *Applegate v. Moss* where a builder constructed a house on foundations which did not comply with the contract terms. The house was finished in 1957 but it was 1965 before the defects began to manifest themselves. The house was declared unsafe for habitation. Although eight years had elapsed, and normally the plaintiffs would have been statute barred, the time was extended to run from the date when they learnt that the foundations were defective because of the builder's concealment of facts relevant to the plaintiff's claim – he had covered the foundations up before they could discover how inadequate they were.

These strict time limits do not apply to equitable remedies such as specific performance. But in exercising any discretionary equitable relief, the court works on the maxim that delay defeats equity. It will be a question of fact in each case whether a plaintiff has unduly delayed.

6

Special contracts

Sale of goods

A contract for the sale of goods is defined by the Sale of Goods Act 1979 as one where: 'The seller transfers or agrees to transfer the property in goods to the buyer for a money consideration called the price.' The Act covers a wide range of transactions from selling loaves of bread to buying cars. It must be read in conjunction with all the basic rules of contract, as the Act is not a complete code in itself. Its significance lies in the fact that it sets out:

- The terms to be implied into a sale of goods transaction.
- The extent to which those implied terms can be excluded, subject to the Unfair Contract Terms Act 1977.
- The rules for determining when ownership and risk pass from the seller to the buyer.
- The remedies for the buyer and seller where breaches of contract have occurred.

The Act does not apply to hire purchase transactions, nor to contracts of exchange (e.g. trading stamps for goods), contracts for work and materials (e.g. installing central heating), or contracts for the supply of services, where separate statutory provisions apply.

Implied terms

It is quite common for people to enter into contracts to buy goods without ever speaking to the seller e.g. when buying from a vending machine, or in a self-service store. If asked what were the terms of their contract, they might reply 'none'. However, such transactions are covered by the Act, and the following terms are automatically included for the buyer's protection.

1   Quality of the goods

Section 14 provides that goods sold in the course of a business must be of merchantable quality (i.e. fit to be sold), bearing in mind the description applied to them, the price paid, and other relevant circumstances. This condition does not apply if:

(a) defects were specifically drawn to the buyer's attention before the contract was made. If a buyer buys a washing machine at a reduced price, having been told that the reduction is because the cabinet is dented, he cannot subsequently try to reject the washing machine because of this damage.
(b) The buyer examined the goods before the contract was made and the defects ought to have been revealed by that examination.

One of the practical problems of applying the rule about merchantable quality is the question of how long the goods should remain merchantable. How long should a pair of shoes last? If they leak at the first wearing, clearly they would seem not to be of merchantable quality. But what if they leak after six weeks? How often did the buyer wear them in that time? In what weather conditions? Whether goods are merchantable is a question of fact and, in disputes, it would need to be answered on the idividual circumstances.

2   Fitness for purpose

Section 14 further provides that where goods are sold in the course of a business, and the buyer makes known the purpose for which he requires the goods, then the goods must be reasonably fit for their purpose. What must a buyer do to 'make known the purpose' for which he wants the goods? In most cases, where goods have one common purpose, and that is what the buyer wants to use them for, then he need do nothing in particular, as he is regarded as impliedly making known the purpose. It is only where he wants to use goods for some unusual purpose that he must make that purpose known in order to benefit from this condition. The protection of this rule about fitness for purpose will not apply if the buyer did not rely on the seller's skill and judgment. This might be shown by the buyer specifically asking for goods by their brand name. In such a case, the inference is that the buyer knows that such goods will satisfy his purpose, i.e. he is relying on his own skill and judgment.

One obvious advantage of these clear duties imposed on the seller of goods is that the buyer has rights against someone whom he can identify and locate. In practice, the seller may try to indicate that he is not liable and that the buyer will have to take the matter up with the manufacturer. The buyer could possibly have some legal action against the manufacturer as well by virtue of the tort of negligence or under the Consumer Protection Act 1987, but he should not be fobbed off by the seller in this way. The seller is under a strict liability to sell goods which are of merchantable quality and reasonably fit for their purpose.

In cases covered by s.14 these conditions are important consumer protections, and they limit the operation of the usual principal of *caveat emptor* (let the buyer beware). That principle is still significant in cases not covered by s.14 e.g. private sales of secondhand goods, because s.14 specifically states that in circumstances outside the rules set out above, there is *no* implied condition or warranty about the quality or fitness for any particular purpose of goods supplied under a contract of sale.

3   Sales by description

Section 13 provides that if goods are sold by description there is an implied condition that they must correspond with that description. There is obviously a sale by description in any case in which the buyer has not seen the goods, but they have been described to him, e.g. goods selected from a catalogue or by reference to a price list. The Act specifically states that there can still be a sale by description even where the goods are displayed and selected by the buyer. The importance of the protection under this section is that it gives a right to a buyer to reject the goods even if they are, in themselves, entirely satisfactory. For example, a buyer who orders a five gallon can of white spirit can reject the goods if the seller supplies five separate one gallon cans, even though the white spirit itself is perfect.

4   Implied terms about title

A person buying goods is naturally anxious to become the proper legal owner of them. Section 12 provides that there is an implied condition that the seller has the right to sell the goods, or will have when the time comes to pass ownership. This condition can never be excluded.

5   *Sale by sample*

The mere fact that a buyer sees a sample during the course of negotiations does not necessarily make the transaction a sale by sample. What is necessary is that the sale should be made by reference to that sample. The parties may well indicate this, e.g. when the buyer orders goods 'equal to sample'. In such a case s.15 then implies conditions:

(a) That the goods supplied will correspond with the sample.
(b) That the buyer should have an opportunity to compare the goods supplied with the sample.
(c) That the goods will be free from any defect rendering them unmerchantable which would not be apparent on a reasonable examination of the sample.

6   *Implied terms about payment and delivery*

Although the parties may not have negotiated specifically about any of the previous terms, it is likely that they will have thought about payment and delivery. This is reflected by s.10 which applies 'unless a different intention appears'.

Section 10 states that stipulation about time of payment are not 'of the essence', which means that any agreement as to when money is due does not go to the root of the contract. In practice, a buyer who fails to make payment on time can be sued for damages for non-payment, but his behaviour will not allow the whole contract to be repudiated.

As to the time of delivery, s.29 makes it clear that if no time is fixed, delivery must be within a reasonable time if the seller is obliged to send the goods. It is important to note that there is no general rule that a seller must send the goods. Whether it is for the seller to send or the buyer to collect is a question to be determined by the contract. In other words, what was expressly or impliedly agreed between the parties? In many cases, the operation of these rules will be straightforward. Suppose that a buyer purchases a deep-freeze cabinet from a shop which promises, as part of the bargain, 'free delivery within twenty miles'. The buyer lives within the twenty mile area, and agrees a day when the goods will be sent by the seller. In this case, by the terms of the contract, the seller is bound to send the goods. If he fails to send them on the appointed day the provision about the delivery date may be a major term, the breach of which would entitle the buyer to repudiate the contract. Alternatively the failure may be a breach of a minor term, merely entitling him to sue for damages. The solution will depend on the weight attached to the term by the parties themselves. Their contract may make it clear that delivery dates are vital and must be complied with.

Unless otherwise agreed between the parties, delivery of the goods and payment of the price are concurrent conditions (s.28). It is very common practice to exclude the operation of this rule, e.g. in cases where goods are bought on account and a bill is rendered at the end of the month.

Exclusion of implied terms

Notwithstanding the extensive 'writing-in' of terms into contracts for the sale of goods, the Sale of Goods Act (SGA) provides by s.55 that any or all of these implied terms may be excluded, subject to the Unfair Contract Terms Act 1977 (UCTA). When considering the relevance of UCTA to sale of goods transactions, a distinction must be drawn between those buyers who 'deal as consumer' and those who do not. The UCTA identifies dealing as a consumer occurring when:

1 A person dealing as a consumer *does not* make the contract in the course of business.
2 The seller *does* make the contract in the course of a business.
3 The sale is of goods of a type ordinarily supplied for private use or consumption (UCTA 1977, s.12).

So, a housewife buying a loaf of bread in a baker's shop deals as a consumer. A contractor buying supplies from a builders' merchant is an example of a buyer not dealing as a consumer.

One party dealing as consumer (UCTA 1977, s.6)

The rule in such cases is that there can be no exclusion of any of the terms implied by SGA 1979, ss. 12-15 (i.e. no exclusion of the terms relating to title, sales by description, merchantable quality, reasonable fitness for purpose or sales by sample). Any attempt by a seller to exclude or limit his liability in these areas will be ineffective.

Neither party dealing as consumer (UCTA 1977, s.6)

Although no exclusion or limitation of SGA 1979, s.12 (title to the goods) is allowed, the seller may limit or exclude his liability under SGA 1979, ss. 13-15, if the contract term by which he imposes the limitation satisfies the requirement of reasonableness, i.e. if, given what the parties knew or ought to have known when they made the contract, it was a fair and reasonable term to have included. UCTA 1977 contains guidelines for the application of the reasonableness test, which suggest that a court should consider:

- The relative strength of the bargaining position of each party.
- Whether the buyer received an inducement to agree to the term.
- Whether the buyer knew, or ought reasonably to have known, of the existence of the term.
- Whether the goods were manufactured, processed or adapted to the special order of the buyer.

Passing ownership and risk

A contract for the sale of goods is defined by the Sale of Goods Act 1979 as one where the seller transfers or agrees to transfer the property in goods for a money consideration called the price (s.2). In this definition the word 'property' is used to mean ownership. It is important to realize that ownership can pass at a different time from possession. When making the contract the parties could agree to ownership passing immediately, but no delivery of the goods (i.e. transfer of possession) may take place until a later date. It is important to establish the exact time at which the buyer becomes the owner because:

1 The buyer can only effectively transfer ownership to a third party after he has become the owner.
2 As a general rule, risk passes with the ownership, irrespective of whether the goods have been delivered. This means that if goods should be insured, the buyer should do so, despite the fact that he has not yet received them. If the goods are lost or stolen at this stage, the loss will fall on the buyer. But the seller who remains in possession is under a duty to take reasonable care of the goods.

The parties are free to fix for themselves when ownership will pass but if their contract does not deal with this point, SGA 1979 provides rules to cover the various situations which can arise. The following points should be noted:

1 The time when ownership can pass depends on how the law categorizes the goods in question. If they are unascertained (goods mixed with others and not yet separated or identified as fulfilling the buyer's contract) no property can pass until they become ascertained (goods identified in accordance with the contract after the contract is made). For example, if a builder orders a quantity of

timber from a timber merchant who has huge stocks, the goods are unascertained until the merchant selects timber of the correct quantity and specification. Once he makes the selection, the goods become ascertained. Goods may also be specific. These are goods identified and agreed upon by the parties at the time when the contract is made.

2   Ownership of specific or ascertained goods passes at the time agreed by the parties. If they do not make their intention clear, the rules of SGA 1979, s.18 will be applied. These can be summarized as follows:

(a) In the case of a sale of specific goods which are fit for their purpose and ready to be delivered, ownership passes when the contract is made.

(b) When specific goods have to be put into a deliverable state (e.g. they must be repaired, cleaned, tested or weighed), ownership passes when this has been done, and the buyer has notice to that effect.

(c) In a sale of unascertained goods ownership passes once appropriate goods are set aside in fulfilment of the particular contract.

It will be seen that it is better for the parties themselves to fix when ownership will pass, as the operation of these rules leaves a buyer with little control over the timing.

Recently sellers have tried to lay down more precise rules in the contracts, to try to retain ownership of goods until the buyer has paid for them. This can be particularly useful when a buyer becomes insolvent, as the seller can insist that he still owns the goods in question and can take them back. Otherwise he would simply rank as an ordinary creditor in a bankruptcy or liquidation, with little hope of being paid in full. Reserving ownership of goods which are now in the buyer's possession is not without practical problems. One of the first significant cases on this point was *Aluminium Industrie Vaassen BV v. Romalpa Aluminium*. Indeed, it was from this case that 'retention' clauses began to be known as Romalpa clauses. AIV had sold aluminium to Romalpa, on terms that ownership would only vest in Romalpa once the goods had been paid for; that if the foil was used in manufacture, the end product would belong to AIV; and that if this end product was then sold, the proceeds would be due to AIV. This clause was held to be valid and was enforced by the court. Their reasoning was based on the fact that Romalpa were not owners but merely bailees under a bailment of the foil. A bailment is a fiduciary relationship, a relationship of trust which would allow the bailor to recover his goods, and also give him the right to trace the proceeds of sale.

This case appears to hold out important advantages for retention of ownership clauses, but it must be viewed in the context of later decisions, where the court reached a different conclusion. In *Borden UK Ltd v. Scottish Timber Products Ltd*, the material supplied under the contract was resin to be used in the manufacture of chipboard. An 'ownership retention clause' was inserted. When Scottish Timber went into receivership, Borden wanted to trace their resin (which was now in manufactured chipboard) and trace the proceeds of sale of chipboard which contained their product. They failed on both counts. There could be no bailment here as a bailment implies a right of redelivery. Borden were supplying small quantities at short, regular intervals and must have realized that their product was being incorporated immediately into the manufacturing process. If the clause was intended to create some kind of charge over the chipboard, it needed to be registered, and it was not.

The difference between the cases seems to rest on the fact that no mixture took place in Romalpa, whereas that was inevitable in Borden. Romalpa clauses could still be effective, as long as the seller makes clear that the buyer is a bailee, and no mixing occurs.

Remedies

The remedies available for breach depend on which party is in breach, and what type of breach has been committed:

1   *Seller in breach* – where the seller commits a major breach, e.g. by supplying goods which are defective, and not therefore of merchantable quality, the buyer ordinarily has the right to repudiate the contract (put an end to it), usually by rejecting goods. He also has the right to sue for damages. In practice, the buyer may choose not to reject the goods, and indeed in some cases the Act specifies that he cannot reject them. This is likely to happen when the buyer has purchased specific goods (goods which were identified by both parties at the time when the contract was made), where he had a reasonable chance to inspect the goods, and where he has now accepted them. He may have indicated his acceptance by selling part of the consignment of goods to a third party. In these cases the right to reject is lost, and the aggrieved buyer must content himself with an action for damages.

2   *Buyer in breach* – the most likely situation is that the buyer has failed to pay for the goods. The seller's remedy will then depend on

whether he is still in possession of the goods. If so, he can exercise his right of lien over the goods (i.e. holding on to them) with a view to ultimately exercising his right to resell them. If delivery has already been made to the buyer, then the seller must sue for the price of the goods.

Supply of goods and services

New provisions were enacted in the Supply of Goods and Services Act 1982 (SGSA), relating to contracts under which ownership in goods will pass, where the contract also provides a service element. The Act also regulates contracts for services only. Obvious examples of contracts falling within the Act are builders who supply materials and do the work and garages who supply parts and undertake the repair. Less obviously, the supply of goods provision may be important where a 'free gift' comes with a contract: 'Buy a luxury fridge/freezer during January and get this electric coffeemaker free.' The coffee-maker is not a 'sale of goods' because there is no money consideration given for it. But it is a supply of goods.

The Act deals separately with the supply of goods and the supply of services. Where the goods are supplied under a work and materials contract, a number of terms are implied:

1 An implied condition that the seller has a right to transfer the ownership of the goods (s.2).
2 Where goods are transferred by description, there is an implied condition that the goods must correspond with their description (s.3).
3 The goods transferred must be of merchantable quality, and reasonably fit for their purpose (s.4). These conditions apply only where the goods transferred are supplied in the course of business.

These conditions are couched in terms very similar to those used in the Sale of Goods Act 1979. Cases interpreting and applying those rules will no doubt be helpful in clarifying the 1982 SGSA provisions. Very similar terms are incorporated by ss. 7–9 in contracts for the hire of goods. These are significant nowadays, as hiring cars, office machinery and heavy plant is very common in business.

As usual, the possibility of excluding these implied terms is limited by the operation of the Unfair Contract Terms Act 1977. Generally in consumer transactions these protective conditions cannot be excluded, but in business transactions an exclusion clause may be acceptable if it satisfies the requirement of reasonableness under the 1977 Act (see page 88).

Supply of services

The 1982 SGSA does not define what is meant by a service, except to make clear that the services provided by professions such as architects and surveyors are included. Obvious examples are activities like car servicing, boiler maintenance, dry cleaning and watch repairing. In any of these cases the customer will feel aggrieved if the job is not done effectively, if it costs too much or if it takes too long. In essence, those are the three areas where the Act now prescribes implied terms.

Exercising reasonable care and skill

Section 13 states that if a supplier of a service is acting in the course of business there is an implied term that he must carry out the service with reasonable care and skill. One interesting feature of this section is that it does not prescribe whether the term is a condition (major term) or a warranty (minor term). The standard laid down is apparently imprecise, but it means that a builder must exercise the care and skill of a reasonably competent builder, a surveyor must exercise the care and skill of a reasonably competent surveyor, and so on. The standard is thus set objectively. It is no use asking whether the builder did his best, or even whether he tried reasonably hard given his limitations! He must be measured against a mythical, reasonably competent builder. The courts will not find this new provision difficult to apply as s.13 merely codifies the existing common law rules, i.e. similar duties would previously have been implied into such contracts by the courts. As soon as the idea of 'reasonable care and skill' is introduced it is clear that there is the possibility of a claim in the tort of negligence too. Usually it is more straightforward to sue in contract, as the relevant duty is owed by virtue of the contract and need not be specifically proved. The singular advantage of codifying the 'reasonable care and skill' requirement in s.13 rather than relying on a judicially implied term, is that it makes the position between the parties much clearer and more certain.

The time for performance

Section 14 provides that there is an implied term that a supplier acting in the course of business, where no time is fixed by the contract, must perform the service within a reasonable time. Establishing what is a reasonable time is a question of fact, which can sometimes be implied from the nature of the contract. If a firm is engaged to come and spray fruit trees when they are in blossom there is only a short span of time within which the contract can be performed.

The cost of the service

Section 15 provides that where the contract does not fix the charge or provide a method of fixing it, the customer must pay a reasonable charge. What is reasonable is a question of fact.

It is possible to exclude the terms implied by these sections, but again, only within the limits provided by the Unfair Contract Terms Act 1977. It should particularly be remembered that where, by negligence, a person causes death or personal injury, he cannot exclude or limit his liability by a contract term (s.2).

Hire purchase, credit sales and conditional sales

It is often the case that a buyer can only afford to purchase goods if payment can be spread over a period. Historically, hire purchase developed at the end of the nineteenth century as a means of allowing people to buy more expensive durable goods like pianos and sewing machines by spreading payments out over a period, and yet achieving a measure of protection for the seller who remained the owner of the goods until the last payment was made. If a buyer fell into arrears with payments, the seller could 'snatch back' his goods. Where a buyer found that he had overcommitted himself financially, he could usually terminate the agreement, but often on terms which were disadvantageous to him. Recognizing these evils, and the potential inequality of bargaining power between the buyer and the seller in such transactions, Parliament passed a series of Hire Purchase Acts, the rules from which are now consolidated in the Consumer Credit Act 1974.

A number of different ways exist for a customer to buy on credit. Traditionally the law provided several types of transaction, which give flexibility about the terms incorporated and which vary in the protections afforded to the customer. The supplier could choose to use:

1   A hire purchase agreement, where the customer hires goods for a period, with the opportunity to exercise an option to purchase at the end of the period. In this type of agreement, the supplier remains the owner of the goods until the option is exercised. The hirer may terminate the hiring agreement without exercising the option, although this would not usually be wise, as it would prove to be a costly way to hire goods. As the goods remain in the ownership of the supplier he has certain rights to seize back the

goods if the hirer defaults on payment. In this type of transaction, terms about merchantable quality and reasonable fitness for purpose are implied in a form similar to the implied terms of the Sale of Goods Act 1979. HP agreements are controlled either by the Consumer Credit Act 1974 or by rules of common law.

2   A credit sale agreement. These extend credit to the buyer of goods e.g. where he arranges to pay by instalments, but the ownership in the goods passes to the buyer immediately. They are governed mainly by the Sale of Goods Act 1979.

3   A conditional sale agreement, where ownership of the goods remains vested in the seller, but the buyer has no right to terminate the agreement. Because credit is extended to the customer, the Consumer Credit Act 1974 may apply.

Of course, these types of contract are not the only ways in which credit may be given. There has been a dramatic rise in the use of credit cards – either those issued by particular stores for use in their own shops, or those issued by credit card companies for use in any accredited outlet of the company. In either of these cases the sum owed can represent many different contracts made by the debtor. Sometimes, by the terms of his agreement with the credit card company, the debtor must repay at regular monthly intervals and may not exceed a fixed credit limit. In other cases the debtor may owe up to a fixed credit limit and may choose whether to settle in full at the end of the month, in which case he pays no interest, or he may pay part of what he owes and run up interest on the balance.

Inevitably, most organizations which are prepared to extend credit do so only for a return. That return is the interest they charge. It may be thought that evil moneylenders are a thing of the past, but 'loan sharks' are their modern equivalent. The law has long believed that rules are needed to protect people from extortionate bargains, and such rules are all the more vital when seen as part of 'consumer protection'. The rules were dramatically altered by the introduction of the Consumer Credit Act 1974. As its name applies, the Act is of special significance to 'consumers', and the protections of the Act range from licensing people and organizations which offer credit to insisting on sufficiently full information being available, so that a customer can establish the cost of the credit. To give the Act 'real teeth' there are criminal as well as civil sanctions.

For the businessman making contracts to purchase supplies or equipment the Act may be of limited significance. Its main provisions only operate where the credit extended is more than £50 but less than £15,000 and the customer is not a corporation. For a company or an individual seeking credit of more than £15,000 the ordinary common law rules apply, the most important of which is *caveat emptor* (let the buyer beware)!

Where the Act does apply there are some very important benefits for consumers, not least that the organization which extends credit, e.g. the finance house, is liable in respect of breaches of the implied terms with regard to merchantable quality and fitness for the purpose. This could be particularly relevant where the actual supplier of goods is not worth proceeding against.

One aspect of the Act is relevant to all credit agreements, with no financial limit. This is the power of the court to examine credit agreements which are extortionate, and seek to do justice between the parties. Section 38 of the Act specifies some factors which can be taken into account when determining whether the credit bargain is extortionate. These include the prevailing interest rate; the degree of risk accepted by the creditor; the creditor's relationship to the debtor; the debtor's age, experience, business capacity, and state of health; and the existence of any financial pressure on the debtor. If the bargain is found to be extortionate the court can adjust the rights and duties between the parties.

Other methods of consumer protection

Many of the protections discussed in this chapter can only be fully effective if a person is prepared to bring a court action to enforce his rights. But the public is often in fear of the cost of litigation and, especially with smaller cases, there can be a feeling that the time, trouble and effort involved is disproportionate to the size of the claim. An interesting trend in consumer protection is towards state enforcement of duties. Examples of this can be seen in rules such as those covering food and drugs and weights and measures, which create numerous offences for which prosecutions can be brought. A further development is the Trade Descriptions Act 1968, which makes it an offence to apply a false trade description to goods. A common example of an offence under this Act is that of the car salesman who falsifies the recorded mileage of a car by interfering with the instrument. If a prosecution is brought against him the court has power not only to fine the salesman, but also to make him pay compensation to the buyer. From the buyer's point of view the advantage of this is that someone else will take the initiative in bringing court proceedings. The drawback, however, is that compensation may not be nearly so accurately assessed as damages would be by a civil court. Moreover, the buyer may not want money, and might prefer to repudiate the contract and hand back the goods.

The individual's best consumer protection comes from dealing with a reputable trader with high standards who wishes to maintain his reputation. In an effort to improve trading standards generally the Office of Fair Trading was established in 1973, under the control of the Director General of Fair Trading. The Office encourages groups of traders to prepare and abide by codes of practice, and generally seeks to discourage unfair trading practices.

Insurance contracts

When a businessman considers the risks inherent in running his business (e.g. that his workmen may injure third parties, the workmen themselves may be injured, his business premises may take fire, a customer may be injured by a defective product) it takes little imagination to realize that potential claims against him could be enormous. It is true that some organizations are sufficiently large to bear their own risks. This tends to be the case only where the insurance premiums charged are so high that these large organizations find it more economical to meet claims, if and when they arise, out of their own funds. In all normal cases a firm would be wise to secure insurance cover, and in some circumstances the law makes insurance compulsory, e.g. employer's liability and motor insurance.

Commercial insurance is subdivided into fire, life, accident and marine. It is common to speak of life assurance, while using the word insurance in relation to the other classes. The difference is said to be that with assurance, the risk (i.e. death) is bound to happen sooner or later, whereas insurance covers risks which are foreseeable but which may never occur, e.g. a fire or an accident. In practice, the difference is not important.

Two vital principles are fundamental to all insurance contracts.

1   Utmost good faith

A person who seeks insurance usually knows all the relevant facts. On the basis of what he reveals the insurers can decide whether to accept the risk (i.e. give insurance cover) and how much to charge by way of premium. Because of this inequality in the bargaining position of the parties the law imposes a duty on a person seeking insurance to disclose all the material facts to the insurer. The duty of utmost good faith (*uberrimae fidei*) only requires disclosure of facts which are material and which are known or ought to have been known by the insured.

(a) *When are facts material?* The answer seems to be when they would influence a prudent insurer as to whether or not he will accept the risk, or as to the amount of the premium. With motor insurance previous motoring convictions are obviously material. In the case of most types of insurance the fact that another insurer has refused the risk is material. In life insurance previous illnesses may be material.

(b) *Knowledge of the facts.* The duty on the insured is quite strict. He must reveal facts he knows or is presumed to know. He cannot avoid this duty by deliberately keeping himself in ignorance. If the facts within the knowledge of the insured actually reduce the risk, or are facts which are common knowledge so that the insurer would be presumed to know them too, then no disclosure is necessary.

These rules about disclosure recognize the possibility that an insured may be silent despite being under a duty to speak. They are an exception to the general contract rule that silence does not usually amount to misrepresentation. This is normally the case because of the principle of *caveat emptor* (let the buyer beware). Usually it is up to the parties to negotiate their own bargain and if one of them requires information, he must ask the other for it. The law does not generally require the other party to volunteer it. Of course, a person seeking insurance may have made positive statements which turn out to be false. In such a case the normal rules of misrepresentation would operate and the insurance company's remedy would depend on the type of misrepresentation, which can be innocent, negligent or fraudulent.

When there has been non-disclosure of a material fact the remedy of the insurer is to avoid the policy. It is irrelevant that the insurer has not asked a specific question on the proposal form. This rule can sometimes operate very harshly in practice. In one case, *Woolcott v. Sun Alliance of London Insurance,* the plaintiff did not complete the proposal form himself. He was buying a house with the aid of a mortgage from a building society. His mortgage application form indicated that the building society would insure the property. The house was subsequently damaged by fire. When the plaintiff sought to claim on the block policy held by the building society the insurers avoided the policy and refused to pay. The grounds for their refusal were that the plaintiff had been convicted for robbery in 1960 and sentenced to twelve years in prison. They regarded this as a material fact which had not been disclosed to them.

2   Insurable interest

If people could insure goods or lives in which they had no legitimate interest the result would be a wager or gambling agreement. It is a necessary ingredient of an insurance contract that the insured must have an insurable interest, i.e. some foreseeable financial loss or liability.

(a) *Life insurance* – it is accepted that everyone has an insurable interest in his own life and a person may insure himself against death or personal accident to an unlimited extent, so long as he can pay the premiums. In certain circumstances a person may have an insurable interest in the life of someone else, e.g. a wife has an unlimited insurable interest in her husband and vice versa; a creditor has an insurable interest in the life of his debtor, up to the amount of the debt. Parties to civil proceedings in the courts have an insurable interest in the life of the judge who is hearing their case, as they stand to lose large sums of money if he dies and the hearing has to begin again in front of a new judge.

(b) *Property insurance* – the owner of property has an unlimited insurable interest up to its full value. In other cases, where a person is not the owner, the law allows insurance to the extent of that person's interest or liability. For example, a building society could insure a building for the amount loaned on mortgage. Where goods are concerned a buyer can insure before he takes delivery, or a warehouseman can insure other people's goods entrusted to him for storage.

(c) *Liability insurance* – where a person can foresee liability, (e.g. arising out of his occupation of premises, or use of a vehicle) he has an insurable interest. The law does not allow him to insure against criminal liability, as that would be contrary to public policy. So a motorist cannot insure against being fined for careless driving.

The insurance contract

Subject to the two principles discussed above, the usual rules about the formation of a contract apply. The following points should be noted:

1 *Agreement* – this usually results from the person seeking insurance completing a proposal form (the offer) which is then accepted by the insurers.

2 *Consideration* – insurance contracts are not usually made by deed, so consideration is necessary. This usually consists of paying a premium in return for the promise of a payment out whenever the risk occurs.

3 *Form of the contract* – as a general rule contracts of insurance do not need to be in writing. An oral contract could be valid and

enforceable. In practice it is usual to record the terms of the agreement in a policy. Should any dispute arise over the risks which are covered the words of the policy must be construed (i.e. interpreted) to see whether they cover the facts of the case. It is usually said that the words of a policy should be read so as to give effect to the intention of the parties. This suggests that both play a part in drawing up the policy, whereas the truth is that it will usually be a standard form contract drawn up by the insurers. Mindful of this, the courts will construe any ambiguity against the insurers. It should also be remembered that the Unfair Contract Terms Act 1977 does not apply to insurance contracts. In theory, therefore, insurers are free to limit or exclude their liability.

4   *Terms of the contract* – one feature of insurance contracts is that all terms, major or minor, tend to be called warranties. This is particularly confusing because of other meanings which the word can carry, e.g. in the sense of a guarantee. In any contract situation it is always a difficult question to determine whether a statement which has been made is so important that it becomes part of the contract (i.e. becomes a term), or is of lesser importance so that it is merely a representation. A person seeking insurance may make a number of statements in answer to questions on the proposal form, e.g. stating that he has no motoring convictions, or that he has never had an operation. Insurers have been in the habit of making such statements form the basis of the contract, by including a note on the proposal form (which is then signed by the insured) to the effect that all the answers will be regarded as warranties. This practice puts the insurers into a most powerful position in relation to the insured. Should there be anything wrongly answered on the form, then, even if the insured has been acting honestly, and even if it is immaterial, an insurer can avoid liability on the whole contract by treating the error as a breach of warranty. This tactic has resulted in one judge commenting: 'I wish I could adequately warn the public against such practices on the part of the insurance offices.' Insurance contracts are not controlled by the Unfair Contract Terms Act 1977, but insurers do now adhere to a 'Statement of Insurance Practice' which resolves some of these difficulties. Although this 'Statement' was issued following consultations and discussions with the Department of Trade it is not legally binding upon insurers. Some changes in the law may be expected, since the Law Commission has already made recommendations with regard to non-disclosure and breaches of warranty. The 'Statement' is limited in its scope to private consumers. This seems in line with the thinking behind the Unfair Contract Terms

Act 1977, in which protection is given mainly to persons dealing as consumers. The insurance industry has been sufficiently worried about customer complaints that it has cooperated to appoint an Insurance Ombudsman, who will look into customers' grievances.

5 *Duration of the policy* – often an insurance policy runs for a fixed period, usually a year. There are cases where insurance relates to a specific event (e.g. bad weather insurance for a country show, or insurance against twins being born) and the protection lapses once the date of the event has passed. Where the policy is of a continuing type e.g. life assurance, the insurer must go on accepting the premiums even though the risk inevitably becomes greater year by year. With other types of policy, e.g. motor insurance, the expectation is that it will be renewed, but neither party is obliged to make a fresh contract. If renewal does occur, then the duty to disclose material facts becomes relevant again, because each renewal creates a fresh contract.

Types of insurance

1 Employers' liability insurance

Although sensible employers have always tended to have insurance cover for protection against claims by injured workmen, problems have arisen in the past when some employers had no such insurance, and were unable to meet claims for damages from their employees because they had become insolvent. Although an employee injured in an accident at work may have claims under the Industrial Injuries Scheme, the law also provides that he can claim damages from a negligent employer. That claim is now protected by the requirement of compulsory insurance imposed by the Employer's Liability (Compulsory Insurance) Act 1969. The following main points about the Act should be noted:

(a) All employers (except local authorities, statutory corporations and nationalized industries) are covered by the rules.
(b) Employers must maintain insurance against liability for injury or disease sustained by employees in the course of their employment.
(c) The level of cover required is £2 million in respect of claims from one or more employees arising from any one occurrence.
(d) The insurance must be made with an authorised insurer. This term is defined by regulations.
(e) The employer's duty is to maintain an 'approved policy'. The effect of this rule is to make it illegal for the insurer to limit his liability in certain ways.

(f) The rules are enforced by criminal sanctions. The Act provides for fines of up to £200 per day for failure to comply.

(g) The insurance certificate must be displayed and, if required, produced to an inspector of the Health and Safety Executive.

Limitations on the cover provided under the Act are:

(a) It only protects employees who work under a contract of service or apprenticeship.

(b) Only those incidents arising 'out of and in the course of the employment' are covered. The same phrase is used in the Industrial Injuries Scheme, where its interpretation and application has not been without difficulties.

2 Public liability insurance

The employers' liability insurance rules only oblige an employer to arrange insurance cover against injury to his employees. He may owe liability to a third party who is injured by some activity of one of his employees, e.g. if one of his labourers negligently hits a pedestrian with a plank of wood. In such a case the principle of vicarious liability means that the pedestrian is likely to bring his action for negligence against the employer. It is not compulsory for an employer to insure against this type of liability (usually called public liability insurance), although it is very common in practice. Despite not being required by law, such insurance is often specified in building contracts. For example, if a contractor is working under the JCT Standard Form Contract he is required to: 'Maintain such insurances as are necessary to cover the liability of the contractor in respect of personal injury or death arising out of the carrying out of the works'.

It is not only employers who need public liability cover. Anyone may cause death, injury or damage while going about his or her daily life. For example, a pedestrian may cause a motorist to swerve and crash, while a property-owner could be liable if his chimney were to fall on a passer-by. However, public liability cover is often provided as part of another type of policy, e.g. under a householder's policy.

3 Insurance against damage to property

This type of insurance usually covers fire damage, but will often extend to damage caused by explosion or lightning. The policy may then be further extended to cover other risks to property caused by, for example, storm, flood or impact. This type of insurance is not compulsory by law, and it is essential that a policy-holder should ensure that he has all the desired protection in his policy. For example, a policy could cover damage caused by fire, yet exclude liability if the fire was caused by explosion.

It is now quite common to extend fire insurance protection to cover consequential loss. Should a fire render a building unusable a firm's business activities could be severely disrupted. Insurance cover can be provided to cover loss of profits and additional expenses necessarily incurred, e.g. renting alternative property.

4   Motor insurance

In the case of motor insurance, certain aspects of insurance cover are compulsory. As a minimum a motorist must have a policy which covers:

- Liability for death or personal injury to third parties, including passengers.
- Hospital charges (up to a fixed maximum) in respect of the treatment of an injured party and emergency treatment fees.

It is very unusual for such limited cover to be taken out by a motorist. He would normally also want cover against:

- Damage caused to property belonging to a third party.
- Fire and theft in relation to his own vehicle.
- Damage to the vehicle and to himself.

The insurance companies do not find motor insurance altogether profitable. Premiums charged naturally vary with the risk, and most insurers will take into account the type of vehicle, its value, the age and experience of the driver, the locality in which he lives, his claims record and any driving convictions. Premiums still tend to be expensive and the high cost may be one of the reasons why some motorists fail to insure. When a third party is injured by an uninsured motorist, or a 'hit and run' driver, the victim may claim from the Motor Insurers' Bureau. Every motor insurer must belong to this organization which operates under an agreement made with the Department of Transport.

Claims under an insurance policy

Once the need to make a claim under a policy arises, the question of construction of the contract becomes important. Is the event which has occurred actually covered by the policy? Naturally the insurers will have based their premium on a fixed amount of cover to be provided, and they will not wish to pay out more than is necessary.

If the loss which has occurred is covered by the policy then, in the case of most types of insurance (except life and personal accident), the principle of indemnity operates. This means that the amount paid out by an insurer should be sufficient to cover the loss sustained, but should not allow the insured person to make a profit. However, even in those cases where the indemnity principle is applicable, the following restrictions on it should be noted:

1   The policy itself may provide for a maximum sum insured. This can provide a complete indemnity if the sum insured is adequate, but a property may have been underinsured, and the policy may contain an average clause which will then operate. The object of such a clause is to 'penalize' the person who has underinsured, since this practice is unfair from the insurer's point of view, preventing him from receiving a proper premium in return for the risk he has to bear. Of course, underinsurance is not necessarily caused by deceitful motives. A person may genuinely fail to realize that the rebuilding of his property will cost much more now because of inflation than when he purchased it some years earlier. Generally, average clauses work on a pro-rata basis. If you underinsure by 50 per cent, your claim will be settled on the basis of 50 per cent of the loss sustained. For example, a house which could cost £40,000 to rebuild at present-day prices is insured for £20,000. If it is totally destroyed by fire, £20,000 is the maximum payable. If damage amounting to £10,000 is caused (one-quarter of the true insurance value) the insured will be paid one quarter of the sum insured, i.e. £5,000.

2   The policy itself may be subject to an excess. It is quite usual for the contract to specify that the insured will bear an agreed proportion of each claim, often the first £15 or £25. In such cases, the insurance does not provide a full indemnity.

3   An insurer may not be wholly liable if the property has been insured with more than one company. In such case the contribution principle will operate, whereby other insurers who are covering the same risk share in the cost of paying out. The indemnity principle is thus preserved, as the total settlement figure will only cover the insured's loss and not allow him to make a profit. As with indemnity, the contribution principle is not appropriate in the case of life insurance. Double insurance consists of covering the same risk by more than one policy. This is not the same as reinsurance. As soon as an insurer has taken on a risk there

is always the likelihood that he may have to pay out. In cases where a single accident may be very costly e.g. the loss of a telecommunications satellite, the insurer may wish to spread the risk. In such a case, he can reinsure part or all of the risk with another insurer. If the risk then occurs, the insured claims against the original insurer in full. The original insurer then claims under his own reinsurance policy.

4   When the risk occurs, an insured person may have a right of action for damages against the person who has injured him or damaged his property, as well as the possibility of claiming under his insurance policy. If a motorist has his vehicle negligently damaged by another motorist, the subrogation principle will apply. If the victim decides to claim from his insurers they may in turn claim against the negligent motorist. The practical effect of this would be that one insurance company would be claiming from another. Given the thousands of claims which they deal with, this process would be expensive and time consuming. It is, therefore, common for insurers to make agreements amongst themselves not to claim from one another under the subrogation rules. In the long run, given the amount of business involved and the administrative savings made, this will usually be a perfectly equitable arrangement. This type of agreement between insurance companies results in the 'knock for knock' arrangements found in motor insurance. The practice does not affect the rights of the insured.

Assignment

A policy of insurance is a chose in action i.e. property which can only be claimed or protected by taking action in the courts. As a type of property it is valuable in itself and the insured person may wish to use it as security to raise money, or may wish to transfer the benefit of the insurance to someone else. The assignment may be governed by the rules of the Policies of Assurance Act 1867 in the case of life policies. It must be in writing, and the insurers must be given notice. Note that it is the benefit of the policy which is assigned. Assignments of other types of insurance are effected under the rules of s.136 of the Law of Property Act 1925. This requires the assignment to be absolute, made in writing and notified in writing to the insurer.

7

Special contracts – building contracts

Control of work under a building contract

Many of the examples used so far to illustrate the working of the law of contract have been simple transactions involving small sums of money where the contract is made and performed within a short period of time. Contrast that with a building contract where the work may be massive in scale, taking months or years to complete and costing millions of pounds. The very scale of the work means that many sub-contracts will be involved, as well as the main contract. Despite the complexity of a building contract it is judged by the ordinary general principles of the law of contract. It would be uneconomic to draft a complex new set of terms for every building contract and although this type of contract has not been codified by a statute, standard forms of contract have developed in the construction industry. These have been subject to extensive interpretation by the courts, and amendments to the standard form are issued regularly. Inevitably, the terms of any standard form contract may be seen to lean against the interests of one of the parties, unless representatives of both sides played a part in drawing up the original version.

A building contract is one whereby the contractor or builder undertakes work for an employer or building owner. Building works are normally controlled by JCT contracts, issued by a Joint Contracts Tribunal made up of bodies such as building trades employers, the architects' association and local authorities. JCT contracts come in a number of forms, for use with a local authority or private employer, with or without quantities. These standard form contracts are long and detailed and have been drawn up by bodies representing wide-ranging experience in the building industry. The parties using such a contract may choose to adapt or vary the specific clauses of the contract and they are entirely free to do so, but with the warning that in such a complex document, many of the provisions may be interdependent and both parties should be clear what are the repercussions of the changes they have made.

The employer who needs to undertake building work may be totally inexperienced in this field. He may feel that he should have professional advice in making and carrying through the contract. It is a traditional feature of large-scale building work that the employer engages advisers such as architects and quantity surveyors, who will supervise and control the work in progress. The standard forms are drawn up in recognition of this state of affairs and many tasks within the contract are specifically allocated to the architect. It is important to remember that the building contract is made between the contractor and the employer. The architect is *not* a party to that contract. He has a quite separate contract with the employer and he will often have been employed under the Conditions of Engagement published by the RIBA. These are standard terms providing for the amount to be paid to the architect, and setting out his duties and responsibilities in detail. Where several professional advisers such as structural engineers and quantity surveyors are engaged by the employer, it is usual for them to be under the overall control of the architect. The employer may employ all of these professional advisers under contracts of service but it is more likely that they will be in independent practice, and the employer then engages them under a contract for services.

The professional advisers will undertake significant amounts of work before the shape of the final project is determined. They must establish what the employer wants, the means by which it can practicably be achieved, and whether necessary legal hurdles can be surmounted. Then, the drawings and specifications are prepared and tenders sought. After the contract is placed the architect may be required to supervise the work and certify the payments. Inevitably, the supervision and certification will bring the architect into regular contact with the contractor, but the architect is only the agent of the employer, restricted in his authority by the terms of his engagement with the employer.

Where large-scale building work is undertaken it is common for much of the day-to-day administration to be carried out by a clerk of the works, who is employed by the employer, and not the contractor. His role is significant as he is the person who is regularly on site. He works under the direction of the architect and reports to him anything which is out of line with the terms of the contract.

The architect owes duties to the employer arising expressly and impliedly from his contract, and also by virtue of duties established by the law of tort. He is in the same position as other professional or skilled people in that he will be liable if he does not do his work with reasonable care and skill. A failure to show such care could involve design faults, inadequate site examination, delays in furnishing drawings, disregard of building regulations, an injudicious choice of builder, or lack of adequate supervision of the work. Some of an architect's duties are described as quasi-judicial because certain terms of the standard form contract require him to settle matters between the employer and the contractor. This aspect will be considered later in relation to certification.

Tendering for building contracts

Once it is clear what the scope of the building work is to be, the employer or the architect acting on his behalf will invite contractors to tender. The costs of preparing the tender (the offer) are significant, and this cost has to be borne by the contractor. The tender reflects how keen the contractor is to get the job. Even if he puts in the lowest tender, he is not automatically assured of success. His tender is only an offer and the employer may accept or reject it. Indeed, the employer may reject all the tenders. Price may not be the only factor by which he is judging the offers.

Once a tender is accepted, a valid contract can come into existence immediately, but it sometimes happens that the employer makes acceptance subject to conditions such as the execution of a formal contract or the provision of a surety bond. This can be relevant if the contractor starts work at once, and subsequently it is held that a contract never existed. In each case it will be a question of interpreting the precise words used. It must be remembered that the negotiations for building work may be prolonged and it may be essential, for reasons of time constraints, to get the work under way. This some-times occurs on the basis of a letter of intent, in which one party indicates to the other that it is likely that a contract will be placed, and inviting the other to commence preliminary work. These letters of intent are also found between contractors and sub-contractors, where the sub-contractor has tendered for specialized work, (e.g. heating and ventilation) and the contractor has used that tender as a basis for his own tender. He may then indicate in a letter of intent to the selected sub-contractor that he will place a contract with the sub-contractor if he is successful with his own tender.

Where preliminary work is done on the basis of a letter of intent such work may have to be paid for on a *quantum meruit* basis (as much as it is worth) if no contract is eventually placed. Where a subsequent contract is made the effect of it may operate retrospectively to cover work done under the letter of intent. *Trollope and Colls Ltd v. Atomic Power Constructions Ltd* is a case where this occurred. The letter of intent was sent in June 1959 and the contract was not finally made until April 1960, by which time the contractors had undertaken work worth a considerable amount. They contended that they should be paid for this early work on a *quantum meruit* basis, rather than on the contract price basis. The court did not agree. It was held that when the contract was finally concluded in April 1960 it contained an implied term that the contract would govern what had already taken place.

The JCT standard form contracts

Although the standard form JCT contract runs to some forty clauses it is not in itself the entire contract. It makes provision in clause 2 for the incorporation of 'the contract documents', which include the contract drawings and bills. The parties will also sign 'Articles of Agreement' which is the actual contract between them, and is a deed made under seal. The advantage of making the contract in this way is to extend the limitation period for breach of contract claims from six years in ordinary simple contracts to twelve years for contracts made by deed. The Articles are dated, they name the parties, define and locate the building work, and are signed and witnessed. They impose an obligation on the contractor to complete the work under the Conditions of Contract for the sum agreed (the consideration); specify the architect and the quantity surveyor; and impose an arbitration agreement.

The Conditions of Contract, referred to in the Articles and therefore incorporated into the contract, contain the essence of the agreement. Clause 2 imposes on the contractor the obligation to execute and complete the works in accordance with the contract documents. 'Completing' for this purpose means practical completion, which is the point at which the defects liability period commences. This is a significant moment because the contractor then ceases to owe certain obligations e.g. insurance obligations. As the contractor has to operate in accordance with the contract documents he does not himself undertake any design responsibility. He is not, therefore, undertaking that the building will be suitable for its intended purpose.

The Conditions of Contract are not laid out in a particularly helpful sequence, and the following appraisal of the conditions attempts to impose a more logical order. It is not intended to deal exhaustively with all of the conditions.

Possession of the site

Clause 23.1 requires the contractor to be given possession of the site on the agreed date of possession. He must then regularly and diligently proceed with the work, bearing in mind that the architect can issue instructions to postpone work, which could in turn provide the grounds for the contractor to claim an extension of time, and for loss and/or expense.

On-site provisions

There must be access for the architect and his representatives at reasonable times (clause 11). The employer may appoint a clerk of works to act as an inspector on his behalf. The clerk of works will be under the supervision of the architect but must be facilitated in the performance of his duties by the contractor. Directions given to the contractor by a clerk of works are of no effect unless confirmed by an instruction from the architect within two days (clause 12). The contractor is obliged by clause 10 to keep a competent person in charge on the site during working hours. Such a 'site agent' is entitled to receive architect's instructions on behalf of the contractor.

The architect must provide the contractor with all the requisite levels and measurements so that the work can be carried out (clause 7). Materials, goods and workmanship must be as described in the Contract Bills and if requested by the architect, the contractor must produce vouchers to prove that materials and goods correspond with the specification. As a further check the architect may issue an instruction for work to be opened up for inspection or to test goods and materials. The cost of this exercise can be added to the Contract Sum, except that if it proves a contractor to be at fault in some way, he must bear the cost.

Clause 16 deals with materials and goods on the site. Such unfixed goods become the property of the employer only when their value has been included in an interim certificate which has been paid by the employer. Before that time their ownership is determined by the usual rules of sale of goods. Once ownership passes to the employer the contractor is under a duty to take reasonable care of the goods in order to protect them against damage or theft.

Under clause 29 the contractor must allow entry to the site to persons who are directly engaged by the employer and whose work does not form part of the contract work but where provision was made in the Contract Bills for the execution of their work. The employer is responsible for such persons. For instance an archaeologist may be called to the site to investigate a discovery of fossils or antiquities. Clause 34 makes provision for the action to be taken by the contractor if he makes such a discovery.

Progress of the work

It has already been noted that clause 2 requires the contractor to execute and complete the work in accordance with the contract documents. As the work progresses unexpected technical problems may occur, or it may not be entirely clear what work is intended to be done under the contract. In these cases the ability to vary the contract is important. Under the JCT standard form, authority to order variations is vested in the architect who acts by issuing architect's instructions. Needless to say, instructions can be issued for a range of reasons far wider than just ordering variations but it is convenient to consider these items together.

Clause 13 deals with variations. These give valuable flexibility to the contract. It is basically sound to include such a clause as it permits the employer to require a variation as of right, instead of having to rely on the goodwill of the contractor or having to create a quite separate contract furnished with its own consideration to render the variation valid and enforceable. The variations clause clearly demonstrates that the employer is vesting the architect with authority to order variations by which he, the employer, will regard himself as bound. When the term 'variation' is used in clause 13, it means the alteration or modification of the design, quality or quantity of the works as shown in the Contract Drawings and described in the Contract Bills. It also covers the alteration, addition to, or omission of, any obligations imposed by the employer with regard to limitations on working hours or space, or the execution or completion of the work in any particular order. Clause 13 makes clear that variations ordered or sanctioned by the architect will not vitiate the contract, but this does not mean that the architect can order any change he likes. An excessive change would not come within the definition of a variation.

Architect's instructions

Architect's instructions generally, and the power to authorize variations are dealt with by clause 4. The contractor is obliged to comply forthwith with instructions issued to him by the architect, but they must be on a matter where the architect is empowered by the contract conditions to issue an instruction. His instructions can cover a wide range of situations such as variations, antiquities, defects and making good defects, nomination of sub-contractors and removal of items not in accordance with the contract. If a contractor does not comply with an instruction within seven days the employer may engage someone else to do that work, pay him and deduct that sum from money due to the contractor. Where a contractor is not clear under what authority an instruction is given, he can ask the architect to specify his authority and, if dissatisfied, the contractor can seek immediate arbitration.

Under clause 4 an architect's instruction is only valid if it is in writing, but the rules do provide for verbal instructions to be confirmed in writing within seven days by the contractor to the architect. If the architect does not dissent from that written confirmation within a further seven days, this becomes a valid architect's instruction. Alternatively, the architect himself may confirm in writing within seven days or, in cases where a contractor has complied with an oral instruction, the architect may confirm it in writing prior to the issue of the Final Certificate.

Extensions of time

Variations which have been ordered by the architect may be one of the reasons why a contractor needs an extension of time. The power for the architect to grant such an extension is contained in clause 25. This could be vital to the contractor because if he does not complete on time, he is likely to become liable under a liquidated damages clause. Extensions of time may not be exclusively for the contractor's benefit. If the employer has failed in some of his obligations, e.g. failure to allow access to the site at the proper time, he may be keen to see the time for completion extended as he would be unable to rely on a liquidated damages clause if he had been the cause of the delay.

Extensions are sought by the contractor making a written application to the architect, which must set out the relevant events which he considers justify an extension. These 'relevant events' are set out in detail in clause 25 and include exceptionally adverse weather conditions, acts of God (i.e. *force majeure*), civil commotion, strike or lockout, compliance with architect's instructions e.g. on variations, non-receipt by the contractor in due time of the necessary drawings or instructions, exercise by the government of statutory powers which affect supplies of labour, goods or fuel essential to the proper execution of the work, or failure or delay on the part of a statutory undertaker in pursuance of a statutory obligation.

Not only must the contractor set out the appropriate relevant event when he seeks an extension of time, but also he must specify the expected effects and the period of expected delay in completing. If the architect decides to grant an extension he does so in writing, specifying such later completion date as he considers fair and reasonable. In his extension, the architect must state which relevant events he has taken into account and the extent to which he has also taken into account variations previously ordered which have cut down on the contractor's task by deleting work originally specified. If no extension or an inadequate extension is granted, the contractor may go to arbitration.

Insurance

Clause 21 provides that the contractor must maintain insurance in respect of liabilities imposed by clause 20, that is liability for third party claims in respect of personal injury and damage to property where the contractor is at fault. Clause 22 determines who should take out an insurance against 'all risks' where the contract relates to a new building. The employer should insure against the specified perils when the work involves alterations or extensions to an existing building. Clause 22 requires the insurances to be effected by joint names policies.

It is eminently sensible to include provisions about insurance in the contract as building work necessarily involves risk. Harm could be caused to people coming onto the site, passers-by, neighbouring landowners or workmen employed on the site. Some insurance is compulsory by law, e.g. employers' liability insurance. Liability for damage or injury may lie on the contractor, or on the employer, sometimes directly and sometimes vicariously, and on some occasions, the contractor and employer may be jointly liable.

Payment for the work

One particular feature of building contracts is that they commonly provide for payment for the work to be made in stages. This is vital when the contractor's expenses and outgoings will be considerable and the overall time for completion may be lengthy. To provide for payments at intervals a system of certification is used. Clause 30 provides for the architect to issue interim certificates, usually at monthly intervals, and the employer must pay the sum due within fourteen days. The architect can seek interim valuation from the quantity surveyor whenever he considers it necessary to determine the amount due on an interim certificate. Following the decision in *Sutcliffe v. Thackrah*, he would be wise to adopt this course. There, the architect issued interim certificates on which the employer paid the contractor. The contractor was subsequently dismissed by the employer and became insolvent. The employer discovered that the architect had certified defective work and work that had not been done at all. The consequence of this certification was that overpayments had been made. The House of Lords held that the architect could be liable for damages for his negligence.

When issuing an interim certificate the architect establishes the amount due by calculating the gross valuation, less any retention and the amount of any previous payments. Gross valuation covers the total value of the work properly done by the contractor, together with the value of materials and goods on site. The retention will usually be a maximum of 5 per cent but some items are not subject to retention e.g. direct loss due to discovery of antiquities, or losses falling under clause 26.

Clause 26 deals with the contractor's claims for loss and expense where the progress of the work is likely to be materially affected by factors such as not receiving properly requested instructions or drawings in time, or any other of the 'matters' listed in clause 26. If the contractor is aware of such losses or expenses he must make written application to the architect who may determine the amount of such loss and add to it the contract sum. A claim by a contractor under clause 26 is without prejudice to other rights. For example, if the contractor is basing his claim on the architect's failure to provide him with the necessary drawings that would be a breach of contract entitling the contractor to sue the employer for damages.

If sums are added to the contract sum by virtue of clause 26, then clause 3 provides that the adjustment can be included in the calculation of the next interim certificate.

Practical completion and final payment

Once the architect considers that the work is at the stage of practical completion, where the building can function properly and any outstanding work is only minor, he can then issue a certificate of practical completion. This heralds the commencement of the defects liability period, usually fixed by the contract as six months. The architect will deliver a schedule of defects to the contractor no later than fourteen days after the end of the defects liability period and the contractor must then put the defects right at his own cost, unless the architect is prepared to instruct otherwise. (Of course, these instructions can only relate to defects which manifest themselves within this period. Any which become apparent later must be the subject of a claim for breach of contract under all the normal rules of contract, including limitation periods.) Once defects have been made good, the architect issues a certificate of completion of making good defects. The obligation to make good defects under clause 17 is confined to defects caused by materials or workmanship not in accordance with the contract, or frost damage occurring before practical completion, this being deemed to be the contractor's fault. These certificates of practical completion and on making good defects are significant because they operate to release the retention money, half at each stage.

Non-completion and breach

By the terms of clause 23 the contractor must complete the works on, or before, the completion date. By clause 24 the architect must issue a certificate of non-completion if the contractor does not complete in time, although the time may have been extended by architect's instructions. Once the architect has issued the certificate of non-completion, the employer may, after written notification to the contractor, deduct or recover liquidated damages calculated at the rate stated in the appendix to the standard form.

The provisions of clauses 23 and 24 relate only to delays. It is more likely that other breaches of contract will occur, some quite trivial and others causing significant loss. As an ultimate sanction, clauses 27 and 28 provide for determination by the employer or contractor respectively. But it must be borne in mind that there are arbitration arrangements under Article 5 and clause 41. Many disputes between the parties during the currency of the agreement could be resolved through those procedures. Other provisions may assist in remedying minor breaches. For instance, under clause 8 the architect can order the opening up and testing and, if necessary, the removal of any work consequently found to be defective.

Clause 27 is principally relevant when the contractor cannot go on with performance or where he has committed major breaches. It will operate automatically to determine the contract if the contractor goes into liquidation. In other situations, such as failure to proceed regularly and diligently, or persistent failure to remove defective work, the architect may serve a notice specifying the fault. If the contractor continues the default for fourteen days the employer may send notice by registered post within the next ten days to terminate the contractor's employment. If he takes such a step the employer would then have to engage other contractors to complete the work. Any extra cost incurred in their engagement can be recovered from the original contractor. Clause 27 specifically provides that notice by the employer must not be given unreasonably or vexatiously.

Clause 28 deals with the contractor terminating his employment with the employer. Nothing in this clause affects other rights and remedies of the contractor. The contractor effects the determination by serving notice on the employer or the architect. He may do so if the employer fails to honour a certificate, or if the work is suspended for various reasons, and for longer than a certain period, stated in the appendix. The contractor is then entitled to be paid for work done and materials supplied, and for any loss caused to him.

Clauses 27 and 28 merely have the effect of determining the employment of the contractor. They do not terminate the contract as a whole, and many of the other terms governing the rights of the parties will still be relevant. The ordinary rules of breach of contract will govern all other situations where either party alleges that the other has not complied with his obligations under the contract.

Sub-contracts

In a large building contract the main contractor is likely to organize that some aspects of the work will be performed by sub-contractors. He undertakes the main contract with the employer and then in turn enters into separate contracts with all the individual sub-contractors. For the employer the advantage of this system is that he gets his work done by making only one contract himself, and obligations in respect of the whole job are owed to him by the main contractor, who remains responsible for the work which he lets out on sub-contracts.

Generally, the main contractor may only sub-contract to the extent permitted by his contract with the employer. Sub-contractors will be paid by the main contractor and have no rights against the employer because they do not enjoy privity of contract with him. The employer can enhance his position by insisting on choosing the sub-contractors, in which case they will be known as nominated sub-contractors. When a sub-contractor is nominated in this way, there is the advantageous provision that, should the main contractor fail to pay him within a stated time of certification (seventeen days), then the employer may pay him directly.

Of course, while there may be advantages for the employer in having no direct contract with sub-contractors, this has inevitable drawbacks, principally the difficulty of incorporating the terms of the main contract into the sub-contract. It may be possible to to this, in so far as it is appropriate, by obligating the sub-contactor not to perform in such a way that he causes the main contractor to be in breach. If a subcontractor does default on his obligations the main contractor will be liable. The choice of sub-contractors is thus seen to be of vital importance as a contractor will be anxious in case the sub-contractor causes delay or becomes unable to complete his contract. If anything goes wrong the contractor may be involved in two legal actions: being sued by the employer under the main contract, and then himself suing the sub-contractor under the separate sub-contract.

One difficult problem involving renomination of sub-contractors used to arise where the original nomination failed for some reason e.g. liquidation of the nominee. The employer might then be anxious that if he renominated he would obligate himself to pay any higher charges of the new nominee. It was thought that he could avoid this burden by not renominating, but the House of Lords held, in *Bickerton v. North West Regional Hospital Board*, that the employer was under an implied obligation to renominate. The JCT standard form was altered to take account of this decision. The Joint Contracts Tribunal has also produced standard forms of collateral agreement, to be entered into by nominated sub-contractors and employers, thus creating a direct contract between the two where no privity otherwise existed. This is incredibly cumbersome, as there will be three contracts – employer and main contractor; main contractor and sub-contractor; and sub-contractor and employer – with all the attendant problems of knowing who to sue in respect of breaches. The consideration for the collateral agreement between the employer and the sub-contractor is that the employer promises the nomination and the sub-contractor promises to warrant his work.

8

Employment law

Employment and self-employment

With a working population in this country of about 24 million people, the rules governing employment are of considerable importance. The past thirty years have seen a massive increase in new employment rights created by Acts of Parliament. Previously, the law of employment was developed largely through case law, and it reflected the attitude that employers could 'hire and fire' at will, with no recognition of the inequality of bargaining power between employers and employees. To some extent that inequality was remedied by the growth of the power of the trade unions. However, the trade unions have themselves been subject to major changes within the last decade, which have curtailed their activities on behalf of their members, and further changes continue apace.

Most of the important protections of employment law are enjoyed by persons employed under a contract of service. This type of contract can be contrasted with a contract for services which, simply stated, is the distinction between the status of an employed person and that of a self-employed person. It is necessary to make this distinction because:

1 Statutory rights (e.g. the right not to be unfairly dismissed and the right to be compensated for redundancy) only apply to persons employed under a contract of service.
2 Employees under a contract of service are Class 1 National Insurance contributors, and therefore eligible for a wider range of social security benefits than self-employed Class 2 contributors. Class 2 contributors are not eligible for unemployment benefit or disablement benefit.

3 The tax arrangements for the two groups of workers are different. Employees pay tax by means of the PAYE system, whereas the self-employed pay tax by half-yearly instalments in arrears under a different tax schedule.
4 The duties implied by law between the parties to the contract are different, tending to be more onerous between employer and employee in a contract of service.

It will be seen that many of the reasons for distinguishing between contracts of service and those for services have financial implications for the employer as well as the employee. It may seem cheaper for the employer to encourage his workforce to become self-employed, and by that means avoid the increasingly strict statutory control over contracts of service. However, it is not enough for the parties simply to change the name of their relationship. It is a question of fact whether the contract is one of service or for services. In those cases where the courts think a change has been made simply to take advantage of favourable rules they may find no alteration in the true nature of the relationship.

When the courts have to determine which relationship exists between the parties there has been considerable difficulty in establishing a simple test by which the decision can be made. Traditionally the courts used a simple test of control. Could the employer tell the employee what to do *and* how to do it? If so, there was a sufficient measure of control to give rise to the closer contract of service. The drawback with such an unsophisticated test is that it is quite inadequate to cope with more complex employment situations. The test is only concerned with the ultimate possibility of exercising control. The fact that an employer chooses to let an experienced employee get on with the job is irrelevant. Even so, the test proved to be over simple and by the late 1940s the courts were searching for another test. It is only fair to say that even today the control test still gives a reliable answer in simple employment relationships.

In more complex situations the judges thought an answer might lie in asking whether a person's work was done as an integral part of the employer's business. This 'integration' test was not entirely satisfactory, and at times highly artificial. More recently the judges have come to the conclusion that there is no simple question which will provide a conclusive answer. Rather, it is a matter of looking at all the surrounding circumstances, and the modern approach is said to be a mixed or multiple test. Using this approach, the court will consider a range of factors, including:

- What are the employer's powers of selection and dismissal?
- What measure of control is exercised by the employer?
- What agreement is there about the method and amount of re-muneration?
- What arrangements exist for the payment of tax and National Insurance contributions?
- Who supplies tools and equipment?
- Does the employee bear any economic risk in the enterprise?
- Does the employee hire his own helpers?
- Does the employee have any responsibility for investment and management?
- Can the employee profit from sound management in the perfor-mance of his task?
- How do the parties themselves view their relationship?
- How are the employees usually engaged in the trade or industry?

The mixed or multiple test may in reality be a kind of 'reasonable man' approach. The difficulty in practice is that a situation may arise where the questions listed above give equivocal answers. Consider the example of *Ready Mixed Concrete Ltd v. MPNI*. On the one side, the man in question had to wear a uniform, obey the orders of a foreman and obey company rules. All of these features of his contract pointed towards it being a contract of service. By contrast, he was buying the lorry under HP arrangements with the company, and had to bear the cost of servicing it. He also paid his own tax and National Insurance contributions. On these facts he could be seen to be taking some risk. When all the circumstances were taken into account the court found that he was self-employed.

It is matterless what the parties call their arrangement although, when the factors are very finely balanced, some assistance may be given by looking at what the parties have chosen to call it. This must be treated cautiously though, as two contrasting cases will show. In *Massey v. Crown Life Insurance Co.* one of the branch managers approached Crown Life to suggest a change in his status from employment to self-employment. He took advice about the conse-quences of the change and his new status was confirmed between the parties, and in a letter sent to the tax office. Subsequently the manager had occasion to regret his decision when certain employment rights were no longer available to him. He sought to prove that, in reality, he was still engaged under a contract of service. The Court of Appeal did not agree. Given how carefully the question of change of status had been approached, the statement by the parties that he was self-employed was of great weight and significance. Compare Massey's case with *Ferguson v. Dawson and Partners Ltd*. Ferguson was injured on a building site and wished to sue his employers for breach of statutory duty. To succeed in his claim he needed to show that he was engaged under a contract of service. The evidence showed that Ferguson had been brought along to the site by some of his friends and had been taken on in an extremely informal manner by the foreman who had informed him that he would be working 'on the lump', i.e. on a self-employed basis. No doubt Ferguson was happy with that situation while everything was going well as he had scope to keep ahead of the tax man and avoid paying appropriate National Insurance contributions! Despite the agreement of the parties to the 'lump' arrangement, the Court of Appeal held that the reality of this situation was a contract of service. It had none of the carefully worked out and evidenced formality of Massey's arrangements, so the view of the parties could hardly be decisive.

Although there are numerous Acts of Parliament conferring rights on employees, none of them gives an exhaustive definition of a contract of service. One usual formulation is to define an employee as a person who works under a contract of employment. That in turn is defined as a contract of service whether express or implied. And as that phrase is not further defined, the rules developed by the judges remain significant.

Creation of a contract of employment

Although contracts of employment are governed by the ordinary rules of contract it is important to consider the role and impact of collective bargaining. This is the name given to negotiations between trade unions and employers, usually concerning the establishment of better terms and conditions of employment for union members. Where a union (or group of unions) has established bargaining rights with an employer (or group or federation of employers), their joint negotiations may result in a collective agreement, which in practice fixes the terms of the employment of relevant employees. Such agreements, together with the increased statutory control of employment, now severely limit the true 'freedom of contract' of the actual parties, the employer and the employee. An employee may ask, 'How can an agreement (the collective agreement), to which I was not a party, affect my individual relationship with the employer?' The answer is that the collective agreement itself cannot alter the terms. But such agreement may well become 'incorporated' into the contract, thereby altering it and have direct force and application to the employer and employee as a result. Two simple methods by which incorporation could occur are:

1   Express incorporation where, by the terms of the original contract, the parties agree to be bound by the appropriate collective agreement for the time being in force.
2   Incorporation by usage, where the employer and employees have acted on the strength of the terms of the collective agreement, e.g. the employer has paid the increased hourly rate referred to in the collective agreement and the employee has accepted the increase.

About half of the working population belongs to trade unions, but the impact of bargaining procedures is much more widely felt. It is estimated that the terms and conditions of about three-quarters of the working population are affected directly or indirectly by such collective agreements.

Inevitably, a collective agreement will not be an exhaustive statement of all the terms of the contract. Indeed, it has already been indicated that collective negotiation has no place in some contracts. In the higher echelons of employment, where staff have desirable skills and talents to offer, the terms of the contract may be fixed by much more individual negotiation. In either case, many of the terms will be implied into the contract by statute or by common law. There is even scope for terms to be implied by custom. These will be considered in detail later.

Form of the contract

Apart from exceptional situations, such as that of apprenticeship, there are no rules requiring a contact of employment to be made in writing. However, since 1963, many employees have enjoyed the right to receive a written statement containing the main terms of their contract. The Employment Protection (Consolidation) Act 1978 (EPCA) requires an employer to issue this statement within thirteen weeks of the start of the employment and it must contain:

1   Names of the parties and date of commencement of employment.
2   The job title.
3   Details about pay, including the amount or method of calculating the amount and the intervals at which it is to be paid. (A separate right for employees to receive an itemized pay statement, setting out the purpose and amount of deductions, is established by EPCA 1978.)
4   Details about hours of work, and overtime arrangements.
5   Details about holidays and holiday pay.
6   Details of rules covering sickness and sick pay.
7   Details about pensions.
8   Details about disciplinary rules and grievance procedure.

9   Details about the period of notice to be given by employer or employee to terminate the contract.

The EPCA 1978 specifically states that if there are no agreed particulars under any heading, that fact must be stated. This rather emphasizes a feature of employment which is not always appreciated. Holidays are usually a question for agreement between the parties, and (except in cases covered by the Wages Councils system) if no holidays have been agreed, then none are due. Holidays with pay in the construction industry might be a problem because of the fact that employees tend to move from employer to employer. This problem is resolved for those who participate in the special Holiday Stamp Card Scheme, negotiated by collective agreement and administered through a separate independent company.

The value of the written statement is that it is evidence of some of the terms of the contract, and may allow disputes between the parties to be quickly and simply resolved. But not all employees are entitled to receive a statement and in particular the following are not eligible:

1   Part-time employees. For this purpose part time means working less than sixteen hours per week. (If the employee is a long serving part-time worker (over five years) that figure is reduced to eight hours.)
2   Crown servants, employees working under certain fixed-term contracts, employees who ordinarily work abroad and employees who are husbands or wives of the employer.
3   Employees who have a written contract, or alternatively have been referred by their employer to some document containing the terms, which the employee has reasonable opportunities to read, or which is made reasonably accessible to him. An employer who chooses this technique can also save himself from individually notifying employees of changes by indicating in advance that these will be shown in the document held by him. This procedure is not nearly so satisfactory from an employee's point of view.

The EPCA 1978 requires the information to the employee to be kept up to date. If an employer fails to give a statement as required by these rules, the sanction is rather ineffective. The aggrieved employee may complain to an industrial tribunal, which has power to determine what the written statement should contain. Unfortunately, the tribunal has no enforcement powers and if the employer continues to default by refusing to comply with the statement issued by the tribunal, the employee will have to enforce his terms by a separate action in the County Court.

Duties of the parties

Once a contract of employment has come into existence, the very nature of that relationship imposes certain duties on both parties, whether they expressly negotiated on these points or not. These duties are summarized below.

Employer's duties

1 *A duty to pay the agreed wages* – There is no general minimum wage legislation in this country. The amount of the wages is fixed by the parties, although in many cases this will be significantly influenced by collective bargains negotiated within that type of employment. The amount may also need to reflect the policy of the Equal Pay Act 1970. The Act implies an 'equality clause' into all contracts of employment, whereby men and women who are engaged on 'like work', or 'work rated as equivalent' or 'work of equal value', should receive equal pay and equal treatment with regard to terms and conditions. Employees prejudiced by breach of these rules can bring a claim in the industrial tribunal. English law has long concerned itself with *how* wages are paid, rather than how much is paid. The old Truck Acts 1831–96, regulating deductions from wages and methods of payment to persons employed in manual labour, have now been repealed but in their place the Wages Act 1986 covers all employees. The Act is largely concerned with deductions from wages for reasons like bad workmanship. Such deductions are permitted so long as they are made under the terms of the contract, and those terms must have been notified to the employee in writing. Of course, an employer may always deduct those amounts which are permitted or authorized by statute, e.g. tax and social security contributions. There are also court orders which permit deductions from earnings, called attachment of earnings orders. The actual method of paying the wages, e.g. cash, cheque or directly into a bank account, is a matter for agreement between the parties. Once the method is fixed one party may not change it unilaterally without the consent of the other.

2 *A duty to indemnify the employee for expenses reasonably incurred during the employment* – this point will often be covered by express terms about expenses. In other cases, if an employee is out of pocket as a result of his work, much may depend on how the expenses arose. Where the employee is doing his work in a lawful way and acting under his employer's authority, he should be reimbursed. If, however, the employee chooses an unlawful method of perfor-

mance e.g. employed to drive but driving in excess of the speed limit, then the employee must bear the cost. A more specialized aspect of the duty to indemnify is the rule that if an employee commits a tort in the course of the employment, the employer is usually vicariously liable. The full extent of this rule is considered in Chapter 9.

3   *A duty to take reasonable care for the safety of the employee* – this duty is linked with the whole question of health and safety and is considered in detail in Chapter 10.

4   *A duty to show mutual respect to the employee* – this is an example of a duty which has emerged more recently in employment law, largely from suggestions made in cases being heard before industrial tribunals. It can be said to mean that the employer must treat his employees with appropriate respect and consideration. It is an example of how far the law of employment has moved in recent years from the old philosophy of the employer being able to 'hire and fire' at will.

It is usually argued that in most cases an employer is under no legal duty to provide work. An old case contains the comment: 'If I pay my cook she cannot complain if I choose to eat all my meals out'. In a number of important ways this rule is of practical significance:

1   It allows an employer to pay wages in lieu of notice. He does not usually have to provide work.

2   When there is no work an employer may lay off his employee, although where this occurs over a sufficiently long period the employee may be eligible to claim a redundancy payment.

3   If no work and no pay are available this may amount to the employee being suspended. The usual rule is that an employee may only be suspended without pay if his contract expressly or impliedly provides for this. Suspension with pay normally causes no problems because the employer is under no duty to provide work.

4   If an employee has no work and no pay the employer may have a statutory duty to pay him guarantee payments of fixed amounts for a specific number of days (EPCA 1978).

An employer is under no duty to provide a reference or testimonial, even though an employee may suffer in consequence of this decision. This can be particularly harsh when an employee secures a new job which is dependent on satisfactory references. The employer may feel justified in refusing to give a reference because anything he writes could open up possibilities of legal liability. For example, the employee may sue if the reference is seen to be defamatory. Employers should have little to fear on this point, as an action for defamation can be defeated by the defences of truth or qualified privilege, i.e. the employer can show that without malice or bad motive he was simply communicating information to a person who had a genuine interest in receiving it. Nowadays, an employer is more likely to fear that statements in a reference could expose him to liability for negligent mis-statement. This issue is considered in more detail in Chapter 9. Moreover, an employer may be estopped from denying the truth of statements made in a reference. This can be relevant in cases in the industrial tribunal for unfair dismissal. If the employer has written a glowing reference in the hope that a mediocre employee will move on, he may subsequently wish to dismiss the employee. In any later proceedings it will be difficult for the employer to deny the truth of that glowing testimonial!

Employee's duties

1 *A duty to render personal service.*
2 *A duty to render faithful service* – this means that if the employee in any way damages his employer's interests he is effectively in breach of his duty. Where such a breach occurs there may be justification for the employer to dismiss the employee. Sometimes a breach may cause an employer serious on-going harm, and he may wish to seek an injunction to restrain the particular activity of the employee. In other cases it may also be appropriate for the employer to seek damages from the employee. Some areas of particular importance emerge from this general duty of faithful service:

(a) The employee should not put himself in a position where his duty to his employer conflicts with his own self-interest. In *Boston Deep Sea Fishing Co. v. Ansell* an employee placed orders for supplies on behalf of his employers. He chose to give the orders to firms which rewarded him for putting business their way. Those firms may well have had the competitive edge anyway, but the 'rewards' may have clouded Ansell's judgment. He was dismissed for this breach of duty.

(b) The employee should not make a secret profit from his employment. This will often be closely linked with the duty in (a). In Ansell's case he had failed to disclose to his employers what he was making 'on the side'. That was quite a crude example of this problem which crops up regularly in business and commercial life. An employee who is in a position to place

large orders for supplies may be courted by hopeful companies. He should take care in accepting any gifts or favours, for
he lays himself open to being in breach of his duty, even if his
judgment was not affected. Many large organizations tackle
the problem by imposing express rules in the contracts of
employment, forbidding acceptance of gifts.

(c) The employee must not compete against his employer. An
example of such competition might be the employee working
as a boiler service engineer who suggests to customers that
they approach him personally in his off-duty hours, and he
will then undertake their work on his own behalf. In a case like
this the employee could be restrained by an injunction and his
behaviour would almost certainly warrant dismissal. The
reason here is obvious. His spare-time activities are seriously
detrimental to his employer. There is nothing to prevent an
employee engaging in a second job as spare-time work so long
as it does not interfere with the duties he owes to his
employers. This rule, that an employee must not compete
against the employer, is also relevant when the employment
terminates. In appropriate cases, the duty of faithful service
can continue to be owed *after* the employment relationship has
ended. In such cases it is common to include a 'restraint of
trade' clause in the contract, which will be enforceable against
the employer so long as it is reasonable (see page 101).

Patents, designs and copyrights

The issue of competing against the employer can also arise where
an employee invents something in the course of his employment. It
could be very unfair if he then leaves his job, and seeks to patent
the invention and profit from it. The rules covering such a situation
are now contained in the Patents Act 1977. Before the Act was
passed, an employer who thought it likely that an employee might
invent something would put an express term into the contract,
requiring the employee to assign (transfer) the rights in the
invention to the employer. This often produced a very unfair
result, with the employee personally getting no reward even if the
employer made handsome profits out of the invention. The 1977
Act aims to deal with questions of ownership of the invention and
the right of the employee to be rewarded. The invention belongs to
the employer if it was made by an employee in the course of his
normal duties, or in the course of duties specifically assigned to
him (s.39). Any other inventions belong to the employee. If an

employer then exploits the invention of an employee, the employee can receive compensation from the court if he can show that a patent has been granted which is of 'outstanding benefit' to the employer (s.40). The Act states that the compensation must secure for the employee a 'fair share' of the benefit derived by the employer, bearing in mind the nature of the employee's duties, the effort, skill and advice of others, and the contribution of the employer in terms of facilities and other assistance. Any attempt to reduce the rights of the employee by agreeing otherwise in his contract is absolutely unenforceable.

Similar problems can also arise in relation to copyright. The Copyright Act 1956 has just been repealed and replaced by the Copyright Designs and Patents Act 1988 which developed out of a government White Paper on intellectual property and innovation. Not surprisingly, the period since the 1956 Act has seen much change and progress, especially in the computer field, and new rules were needed to take account of these changes. Where a literary, dramatic, musical or artistic work is made by an employee in the course of his employment, his employer will be the first owner of any copyright in the work. The work in question could be sales and promotional literature, or a users' manual, or an installers' guide. It is important to bear in mind that such apparently mundane publications are governed by these rules in the same way as novels and pop songs. So complex is this area that the general public is only likely to be aware of the controversy about whether the Act should have included a levy on blank recording tapes.

Design rights are dealt with slightly differently by the new Act. Designs are protected on principles similar to copyrights but lasting only for fifteen years as against the fifty-year period for copyrights. The designer is the first owner of any design right in a design, but if the design has been commissioned for a fee, the person who commissioned the design is entitled to any design right in it. Generally, the rules are the same as those for copyright – when the design was created in the course of the employment the employer will be the first owner of any design right in the design.

3 *A duty to obey the lawful and reasonable orders of the employer* – for an order to be lawful it must not contravene the general law nor must it be contrary to what was agreed by the parties. An employee could therefore refuse to obey an order which required him to contravene safety regulations, or one requiring him to work in another part of the country when his contract plainly does not anticipate that he should be mobile. It may be more difficult to determine whether an order is reasonable. Each case will turn on

its own individual facts. Clearly an order is not reasonable if it exposes the employee to grave risk. Where the employee refuses to obey a lawful and reasonable order he is in breach of his contract, but that may not necessarily be a 'fair reason' for dismissing him. In *Wilson v. IDR Construction Ltd* the employee refused, in breach of his contract, to move to another construction site. Given his past work record, the genuine reason the employee gave for not wishing to move, and the employer's failure to allow the employee to explain, it was held to be unfair to dismiss him for that reason. Cases like this highlight the significant difference between a common law breach of contract and the statutory protections for unfair dismissal. 'Technical' breaches have to be viewed in the overall context of the contract.

4   *A duty to carry out his duties with reasonable care and to take reasonable care of the employer's property* – again, any behaviour short of reasonable care is technically a breach of the contract but whether it would justify dismissing the employee depends on all the circumstances. In any well-structured employment situation the disciplinary procedure drawn up by the employers should provide for sanctions such as written warnings, so that every act of misbehaviour does not necessarily warrant dismissal.

Statutory rights for employees

The duties previously considered arise by virtue of the employer/employee relationship. The past thirty years have seen an explosion of new rights and duties created by statute, but it should be remembered that Acts of Parliament had played an important role in some spheres of employment for much longer, e.g. health, safety and welfare, and methods of paying wages.

The new statutory rights are mainly granted to employees, thereby redressing to some extent the inequality of bargaining power between a single employee and a powerful employer. Some important examples include:

- The right to a written statement of terms.
- The right to receive an itemized pay statement.
- The right, in appropriate circumstances, to receive a guarantee payment or a medical suspension payment.
- The right to a minimum period of notice.
- The right not to be unfairly dismissed, or made redundant, without compensation.
- The right to request written reasons for dismissal.

- The right to maternity leave or maternity pay.
- The right not to be discriminated against.
- Rights in connection with trade union membership.

Most of these statutory protections are confined to persons who work under a contract of service, and each right has a number of qualifying conditions attached to it.

Generally, each right will lay down a 'working-in' period, i.e. a period of continuous service which must have been served before the right accrues. These working-in periods vary from four weeks in the case of guarantee payments to two years for redundancy payments. The concept of 'continuous service' is, therefore, vital to establishing eligibility. In any normal working life there will be times when an employee is not at work, e.g. through holidays or leave of absence or illness. If continuity of service was broken on each occasion, none of these statutory rights would ever be earned. The law provides that where a week is covered by the contract of employment, it will not break the continuity of service. As a general rule, the week in question must always be a week where the employee was contracted to work for sixteen or more hours, but exceptionally, where an employee has worked part time for more than five years that figure is reduced to eight hours per week. (There is a significant problem in employment law that many of the statutory protections do little to help part-time workers.)

Not only must the rules establish when there is continuous employment, they must also determine whether the weeks in question count in, or not. Take the example of someone employed for just over two years who now needs to consider eligibility for a redundancy payment. During that two years the employee in question has six weeks of paid holiday, two separate weeks of sickness, one week's absence with the permission of the employer when the employee's mother died, and five weeks spent on strike. It could be critical to the 104 week working-in rule to establish which of these periods count in and which do not. In fact, all of them except for the period on strike would be added in. By law, strikes do not break continuity but the time spent on strike (or absent from work through a lock out) cannot be counted in.

Rules exist to govern the continuity of employment where a business is sold. Where the business is sold as a going concern, employment with the old and the new owner can count as one continuous period. Inevitably the rules about continuity are complex but the employee gets the benefit of a presumption that his service is continuous; it is for the employer to prove a break in continuity. The rules are contained in the Employment Protection (Consolidation) Act 1978.

Protection against discrimination

The principal protections against discrimination in employment are contained in the Sex Discrimination Acts 1975 and 1986, the Equal Pay Act 1970 and the Race Relations Act 1976. The Sex Discrimination Act 1975 (SDA) works on a model of defining discrimination, stating where it will be unlawful, determining what defences might be available and establishing procedures for enforcement.

1   Section 1 of the Act states that a person discriminates against a woman on the grounds of sex if he treats her less favourably than a man of the same marital status. This is *direct discrimination*. The Act also recognizes that discrimination can be much less obvious, and has identified *indirect discrimination*. This occurs where a requirement or condition is applied equally to men and women, *but* the proportion of women who *can* comply with the requirement is considerably smaller than the proportion of men, the condition is not justifiable *and* the condition is to the detriment of the person complaining because she cannot comply with it. (Although these examples are couched in terms of discrimination against women, it must be remembered that the Act is drafted to protect 'persons' from discrimination. In the right set of circumstances a man could allege discrimination.) An example of indirect discrimination occurred in the case of *Price v. Civil Service Commission*, where applicants for the particular branch of the Civil Service had to be under twenty-eight years old. Mrs Price complained that the proportion of women who could satisfy this requirement was smaller than the proportion of men, because a significant number of women in their twenties would be out of the job market bearing and rearing children. This argument was answered by the Civil Service seeking to show that, statistically, there were roughly equivalent numbers of men and women who could come forward. The tribunal determined that the phrase 'can comply' in s.1. of the Act must be interpreted in practice and not in theory for indirect discrimination.

2   Once discrimination is established, the next stage is to establish which acts of discrimination are rendered unlawful by the SDA. So far as employment is concerned, it is unlawful to discriminate against an applicant on grounds of sex in selection arrangements and job offers; and once in employment it is unlawful to discrimi-

nate in access to promotion, training or other benefits or facilities
(s.6). It is also true that an employee dismissed on discriminatory
grounds could complain under SDA but for technical reasons
connected with the burden of proof, a dismissed employee may be
better off using the ordinary rules of unfair dismissal (see page
171).

3   Exceptionally, where an unlawful act of discrimination has
occurred, the employer may be able to excuse himself by pleading
that being a man or being a woman was a genuine occupational
qualification in the particular case (s.7). This defence is limited to
the situations specified in the Act, e.g. a man or a woman is needed
to preserve decency or privacy, or where the work is to be
performed outside the UK in a country whose laws or customs
preclude one sex from performing the duties.

4   Where a person wishes to pursue a claim for sex discrimination it is
possible to complain to the Equal Opportunities Commission, who
may carry out an investigation into an employer's policies, and
who may give advice and assistance to individual claimants. In
exceptional cases, where a major point of principle is at stake, the
EOC may finance the bringing of a case. This could be especially
useful when it is borne in mind that individual claimants are not
eligible for legal aid for industrial tribunal cases.

The more usual enforcement procedure is for an aggrieved person to
commence proceedings in the industrial tribunal, usually within three
months of the date of the act of discrimination. In appropriate cases, a
successful claimant can be awarded compensation up to a current
maximum of £10,000. A serious problem facing the claimant is that he or
she will have to bear the burden of proving discrimination. Many
cases collapse before they are due for hearing because of the difficulties of obtaining evidence, and the pressure a claimant feels under,
particularly where he or she is still in the employment of the employer
being complained about.

The SDA is drafted in such a way that it appears to be designed to
protect women. In fact, it is designed to protect people who are
discriminated against on grounds of sex or marriage. Although the
rules contained in the Acts are the first line of attack for an aggrieved
person, there are also European Community rights, which have
played a significant part in the development of this area of law. Where
discrimination relates to the amount to be paid for the work the issue
will be resolved under the Equal Pay Act 1970. That Act provides for
equal treatment regarding terms and conditions whenever men and
women are doing like work, work rated as equivalent or work of equal

value. An employer can pay at different rates, only if he can show that he is doing so because of a 'genuine material difference' which is not just the difference in sex. The employer may point to factors like length of service, previous experience or additional qualifications. Equal pay disputes are also resolved in the industrial tribunal.

The scheme of the Race Relations Act 1976 is very similar to that of the Sex Discrimination Act 1975

Termination of contract of employment

The parties to a contract of employment do not usually fix a date for its termination, unless they have negotiated a fixed-term contract. If the duration of the contract is not fixed, the law provides for either party to end the contract by giving notice to the other. Many cases are now covered by rules providing for fixed minimum periods of notice, although it is still open to the parties to agree longer periods if they wish. The EPCA 1978 provides that if an employer wishes to terminate, he must give a minimum of one week's notice for each year of continuous employment, up to a maximum of twelve weeks' notice. If an employee wishes to terminate he must give a minimum of one week's notice, although the contract may specify a longer period. If an employee fails to give the proper period of notice he is in breach of his contract. Theoretically he could be sued for damages by the employer. This may seem a little unlikely, but it should be remembered that the employer may be holding moneys due to an employee, e.g. accrued holiday pay, bonuses or expenses, or a week's pay lying on. The employer could certainly delay making those payments to the employee. What is more, the employer could also refuse to give a reference.

There are no particular legal rules about how notice must be given to be effective. This depends on the terms of the contract. It is common to require notice to be in writing, and often the contract will specify that the period of notice must be calculated by reference to a pay day. So a weekly-paid employee who normally gets paid on a Thursday must give notice to expire on a Thursday.

Nothing in these rules prevents either party from terminating with no notice at all, if the behaviour of the other party justifies such action. When an employee receives no notice, this is referred to as summary or instant dismissal. The question will often arise whether such behaviour on the part of the employer is appropriate. An employee who is the victim of such action may be able to pursue a claim for unfair dismissal.

Unfair dismissal

A statutory right to claim for unfair dismissal was introduced in 1971. Before then, an employee who had been dismissed was limited to a claim against his employer in a civil action in the County Court for wrongful dismissal. In many cases, such an action was worthless because the County Court could only award damages, and these were often limited to an amount equal to the ex-employee's wages for the period of notice he should have received. If proper notice had been given, there was little point in an employee bringing an action for wrongful dismissal. However, this common law remedy is still available and may sometimes be useful. This is particularly likely to be the case where the employee is highly paid, as there is no maximum limit on damages for wrongful dismissal; or where the employee is outside the three-month time limit for pursuing a claim of unfair dismissal; or where the employee does not yet have a sufficient period of continuous employment to be within the statutory unfair dismissal rules.

Prior to 1971, even where the proper notice had been given, an employee might still feel a sense of grievance about the dismissal, especially if there had been no good reason for it. The common law attitude at that time still reflected attitudes that the employer could 'hire and fire' at will. A long-serving and loyal employee could be dismissed for no reason at all, and would have no claim, so long as the employer had given the appropriate period of notice. Unfair dismissal protection was created to change this situation. An employee now has a statutory right not to be unfairly dismissed. An aggrieved employee can seek a remedy in the industrial tribunal. The remedy emphasizes an idea which has developed in employment law, that an employee has a 'property right' in his job. If this is lost when the employee is not at fault (e.g. unfair dismissal or redundancy), then he should be protected or compensated.

The current rules on unfair dismissal are now to be found in EPCA 1978 as amended by the Employment Acts 1980, 1982 and 1990. Employees who may claim their protection are those working under contracts of service, except:

- Part-time employees.
- Persons employed outside the UK.
- Persons over retiring age (either the statutory retiring age or that fixed by the employer).
- Persons engaged on certain types of fixed-term contract.
- Persons who have not yet served two years continuously with their employers.

Fair reasons for dismissal

The Act has given employees who are within its scope the right not to be unfairly dismissed, and lists the reasons why a dismissal may be fair (s.57):

1 *Reasons connected with the employee's capability or qualifications* – capability is broadly defined to include skill, aptitude and health, amongst other things. Qualifications includes degrees and diplomas as well as technical or professional qualifications relevant to the particular job.

2 *Reasons connected with the conduct of the employee* – misconduct may range from very trivial acts to acts which can be classed as gross. Inevitably, these will vary in different employment situations. Swearing may be regarded as fairly trivial on a shopfloor of a factory or construction site but may be regarded as extremely serious on a hotel reception desk or in the offices of a professional person. Generally, the more senior an employee, in terms of age and position in the firm, the more the employer can expect from him. The misbehaviour may take place at work, but in appropriate cases, an employer may dismiss because of conduct occurring outside work, where the conduct could have an adverse effect on the employer's business.

3 *Redundancy, where the employee was fairly selected for redundancy* – the ideal situation for an employer faced with inevitable redundancies is to deal with the problem by reference to an established procedure, agreed at some previous time with the appropriate unions. Otherwise, he may be able to show he acted fairly by applying the principle of 'last in, first out'. This approach may still leave the employer having to choose some from a group who all commenced work together. In that case, he could take account of experience and ability, and the hardship likely to be caused by the redundancy. An employee who thinks he was unfairly selected can claim unfair dismissal.

4 *Where the continued employment of the employee would cause the employer to be in breach of a statutory duty.*

5 *Some other substantial reason justifying dismissal* – it is difficult to spell out in detail in the Act all the circumstances where dismissal can be fair, so some residual provision is inevitable. Under this heading, a number of cases have involved employees unreasonably holding out against variations to their contracts of employment. The employer cannot unilaterally change the terms of employment. Indeed, to attempt to do so would be a breach of contract. But where the commercial needs of his business dictate that he must

run it in some different way, he may need to approach employees to seek their approval for altered working hours, or new shift patterns. In such cases, if the employer has set about negotiating the changes in a reasonable way, and one employee holds out against the change, the employer may have little alternative but to dismiss that employee.

Establishing a reason capable of being fair is not sufficient in itself. The employer must also prove that it is fair in all the circumstances of the case to use that particular reason for justifying dismissal. For example, swearing at the employer is a reason capable of being fair, but whether it is fair to dismiss for swearing in any particular case would depend on the words used, the circumstances surrounding the offence, any provocation, previous treatment of employees for swearing, any works rules, any warnings received by the offending employee, and any other relevant factors. The key question facing the industrial tribunal is to determine whether the employer behaved as a reasonable employer would have done. One factor which may be relevant is the extent to which the employer followed his own disciplinary practices and procedures. These should form part of the information given to employees in their written statement. A sensible employer will have disciplinary procedures suitable for his working situation which are in general conformity with the guidelines issued by ACAS (Advisory, Conciliation and Arbitration Service). The House of Lords has confirmed that, in unfair dismissal cases, if the procedure is unfair then the dismissal itself will also be unfair – *Polkey v. A.E. Dayton Services*.

Definition of dismissal

To be able to proceed with a claim for unfair dismissal, an employee must show that he has been dismissed. There can sometimes be doubt whether a dismissal has occurred. Take the case where an employee simply walks out, or an employer asks the employee for his resignation and this is reluctantly given. Section 55 defines dismissal as:

1 Termination of the contract by the employer with or without notice, or
2 termination by the employee in circumstances justified by the employer's conduct. This situation is called constructive dismissal. The employer's behaviour must amount to a breach which is sufficiently grave so that it entitles the employee to treat himself as discharged from further performance of the contract. Not every breach by an employer can be regarded as so significant. Much will

depend on the factual circumstances, but a simple example is the case where the employer proposes to reduce an employee's wages without negotiation. It will always be a question of fact whether a constructive dismissal has occurred.

These cases pose a real dilemma for an employee. He is faced with some kind of breach by the employer, (e.g. the unilateral imposition of a new shift system) and if he leaves, there is the complication of needing to prove constructive dismissal. If the employee delays taking any action the employer could argue that he had impliedly consented to the change by staying on and working under the new arrangements.

Disciplinary rules

The importance of the rules about unfair dismissal can best be appreciated when it is realized that well over 30,000 applications are filed annually by employees who wish to claim against their employers. The very existence of a right to claim, coupled with the possible cost of the claim to the employer if his employee succeeds, has forced employers to give more detailed consideration to their internal disciplinary and grievance procedures. These procedures must be communicated to employees who are entitled to receive a written statement.

When drafting disciplinary rules, employers can seek guidance from ACAS. The rules should aim to encourage better standards in employees, and should not be concerned exclusively with imposing sanctions. Where sanctions are necessary it is better to provide a range appropriate to the different forms of misbehaviour. Not all misconduct necessarily warrants instant dismissal. It may be more appropriate for an employee to receive oral or written warnings, or some other form of 'punishment', such as demotion.

The ACAS Code of Practice on Disciplinary Procedures stresses that disciplinary rules and procedures are necessary for promoting fairness and order in the treatment of individuals. They also help the organization to operate effectively. Employees must know what standard of conduct is expected from them. The responsibility for formulating a policy for maintaining discipline lies with the management, who should aim to secure involvement at all levels when formulating new rules. Rules should not be so general as to be meaningless, but rather they should specify clearly and precisely what is necessary for the efficient and safe performance of work, and the maintenance of satisfactory working relations. Employees should know the likely consequences of breaking the rules, particularly where such a breach is likely to lead to summary dismissal. Disciplinary procedures should be viewed as a means of encouraging improved conduct in individuals. Great emphasis is laid on fairness in operating the procedures. This means telling an individual what the complaint is, and allowing him or her the opportunity to state their case before a decision is reached; allowing the employee the right to be accompanied by a trade union official or a fellow employee; ensuring that no decision is reached until the case has been fairly investigated; and ensuring that the employee is given an explanation for any penalty imposed. An employer should keep proper records of all actions taken under the disciplinary rules. Good employers will normally provide for breaches of the disciplinary rules to be struck from an employee's record after completing a further specified satisfactory period of service.

Remedies for unfair dismissal

Claims by an employee under the unfair dismissal rules are made to an industrial tribunal. An action should usually be commenced within three months of the effective date of termination of the employment. Claims are initially referred to a Conciliation Officer of ACAS, whose duty it is to mediate between the parties to see if a settlement can be reached. At this stage the employer may agree to take the employee back, or may agree to pay a sum by way of compensation which is acceptable to the employee. A large proportion of claims are resolved at this stage.

Before a full tribunal hearing takes place, it may be appropriate to hold a pre-trial assessment to consider whether the case has any real substance. The case is not decided at this stage but if it is clear that one party has no real chance of success, the tribunal may warn that party that costs could be awarded against them. Not surprisingly, a number of applications to the tribunal are withdrawn at this stage. If no withdrawal occurs, the case proceeds to a full hearing. An employee found to have been unfairly dismissed may be awarded:

1 *Reinstatement* – the employee's job is restored and he is treated in all respects as though he had never been dismissed.
2 *Re-engagement* – this gives the employee a job comparable to his former job.
3 *Compensation* – all awards consist of two elements, the *basic* award and the *compensatory* award. The calculation of the basic award depends on a combination of factors, namely age, length of continuous service and the amount of a week's pay. An employee's working life is divided into three periods: years worked between eighteen and twenty-one, years worked between twenty-two and

forty, and years worked between forty-one and sixty-four (sixty in the case of women). A maximum of twenty years of employment is taken into account and a financial cut-off point on what constitutes a week's pay is fixed. This is increased from time to time to take account of rising wage levels. The current figure (1991) is £198. Once the relevant facts are known, the basic award is calculated by awarding half a week's pay for each year of service between eighteen and twenty-one, one week's pay for each year of service between twenty-two and forty and one and a half weeks' pay for each year of service between forty-one and sixty-five. The basic award may be reduced if the employee has caused or contributed to his dismissal, or if the employee has been guilty of bad conduct before dismissal which is only revealed after his dismissal takes effect. The compensatory award is an amount which the tribunal considers just and equitable bearing in mind a claimant's losses and expenses, including loss of future earnings. The calculation is often speculative, since it is impossible to know how long a claimant may remain unemployed. This part of an employee's compensation may be reduced where his conduct has contributed to his dismissal, or, where he has not taken reasonable steps to minimize his losses, e.g. if he has failed to seek new employment. The maximum figure currently for the compensatory award is £10,000, which brings the potential maximum compensation in unfair dismissal cases to over £15,000. To put those figures into a proper perspective, only about 5 per cent of all cases annually result in payments in excess of £6,000. One third of all cases will result in awards of less than £1,000. These maximum figures may be increased exceptionally where additional awards can be made. An additional award is relevant if an employer refuses to comply with an order to reinstate or re-engage the employee. The amount could be between thirteen and fifty-two weeks' pay, over and above the basic and compensatory awards.

Note that both reinstatement and re-engagement are discretionary remedies. The tribunal must consider the wishes of the parties and the practicability of compliance before making such an order. Where either order is made, if the employer refuses to comply with it he will be obliged to pay an additional amount of compensation.

Tribunal procedure

Procedure at the tribunal hearing may be relatively formal, perhaps as a result of the 'adversarial' nature of these proceedings. The tribunal consists of a legally qualified chairman, who sits with two lay members who are intended to be representative of employers and employees, respectively. All three play an equal part in the decision-making process. Evidence is given on oath. Although the tribunal may take a more informal approach than a court, it is usually better to bring witnesses who can speak directly about the facts than to rely on hearsay evidence. Applicants should bring along relevant documentary evidence, such as their written statement of terms, or their written reasons for dismissal, or documents relating to their financial position which may be relevant when calculating the compensatory award. It may be difficult to persuade people to come to give evidence, or to get hold of documents considered vital to the case. In these circumstances an applicant can ask the tribunal to grant a witness summons order, or a discovery of documents order.

The parties will each be invited to present their case and to call any necessary witnesses, who may be cross-examined and who may also be questioned by members of the tribunal. Where an applicant is unrepresented, the members can do much to assist by the type of questions they put. The length of each case will depend on factors such as the number of witnesses and the complexity of the evidence, but it will not normally last more than two days. The tribunal retires to consider its decision, which is given to the parties, with full reasons.

Although large sums of money are at stake, and the law to be applied is complex and constantly changing, no legal aid is available to pay for representation in the tribunal. A claimant who is dissatisfied with the outcome of the hearing may have a right to appeal. Appeals on a point of law lie to the Employment Appeal Tribunal, then in turn to the Court of Appeal and the House of Lords.

Redundancy payments

A dismissal is due to redundancy if:

1 The employer has ceased to carry on business for the purposes of which the employee was employed, or
2 the employer has ceased to carry on business in the place where the employee was employed, or
3 the requirements of the business for employees to carry out work of a particular kind have ceased or diminished.

Where a redundancy situation exists, there is no entitlement to a payment if the employee is dismissed for misconduct, or if he unreasonably refuses suitable alternative employment which has been offered to him in accordance with the Act. Employees who have been given notice because of redundancy are entitled to reasonable time off with pay during working hours to look for a new job or to make arrangements for retraining. What is a reasonable amount of time off will vary according to the differing circumstances of employers and employees. During such absences employees should be paid at their normal rate.

Payments are calculated by reference to rules similar to those used to calculate a basic award for unfair dismissal. Many employees are disappointed at the size of the payment they receive. This may be because they have read about especially generous redundancy schemes operating for particular industries, or because they have failed to understand the basis on which the calculation is made. Vital to the calculation of both redundancy payment and unfair dismissal compensation is the concept of 'a week's pay'. Where an employee has normal working hours and the pay does not vary from week to week, a week's pay is simply the basic weekly wage. Overtime earnings are not included unless overtime is obligatory under the contract of employment. If the employee has variable earnings because of a shift pattern, or piece rates, or productivity bonuses, these are usually averaged over a twelve-week period.

An employer is under a duty to consult with trade unions if sizable numbers are to be made redundant over a short period. This duty is quite separate from his obligation to notify the Department of Employment. If the employer fails to consult, a special protective award may be made against him, which will safeguard the remuneration of employees for the period for which it is made.

Hearing redundancy and unfair dismissal claims forms the largest part of the work of industrial tribunals. However, the trend has been to increase this workload in employment-related spheres. Since 1974, the tribunals have heard appeals against Prohibition and Improvement Notices issued under the Health and Safety at Work etc. Act 1974. The equal pay and sex discrimination rules can also be enforced in the industrial tribunal. Extensions to the work of the tribunals were made by the Employment Act 1980 in relation to unreasonable exclusion or expulsion from a trade union. Despite their wide coverage of employment disputes, the tribunals cannot be regarded as employment courts, since some questions arising from the common law rules with regard to employment are still heard by the County Court. There is a statutory power to transfer jurisdiction in such cases to the industrial tribunals, but that step has not yet been taken.

This brief account of employment law is sufficient to show it to be a complex and constantly changing area. Many firms do not have a legal or personnel department which can guide them through the maze of rules. However, the Department of Employment publishes a large range of explanatory booklets, and the officers of ACAS are always ready to give help and advice on questions which are within their particular sphere.

Employees and the welfare state

Three major hazards for an employee are the prospects of sickness, accidents at work or unemployment. These are all areas where the welfare state has traditionally played a part in supporting people through such crises. There is a trend nowadays to see the welfare state in a more subsidiary role when people are in employment, and to turn initially for support to a more obvious and direct source of assistance – the employer. This is evidenced by the employer's increased responsibilities with regard to statutory sick pay and guarantee payments. However, the traditional role of the welfare state will still be important in many cases and it is useful to have a basic knowledge of the workings of the schemes.

The social security system basically provides benefits appropriate to a claimant's circumstances, often in return for contributions made to the National Insurance Fund. Persons employed under a contract of service are Class 1 contributors, paying earnings-related contributions. Employers also contribute to the scheme in respect of their employees. Class 1 contributors are entitled to the greatest range of benefits.

The modern rules of social security are contained in the Social Security Act 1975. The range of benefits is vast. It encompasses on the one hand the 'traditional' contributory benefits such as unemployment and sickness benefit and retirement pensions, and on the other hand, the newer non-contributory benefits like mobility allowance and non-contributory invalidity pension. With each benefit to be claimed it is important to ask:

1   Whether the claimant is in the proper class to claim the benefit in question. For example, only Class 1 contributors can claim unemployment benefit.
2   Whether the claimant satisfied the contribution conditions, if any. This involves determining the level of contributions paid in the appropriate year or period. For example, in the case of unemployment benefit, a claimant who seeks benefit during the year January to December 1992 will be paid by reference to contributions made between April 1989 and March 1991.

3   Whether the claimant satisfies the 'other' conditions attached to the benefit in question. For example, if he seeks unemployment benefit, he must be unemployed and available for work.

Where a person is not eligible for any national insurance benefits (e.g. because of a deficient contributions record) he may claim under the 'income support system' introduced by the Social Security Act 1986 to replace supplementary benefit.

Unemployment benefit

This benefit can be paid only to a person who:

1   Fulfils the contribution conditions;
2   is unemployed or may be treated as such;
3   has a period of interruption of employment longer than three days (no benefit is payable in respect of the first three days, known as 'waiting days');
4   is available for work; and
5   has not been disqualified from receipt of benefit.

Some of these points have particular relevance to employees in the building industry. Take the case of what constitutes a day of unemployment. If an employee performs no work on a particular day, but that day is covered by a guarantee payment (statutory or contractual) or a payment in lieu of notice it cannot count as a day of unemployment. Conversely, an employee may lose his full-time job but still have some part-time subsidiary or casual job. Holding such a job does not automatically disqualify him from receipt of benefit, provided certain conditions are fulfilled. He should not earn above the fixed daily rate from the subsidiary work, and it should not restrict his ability to return to his normal full-time occupation.

Consider also the requirement that a claimant must be available for work. He must not unduly restrict the type of work he will undertake, and should be willing to take suitable work offered to him immediately.

As one of the main objects of unemployment benefit is to protect a person who loses his job through no fault of his own, there are periods of disqualification from benefit which may be applied in cases where an employee loses the job through his own misconduct or where he leaves his job voluntarily without just cause (disqualification for up to twenty-six weeks). Where unemployment is caused because the employee is 'directly interested' in a trade dispute, the disqualification is for the duration of the stoppage of work.

Where unemployment benefit is payable, it takes the form of a flat-rate payment coupled with appropriate dependants' allowances. Claimants dealing with the DSS should make full disclosure of any income likely to affect payment of benefit, e.g. receipt of wages in lieu of notice or holiday pay or a wife's earnings. Overpayment of benefit may result in a criminal prosecution. In addition, a claim by the DSS for repayment of sums overpaid will be likely to succeed unless the claimant can show that he used 'due care and diligence throughout' to avoid overpayment. In practice, this is very difficult to prove.

Special regulations exist to deal with the problem of overlapping benefits. As a general rule, it is not possible to receive two benefits simultaneously, and the claimant will receive only the higher of the two. Unemployment benefit expires after it has been paid for 312 days and a claimant must then requalify by actually paying further contributions

The industrial injuries scheme

An examination of health and safety issues shows that there is a serious risk of accidents to workers in the construction industry. When an employee is injured at work he may be able to sue his employer for damages, if the employer was negligent. For such a claim to be successful the employee must show fault. By contrast, the Industrial Injuries Scheme is based on a no fault principle. An employee can recover benefits:

1   If he has sustained a personal injury caused by accident arising out of, and in the course of, the employment, or
2   if he is suffering from a prescribed industrial disease.

All Class 1 contributors are within the scope of the scheme, and benefit is not dependent on contributions. An employee is protected from the beginning of his working life, for as long as he remains employed under a contract of service.

The results of the injury or disease can vary. An employee may be off work for a time, but may make a complete recovery. He may be left with some long-term disablement and, over a period, this may improve or deteriorate. He may suffer some disfigurement or he may even be killed. The scheme must be flexible enough to cope with these various possibilities. The main benefit paid out under the scheme is disablement benefit.

Disablement is assessed as a percentage by comparison with the condition of a normal person. For example, loss of a leg below the knee is assessed as 50 per cent disablement, while loss of all useful vision in one eye is assessed as 30 per cent. These figures are fixed by a 'tariff', listing the main types of injury. Other examples are decided by analogy to those listed. One drawback of disablement benefit is that it is assessed purely by reference to the disablement itself, and not to the effect which it has on the earning capacity of the claimant. To overcome this problem, disablement benefit used to be paid with an extra allowance, reduced earnings allowance, which takes account of the claimant's inability to follow his regular occupation, or employment of an equivalent standard. This allowance has been abolished.

Medical questions (e.g. assessing the level of disablement) are decided by Medical Boards, with appeal to the Medical Appeal Tribunal. Legal questions are decided by DSS officers with appeal to the Social Security Appeal Tribunal. The legal questions include the following:

1   Was the injury caused by accident? Sometimes, an injured workman can point to a specific incident, e.g. when he fell from the scaffolding. This is an accident. In other cases, he may be complaining about a sequence of events, e.g. regularly having to lift heavy weights, which ultimately results in strain to his heart. This 'sequence' is called a process and such injuries are outside the scope of the Industrial Injuries Scheme, unless the outcome of the process is a 'prescribed industrial disease'.

2   Did the accident arise out of, and in the course of, employment? When is an employee in the course of his employment? This is never an easy question to answer, and often turns on the individual facts of a case. Persons injured when eating in the works canteen, driving to and from work, taking part in sporting activities on behalf of their firm, or dealing with an emergency may all have valid claims for benefit.

Prescribed industrial diseases

It has been recognized that certain diseases can be caused by working conditions, e.g. coalminers are prone to suffer from pneumoconiosis. Where such an association between working conditions and subsequent illness exists, it is likely that the illness will be listed as a prescribed industrial disease.

The present list contains about fifty industrial diseases, including some recent additions, e.g. occupational deafness. Each disease must have been contracted in the appropriate employment and under the separate conditions listed. Once it is shown that an employee is suffering from a prescribed industrial disease, he is then assessed by a medical board to ascertain the degree of disablement and, on the basis of that assessment, disablement benefit is awarded.

Sickness benefits and statutory sick pay

Before the statutory sick pay scheme was introduced, practices in employment for dealing with employees who were ill varied enormously. Generous employers had negotiated contractual terms for full pay during sickness, often for six months or a year. At the other end of the scale, some employees got nothing at all and were thrown straight onto the welfare state sickness benefit. In order to standardize treatment of employees, and to shift this burden from the state, the new statutory sick pay scheme (SSP) was introduced in 1980. A state scheme still operates to take care of Class 2 contributors and those who fall through the net of SSP.

In order to qualify for SSP an employee must have a period of four or more consecutive days of incapacity for work. No payment is made for isolated days of sickness under the scheme, although the employer may still be bound by the terms of the contract to make the payment for that day. If an employee is eligible to receive SSP the minimum amounts are fixed by statute. There are two levels of payment, depending on the employee's earnings. An employer is free to improve on these minimum payments, and many have contractual arrangements which are better, at least in the short term.

The basic rules for the operation of SSP are very similar to those of sickness benefit. There are three waiting days and it is possible to link together separate periods of illness, if they occur within eight weeks of each other. This would eliminate the need to comply with the waiting days rule again.

Employers will need to indicate to their employees what notice they require of absence through sickness, and at what point they require an employee to submit medical certificates. Many employers rely on a system of self-certification for the first seven days of illness.

If there are disputes between the employer and the employee about SSP these can be resolved through the adjudication procedures provided for sickness benefit. The employee should remember that any payment of SSP is earnings, and liable to taxation. Inevitably, the changed status of these payments means that there is no question of dependants' allowances. The employer is liable to pay SSP for up to twenty-eight weeks of illness and, thereafter, an employee who is still incapable of work must transfer to appropriate benefits in the state scheme. Research undertaken before SSP was introduced showed that the majority of absences from work through sickness lasted less than a month, so SSP can be seen to have taken on a pre-eminent role in providing during illness.

Employees and trade unions

Employees governed by a contract of service may enjoy a further contractual relationship which is of major significance in employment, i.e. membership of a trade union. About 10 million people belong to trade unions in this country, ranging from the very large general unions like the Transport and General Workers Union to small specialist unions with quite small numbers of members.

The position of the trade unions under the law is unusual, some times accounted for because of the history of their development. Trade unions could only begin to exist and operate as they do today once they were freed from the problems of laws like the Combination Acts and the civil and criminal rules about conspiracy. These shackles were not removed until 1871, when the growth of the movement into what it is today could get under way. After conceding the right of trade unions to exist and organize workers, the law originally did very little to interfere with, or control, their internal activities. The result of their early policy of non-interference is that trade unions have kept control of their internal affairs, to a considerable extent, until the passing of the Trade Union Act 1984. That Act now requires unions to hold secret ballots for trade union elections, secret ballots before industrial action, and secret ballots about political funding, if any. Of the statutory rules relating to trade unions, most have been framed to regulate their external activities, e.g. political activities and industrial activities. The main reason why a union engages in industrial action is to support the claims it is making for its members in collective negotiations with employers. The process of voluntary collective bargaining is recognized in this country as the principal means of fixing terms of employment. If a union is to be in a position to bargain effectively with an employer, it must gain recognition for that purpose. Between 1975 and 1980 the rules of the Employment Protection Act 1975 permitted trade unions to use the services of the Advisory, Conciliation and Arbitration Service to gain recognition from employers who were reluctant to grant bargaining rights. These procedures proved ineffective, and were repealed by the Employment Act 1980. Now, a union wishing to be recognized for bargaining purposes must establish that right for itself, by taking industrial action if necessary.

Definition of a trade union

The modern definition of a trade union is found in the Trade Union and Labour Relations Act 1974 (TULRA): 'An organisation consisting wholly or mainly of workers. . . whose principal purposes include the regulation of relations between workers and employers'. It will be realized that trade unions are defined both by reference to their membership and their purposes. No formal act of creation is necessary. Although an organization complying with this definition qualifies for the name 'trade union', the best legal rights and protections are afforded only to 'independent trade unions' (ITUs). The status of being independent is achieved by a trade union applying to an official called the Certification Officer (CO) for a Certificate of Independence.

As a first stage towards achieving certification, a union applies to the CO to be listed. Listing is conclusive proof of status of a trade union. The next is to apply for a Certificate of Independence. The list of advantages conferred by independence is impressive, particularly where the union is also recognized by the employer for bargaining purposes. It includes:

- An independent trade union has the statutory right to receive certain information for bargaining purposes.
- ITUs have the right to be consulted about proposed redundancies.
- ITUs can appoint safety representatives under the Health and Safety at Work etc. Act 1974.
- Members of ITUs may have time off work to take part in union activities.
- Members of ITUs have the right not to be dismissed because of taking part in union activities at an appropriate time.
- ITUs may seek state subsidies for postal ballots.

When the CO considers a union's application for a Certificate of Independence, he must take into account the criteria laid down by TULRA 1974. These provide that the union must not be under the domination or control of the employer, nor liable to interference from the employer. In other words, the advantages of independence should only be conferred on genuine unions, which can exercise a proper, vigorous and independent role on behalf of their members. Unions least likely to gain certificates are 'house unions' or staff associations which have often emerged from a firm's social club.

When the CO assesses the independence of a union he considers:

1   How is it funded? A subsidy from the employer would tend to show control and domination by him.

2   Does the employer provide facilities, e.g. office space, telephones, typing services?
3   What is the history of the union? Did it spring from an organization created by the employer?
4   Is the union based only in one company?
5   How 'robust' is the union in negotiations with the employer?

The CO is also permitted to hear the views of other unions about granting the certificate. Another union may have a vested interest in the outcome, as its own position may be jeopardized by the emergence of a new independent union. This could particularly affect the recruitment of new members.

As the Certificate of Independence is the key to claiming all the statutory rights and protections, a union which is refused this status may wish to appeal against the CO's decision. A right of appeal against the refusal of a certificate lies to the Employment Appeal Tribunal. If the application is still unsuccessful the union may apply again, after it has put right those matters specified as reasons for refusal of the certificate.

The legal status of a trade union

Strictly speaking, a trade union is an unincorporated association but so many special rules have been created in relation to unions, that their position more closely resembles that of a corporation. The trade union is an association of individuals, bound together by their rule book, which is effectively the terms of a contract between all the members. The greatest difficulties caused by lack of corporate status would usually be connected with holding property or making contracts. Special rules in TULRA cover these points. A trade union may make contracts in its own name, and its property will be vested in trustees.

The rule book

Generally a union is free to draft its own rules subject to the following limitations:

1   The rules must not offend the discrimination laws or EEC regulations.
2   The rules may not exclude the principles of natural justice, nor may they seek to oust the jurisdiction of the courts.
3   Every member has a right under the Employment Act 1988 not to be subjected to unjustifiable discipline.

4   The rules of a union which has a political fund must provide for members to be able to opt out of contributing to the political fund.
5   The rules may not exclude the duty of every trade union to secure that its principal executive committee has been directly elected by the membership.

As the rule book constitutes the terms of a contract between the members, the courts have power to enforce the rules if an aggrieved member brings an action. It must, however, be borne in mind that not all the rules may be contained in the rule book; some may exist because of custom or practice.

Membership of a trade union

The right to become and remain a trade union member has been very significant especially when a 'closed shop' was in operation at a place of work. Basically that meant either that the worker must be, or become, a trade union member. The closed shop (which the law calls a union membership agreement) has been gradually eroded by legislation, most recently by the Employment Act 1990. All statutory support for closed shops has now been removed, although they can still exist or be created by agreement between employers and employees.

When an applicant applies to a union for membership, the situation is controlled by the union's rule book (which also controls questions of the discipline of members, including possible expulsion from the union). It has already been seen that trade unions have great control over the contents of their rule book. If the rules are clear, unambiguous and properly applied, there should be no need for recourse to the courts for their interpretation by an applicant refused admission.

As the consequences of an exclusion can be so grave, two possible remedies should be noted:

1   The excluded worker may refer his case to the industrial tribunal, under rules introduced by the Employment Act 1980. These rules provide that (where a union membership agreement is in force) persons have the right not to be unreasonably excluded from membership of the appropriate union. The tribunal must look at the 'substantial merits of the case'. The mere fact that a union has slavishly followed all its own rules is not in itself evidence of reasonableness. If the tribunal finds the claim well founded, it can make a declaration to that effect, although this will not suffice to get the worker into the union. The advantage of getting such an order from the tribunal is that the worker may then apply for an award of compensation against the union. The amount is fixed to try to

compensate him for the loss he will sustain as a result of the union's refusal to admit him. The worker must have taken reasonable steps to keep his losses as small as possible – this is known as the duty to mitigate loss. He may have the compensation reduced if his own behaviour in any way caused the refusal to admit him. Compensation could be in excess of £10,000 in extreme cases.

2   The excluded worker may seek the assistance of the Independent Review Committee (IRC) of the TUC. This is a voluntary body set up by the TUC in 1976 to look into cases where a person has been refused admission or expelled from a trade union where a 'closed shop' is in operation. The worker concerned must have been dismissed, or be under notice of dismissal. This procedure can only cover those unions which are affiliated to the TUC and it is important to realize that it has no legal 'teeth' at all. In other words, if it recommends that a union should admit a member, there is no real sanction it can apply if the union refuses to comply.

The approach of the IRC is quite different from that of a court or tribunal. It is concerned to seek a just balance between the interests of an individual complainant and the interests of the union, seen in the context of the whole trade union movement. This can be recognized as the 'collective-interest approach', compared with the 'protection-of-the-individual approach' of a court or tribunal.

Freedom to join a trade union

The rules which have just been considered operate only when a closed shop exists. Not all workers are faced with such a situation, and normally they are free to join a union if they choose to do so. (The exceptions to this rule are members of the police and armed forces, who cannot form themselves into unions.) What is more, workers are often free to choose between several appropriate unions. This apparent choice may be restricted where the Bridlington Agreement operates. This agreement, made in 1939 between unions affiliated to the TUC, regulates inter-union competition for members, and the transfer of members between affiliated unions. The main object is to prevent unions from 'poaching' members from each other. Where a union wishes to complain about such activities, the dispute will be referred to a Disputes Committee of the TUC. Again, this is a body with no legal sanctions to impose. If it finds the claim of poaching is well founded, it will usually tell the offending union to expel the member in question, in the hope that he will then rejoin his original union. The Bridlington Agreement may contravene Article 11 of the

European Convention on Human Rights which guarantees freedom of association. If this is so, then the Bridlington Agreement cannot affect the rights of individuals to join the trade union of their choice. Nowadays, changes in patterns of employment have resulted in many employers wanting to deal with only one union. In such a case it may be a question of competing unions holding a 'beauty contest' to determine which union should be recognized by the employer. Examples of this have occured in the print and motor industries.

'Union only' contracts

It used to be quite common for organizations like local authorities to demand of all their suppliers that they should allow their workers to be union members. Indeed, some authorities would go so far as to refuse to invite tenders from suppliers who did not comply with this rule. Now, under the Employment Act 1982, any term in a contract for the supply of goods or services is void if it purports to require that work done under the contract shall only be done by unionized or non-unionized labour.

A new tort is also created by the Act. It is a breach of statutory duty if, on grounds of union membership or non-membership, a person:

1 Fails to include a particular person's name on an approved list of suppliers; or
2 excludes a person from tendering; or
3 terminates a contract for the supply of goods or services.

Expulsion from membership

A union's rule book will normally provide a range of disciplinary measures, to cover various acts of misbehaviour by its members. Misbehaviour can range from failure to pay union dues, to breach of vague rules like 'behaviour prejudicial to the union'. The discipline imposed can range from a fine, or temporary withdrawal of benefits, to ultimate expulsion from the union. This would be an exceptionally severe form of punishment where a closed shop operates. The remedies for a worker who wishes to contest his expulsion are:

1 *To bring an action against the union in the ordinary courts* – this can succeed if the union has acted in breach of its rules, or contrary to the principles of natural justice (e.g. by failing to give the expelled worker the opportunity to put his side of the case).
2 *To bring an action against the union in the industrial tribunal* – under ss.3-5 of the Employment Act 1988, where the member has been

subjected to unjustifiable discipline. This is a new feature introduced by the 1988 Act, and could include imposing a fine,
suspension or expulsion on a member for refusing to take part in
industrial action.

Industrial activities of trade unions

Industrial action represents the means by which employees can
collectively bring pressure to bear upon an employer. The theory of
this concerted action is that it produces an equality of bargaining
power between workers and employers which could never exist
between one individual employee and the employer. Common
reasons for using industrial action are support of claims for higher
wages or demonstrating protest at unsafe working conditions.

Although the strike is the ultimate form of industrial action, a union
may achieve results by using a work-to-rule, a go-slow, a boycott of
customers or suppliers, or a refusal to work contractual overtime. If a
strike is considered to be the most appropriate action, it may not be
necessary for the union to call out all its members. Results can often be
achieved quickly with selective stoppages, especially if these are by
key workers, e.g. those operating computers, or involved in the
collection of money for the employer.

All forms of industrial action can give rise to the question: 'Are the
workers concerned in breach of their contract of employment?' The
answer to this is not easy. For example, an employee working to rule
could give little cause for complaint if he was meticulously observing
the rules laid down in his contract; but if he seeks to give those rules an
unrealistic meaning, so that he is wilfully obstructing his employer's
business, then he may be in breach of his contract. If there was a
breach, one of the remedies would be for the employer to sue the
offending employees for damages for breach of contract. However,
any employer conscious of the need to preserve good industrial
relations is unlikely to resort to such action. It is far more likely that an
employer who believes his business interests are being wrongly
interfered with will want to take action in tort against officials and
members. A number of specific torts (e.g. interference with contract,
and conspiracy, often known as the economic torts), relate almost
exclusively to trade union activities. Other torts like trespass and
public nuisance can easily be committed while participating in
industrial action.

An example of a typical situation will show how these possibilities
could occur. A union in discussion with an employer about new wage
rates feels that negotiations are making no progress and that the

employer could offer more. The employees who are union members are called out on strike after a ballot. The union members account for about 60 per cent of the workforce. While some employees continue to work, the effect of the strike is not fully felt, so the union officials organize a picket line and attempt to persuade those still working not to cross the picket line (i.e. persuade them to break their contracts of employment). What is more, officials realize that the impact of their action can be increased by persuading lorries bringing supplies to turn back without making delivery (i.e. causing a breach of commercial contracts). The number of pickets may well get out of control, spilling on to the road and causing it to be blocked, or into the employer's premises, constituting trespass.

The possibility of the employer suing successfully in tort, either for an injunction to stop the commission of the torts, or for damages, is restricted because of the immunities enjoyed by trade union officials and members. Since 1906, these immunities have existed if the person committing the tort was acting in contemplation or furtherance of a trade dispute. Because of the protection it affords against tort actions, this is frequently referred to as the golden formula, although it is subject to recent limitations in its scope. Two elements of the formula require consideration:

- When is there a trade dispute?
- What constitutes acting in contemplation or furtherance of it?

Trade disputes

A definition of a trade dispute is contained in TULRA 1974, s.29. It must be a dispute between workers and their employers, which relates wholly or mainly to one or more of the following matters:

1 The terms and conditions of employment.
2 The physical conditions in which people work.
3 The engagement or non-engagement of workers.
4 The termination of employment or suspension of workers.
5 The allocation of work between workers.
6 The question of discipline.
7 The membership or non-membership of a trade union by any worker.
8 The facilities for officials of trade unions.
9 The machinery for negotiation or consultation relating to any of these matters.
10 The question of recognition of a trade union.

The trade dispute may also relate to matters outside Great Britain. This is of considerable significance where companies may be multi-national, or working on contracts abroad, engaging cheap local labour.

There are many complex cases on the full meaning of the definition, because an employer who sees his business severely affected by industrial action would naturally be keen to prove that the golden formula should not apply on the ground that there was no trade dispute. An interesting example where this argument succeeded involved the BBC. The BBC planned to televise the 1978 Cup Final at Wembley, and to 'beam' their transmission to many foreign countries. An anti-apartheid movement approached the union organizing the TV engineers and asked for support in not beaming the programme to South Africa. If the engineers were to agree to this, and refuse to carry out the orders of the BBC, they would be in breach of their contracts of employment. The BBC in turn would inevitably be in breach of a number of its commercial contracts with countries overseas who would not then receive the programme. Was the proposed action of the TV engineers in contemplation or furtherance of a trade dispute? The Court of Appeal decided that no trade dispute existed here, although the engineers could easily have brought themselves within the definition. If they had asked the BBC to insert a new term in their contracts which provided that they would not be required to take part in broadcasts to South Africa, the BBC would almost certainly have refused. Then the engineers could have said that their dispute was related to 'terms and conditions of employment' (*BBC v. Hearn*).

Contemplation or furtherance of a dispute

Although the judges in the cases have often emphasized that acts can only 'further a trade dispute' if they are not too remote from the dispute, or if they are reasonably capable of furthering the dispute when viewed objectively, these approaches inevitably limit the scope of the golden formula. The matter was considered by the House of Lords twice, in 1979 and 1980, and on both occasions the court confirmed that the proper approach to interpreting the word 'furtherance' is to apply a subjective test. Did the person in question honestly believe that his acts would further the dispute? If so, he must have the benefit of the golden formula, however unwise or damaging his actions may be.

Limitations of the immunity

The whole question of the scope of trade union immunity from actions in tort is politically very contentious, and developments in this field have continued apace. The present position can be summarized as follows:

1   *The position of the trade union itself* – the union can be liable in tort if the act in question is authorized or endorsed by a responsible person in the union, e.g. by the president or general secretary, or the principal executive committee. Where the trade union is successfully sued for damages under the Employment Act 1982, the damages awarded are subject to upper limits dependent on the number of members. A union with less than 5000 members may have to pay damages up to £10,000, whereas a union with more than 100,000 members may have to face a damages bill for up to £250,000.

2   *The need for a ballot of the members* – under the Trade Union Act 1984, immunities will only be extended to industrial action which has been preceded by a secret ballot. The ballot must have taken place within four weeks of the action being taken and a majority of those voting must support the proposed action. Public funds are available to conduct the ballot. Immunities will be lost if no ballot is held.

3   *Secondary action* – when an official or member commits a tort, he will be protected if it is one of the torts protected by the golden formula. Which torts are so protected has varied from time to time. Initially the immunity only covered inducing a breach of contract of employment, but was subsequently extended to cover inducing breaches of commercial contracts. The changes introduced by the Employment Act 1980 seek to limit the golden formula protections. Where a breach of a commercial contract has been induced, the immunity can only operate if the breach is caused by primary, or in limited cases, secondary action. This limitation is designed to protect employers far removed from the actual dispute, who may find themselves being used as unwilling pawns by a trade union experiencing difficulty in achieving its objectives by more direct means.

4   Further restrictions on the immunity from liability in tort are contained in the Employment Act 1988. Thus, there is no immunity for tortious actions where the reason for the action is that the employer is employing a person who is not a trade union member or who is not a member of a particular union. Anyone who commits an industrial tort while seeking to impose or enforce a closed shop will not have the protection of the golden formula.

5   Where the member or official concerned is picketing, limited immunity is granted as long as:

(a) he pickets in contemplation or furtherance of a trade dispute.
(b) He pickets only in the right places – this is now usually limited to the member's own place of work.
(c) He pickets for the right purposes – these are limited to peacefully obtaining or communicating information or peacefully persuading anyone to work or not to work.

One difficulty about the immunity in relation to picketing is that it is extremely restricted, and bears no relation to the realities of the picket line. Although some changes in the law were made in 1980, they did not put right the worst practical problems, namely that there is no right to stop vehicles, and there is no control over the number of pickets. The 1980 changes were principally aimed at putting a stop to secondary picketing, i.e. picketing on premises other than those of the employer in dispute. It was hoped that the other problems could be resolved by the issue of a Code of Practice. This was published by the Secretary of State for Employment in 1981.

By its very nature picketing is a public activity which tends to involve the commission of criminal offences, e.g. obstruction of the highway, causing a breach of the peace. Although the immunity is so worded as to cover criminal behaviour ('it shall be lawful'), the scope of the protection is extremely narrow, as proved by the cases on the point. Thus there was no protection for a picket charged with obstruction because he had tried to detain a lorry driver for long enough to speak to him (*DPP v. Broome*) nor for the pickets who blocked a road by circling round continuously in it (*Tynan v. Balmer*).

Picketing must also be conducted in compliance with the provisions of the Public Order Act 1986. Section 14 of the Act empowers the police to impose conditions on 'public assemblies' i.e. assemblies of more than twenty people in a public place in the open air. The police can issue directions as to the place, the duration and numbers involved. The power of the police exists where it appears that the assembly may result in serious public disorder, serious damage to property, or serious disruption to the life of the community. The police also have power to act where they believe the purpose of the assembly is to intimidate others.

9

The law of tort

Introduction

The basis of liability in tort is probably one of the most difficult legal ideas for the layman to grasp. The word itself is of French origin and means a wrong. Basically, the law of tort is concerned with situations where the behaviour of one party causes, or threatens to cause, harm to the interests of another party. The rules of the law of tort determine when one party can be compensated for the behaviour of another. The law of tort is limited in its scope and although new torts do evolve from time to time, there is not necessarily a legal remedy for every wrong suffered. A plaintiff will only succeed in an action if he can show that the defendant's behaviour falls into a specified situation covered by the law of tort. Those specified situations are then given identifying names such as the tort of defamation, the tort of nuisance, the tort of negligence and the tort of trespass.

Much of the law of tort has developed through the cases. Some of the rules have now been given statutory force, for example the Law Reform (Contributory Negligence) Act 1945, the Occupiers' Liability Act 1984, and the Torts (Interference with Goods) Act 1977. But case law continues to play a very significant role in the development of tort principles. Case law allows the rules to operate very flexibly and to be applied to widely differing situations. The cost of that flexibility will sometimes be a lack of certainty. While the rules are continuing to evolve, it may be difficult to say with any precision whether liability will arise.

Compensating plaintiffs under the law of tort is a long established part of our legal system, with cases dating back to the thirteenth and fourteenth centuries. The earliest forms of tort usually gave protection to the person or to property. These were the various forms of trespass, where the injury which had been inflicted was direct. As society became more sophisticated, the law of tort developed to give protection against less direct forms of harm. Torts such as negligence and the torts designed to protect economic interests then evolved.

Tort distinguished from crime and contract

There are circumstances where exactly the same act or behaviour may give rise to liability in both the law of tort and criminal law. Take, for example, the case of the motorist who causes death by dangerous driving. He may find himself charged with offences in the criminal courts, and at the same time sued for damages on behalf of the deceased victim. Criminal law is concerned with the preservation of order in society, whereas the law of tort is concerned to compensate victims who have suffered harm. Although it is easy to state the differing functions of criminal law and the law of tort, nowadays these differences are blurred in practice. For example, the criminal courts have power in certain circumstances to make compensation orders to victims as well as meting out punishment to the offender.

The same set of circumstances can also give rise to liability in both the law of contract and the law of tort. For example, a person who buys a defective hedgecutter which causes him to cut off his finger may sue the supplier for breach of contract, or the manufacturer for the tort of negligence. The most significant difference between contract and tort is that contractual liability is based on consent between the parties, a form of arranged liability, whereas tort liability is imposed by law. Although this distinction may be true in essence, again the boundaries between the two areas are not so clear. In the law of contract many of the obligations are in fact imposed by law. For example, in a sale of goods situation conditions are imposed by the Sale of Goods Act 1979, and the parties are not free to exclude them. Where tort and contractual liability overlap, a plaintiff can take advantage of whichever claim is more favourable to him. That may depend upon the limitation rules governing time limits for bringing actions and the rules for the calculation of damages. His choice of action may also be governed by any possible defences available to the other party. If he brings an action in tort, the defence of contributory negligence may be pleaded and may largely defeat his claim. That defence is not available in contract.

Although there is considerable emphasis on the compensatory function of the law of tort, an award of damages is not the only remedy when a tort has been committed. A plaintiff may wish to put a stop to some form of behaviour being carried on by the defendant, for example repeated excessive noise. He may ask the court to grant an injuction in his favour. An injunction is an order of the court telling the defendant to do, or refrain from doing, certain things. A defendant who fails to obey an injunction is in contempt of court.

When suing in tort a plaintiff does not have to specify the particular tort on which he is relying. In practice, the conduct he is complaining about may amount to more than one tort. For example, the same behaviour may amount to both the tort of nuisance and the tort of negligence. If more than one tort has been committed the plaintiff will not recover double damages; he will simply have the protection of alternative reasons why he should succeed in his claim.

Tort compared with other systems of compensation

In order to succeed in a tort action the plaintiff must usually show fault on the part of the defendant. To do so, it is likely that he will need to bring complex, lengthy and costly court proceedings. If a plaintiff is successful in those proceedings there is no certainty that the defendant will have the means to satisfy the judgment made against him, i.e. he may be unable to pay the damages. As a general rule in English law, there is no obligation to insure against the possibility of tort claims. (There is an exception to this rule in the provisions of the Road Traffic Act 1972, which compel the owner of a motor vehicle to insure against tortious liability owed to third parties.) In view of the problems of proving fault, it has sometimes been argued that victims of accidents should receive compensation from some kind of central insurance fund on a 'no fault' basis i.e. without having to prove liability against a defendant. A Royal Commission considered this idea and its Report was published in 1978. It recommended that the no fault principle should be extended to apply to motor vehicle accidents, but it did not recommend abolition of tort actions in other cases of personal injury. There is great pressure at the present time to compensate victims of medical negligence on a 'no fault' basis.

There is some experience of operating a no fault insurance system in this country. The Industrial Injuries Scheme, which forms part of our social security system, allows a workman who is injured in an accident at work to receive disablement benefits if he suffered personal injury caused by accident arising out of, and in the course of, his employment, whether or not his employer was at fault. Such an injured workman may also successfully sue his employers for damages in the tort of negligence if he can prove that the employer was at fault. In assessing his damages within the law of tort some account will be taken of social security payments received. The same workman may also have private insurance cover where the payments made to him are unaffected by benefits received under the social security system or through tort damages.

The failure to implement any kind of no fault compensation scheme in this country can be contrasted with the experience of New Zealand. The scheme introduced there in 1972 covers all cases of accidental injury and the common law action for damages in the law of tort has been abolished.

Trespass

Trespass is commonly thought to be a tort relating to land, but the law also recognizes trespass to the person and trespass to goods. Trespass to the person occurs if force is directly and intentionally inflicted on another person. For this purpose force means any physical contact. It would equally be a trespass to punch someone on the nose or to give them a kiss. It is a special feature of all forms of trespass that an action can be brought even if no damage has been suffered. This tort is said to be actionable *'per se'*, of itself, without proof of damage. Of course, a person who has suffered no real harm will usually receive nominal damages. People often consent to actions which would otherwise constitute a trespass to the person, e.g. where one willingly holds out a hand for another to shake it, where a patient willingly opens his mouth to allow a dentist to extract his teeth. Where consent has been expressly or impliedly given it is a complete defence to an action. The defence of consent is usually known by the Latin maxim *'volenti non fit injuria'*, he who consents cannot complain of the injury.

Where there is a trespass to the person, the same behaviour could also be a crime. For example, a punch on the nose could also result in a prosecution for assault.

Trespass to goods

Originally, there were a number of forms of tortious action which could be brought to protect goods. The law in this area was reformed by the Torts (Interference with Goods) Act 1977. Wrongful interference with goods can take the form of trespass or conversion. Trespass to goods is an intentional and direct act of interference by a defendant with goods in the plaintiff's possession. The emphasis here is to protect possession. Frequently, the person in possession will be the owner of the goods in question. The defendant's act must be direct and intentional, so tearing a page from your book, or throwing a stone at your car, or breaking a window are all examples of trespass to goods. In these cases the person inflicting the damage had no intention to deny the other person's right to possess the items. If the defendant does commit some act which denies a plaintiff's right to possess the goods this may amount to conversion. So if the defendant took the book from the plaintiff, rather than simply tearing some pages out of it, he has converted the book to his own use. The principal remedy for any wrongful interference with goods is damages, but where a defendant is still in possession or control of the goods, section 3 of the 1977 Act may permit the plaintiff to obtain an order for delivery of the goods and payment of any consequential damages. Where a plaintiff seeks only damages these are based on the value of the chattel together with any consequential loss suffered.

Trespass to land

This tort consists of an unjustifiable interference with the possession of land. The interference may consist of walking over another's land, or throwing things onto the land, or placing a ladder against the surrounding wall or even swinging a crane jib over the land. For the purposes of this tort, land means the surface of the earth itself, anything which is a fixture on it (for example a building), the air space above it to the extent necessary for the use and enjoyment of the land, and the sub-soil below the land. Aeroplanes flying over land would constitute a trespass if the activity were not permitted by Act of Parliament.

Trespass protects possession of land. Where a person is rightfully in possession he may bring an action against even the owner of the land. An example could occur if the landlord rented premises to a tenant without reserving the right of entry to those premises. If he ever entered without the tenant's permission he would commit trespass. The tort is actionable without proof of damage. In those cases where no harm has occurred the plaintiff may be seeking an injunction, for example to restrain a neighbour who regularly takes a short cut through the plaintiff's garden. Cases such as *Anchor Brewhouse Developments Ltd v. Berkley House Ltd* (1987) show that the courts are prepared to grant injunctions to prevent oversailing by tower cranes, even where no damage is caused.

An apparent trespass may be justified because the person is on the land with express or implied permission or under statutory authority or in exercise of a right of way. An example of an implied permission to enter premises is the open door of the supermarket. Having entered the shop, however, if a shopper creates a disturbance he may be asked to leave. He would then become a trespasser if he refused to do so. There are numerous examples of persons having the right to enter premises without the occupier's permission. Acts of Parliament confer powers on officials such as factory inspectors, gas and electricity board officials and public health officials, who have the right to enter premises if particular circumstances exist. It is not a defence to trespass to plead that the defendant did not know he was trespassing. Even if he has lost his way, he could be liable.

There is a general misconception that trespass is a crime. This is not usually the case but in a limited number of cases Acts of Parliament can make trespass into a criminal offence. Typical examples would be trespass on property belonging to British Rail or British Coal. The notice 'Trespassers will be prosecuted' is, therefore, usually meaningless except in these limited cases. Changes have occurred however, in the law of trespass to deal with the position of squatters and, more recently, itinerant groups of hippies travelling to the Summer Solstice festivals.

It is obvious that construction work could involve constant danger of trespass. A contractor would be wise to seek permission for acts which would otherwise cause a breach of these rules. If court action becomes necessary, a plaintiff who has been dispossessed of his land by a trespasser must bring an action for ejectment and he may combine it with an action for damages. If the plaintiff remains in possession, he may claim damages and, if necessary, an injunction to restrain further acts of trespass. The help of the court is not always needed in cases of trespass. The owner of the land can ask the trespasser to leave. If he does not do so, the owner may then use reasonable amounts of force to eject him. What is reasonable will vary with the circumstances of each case.

Nuisance

For the purposes of the law, nuisances fall into three categories: public nuisance, private nuisance and statutory nuisance.

Public nuisance

Public nuisance is primarily a crime, and consists of generating harm to members of the public. Examples of public nuisance include obstructing the public highway, allowing smoke from a burning field to blow across the highway, polluting a public water supply or creating some projection over the highway. An unruly march or demonstration which causes obstruction of the highway could also constitute a public nuisance. Normally such behaviour is controlled by criminal prosecution, but it may be possible for a person affected by the public nuisance to sue in tort. A plaintiff would need to show that he suffered special and particular harm as a result of the public nuisance, greater than that suffered by ordinary members of the public. Where he can prove this, he may succeed either in recovering damages, or in obtaining an injunction, or both. Sometimes, the behaviour of the defendant will constitute both a public and a private nuisance and in such a case, the individual affected will be in an even stronger position to sue. In one case, quarrying operations had caused all the houses in the neighbourhood to be affected by dust and there was held to be both public and private nuisance. A right to sue for public nuisance may be important in those cases where a plaintiff would have no right to sue in private nuisance, for example in those cases where he has no interest in land to protect.

Private nuisance

The tort of private nuisance is committed when one person unlawfully interferes with another's use or enjoyment of land. The range of activities which can amount to private nuisance is very wide and could include harm caused by smells, fumes, vibrations, noise, dust, encroachment by tree roots, escape of sewage and the keeping of animals. Essentially, the law of private nuisance attempts to reconcile conflicting interests. An Englishman's home is his castle, and he is free to do within it as he pleases, so long as he does not spoil his neighbour's enjoyment of his own land.

In seeking to apply this 'live and let live' approach, and when assessing the reasonableness of a defendant's behaviour, the court takes a number of factors into account. The duration of the nuisance is relevant, not only in establishing the existence of a nuisance but also in determining which remedy is more appropriate – damages or an injunction. Where the occurrence is an isolated event or of a temporary nature, that in itself may be evidence that there is not a sufficiently substantial interference to constitute nuisance. As the court takes all the circumstances into account, duration alone is not conclusive. Consider the case of a firm demolishing a building. If the work will be over in a matter of weeks, it may be reasonable to expect the owners of adjoining properties to put up with the noise and dirt over that time. But if the contractor works twenty-four hours each day, seven days each week, with the constant noise of machinery operating, vehicles coming and going and the glare of arc lamps at night, his activities may well constitute a nuisance. Certainly in *Andreae v. Selfridge and Co. Ltd* a plaintiff hotel owner was able to recover damages from a demolition contractor who had created excessive amounts of noise and dust.

The nature of the locality where the alleged nuisance is occurring will be relevant. One judge summed up this aspect of the tort by saying: 'What would be a nuisance in Belgrave Square would not necessarily be so in Bermondsey'. A person keeping pigs on his land might do so without complaint in the country but might be liable for nuisance if he kept them in a town garden.

Although locality is an important factor, the courts will be more inclined to find a nuisance if the offending behaviour has caused actual harm to property as opposed to mere interference with the occupier's comfort and enjoyment of his land. A plaintiff is far more likely to succeed where he can show actual physical damage. If he is simply complaining about behaviour which causes him personal discomfort in the use of his property, then he must show that his complaint is substantial, and one which ordinary men of ordinary sensitivity would complain about. The essence of nuisance is to achieve a balance. If the defendant has behaved reasonably, the plaintiff cannot complain if he has suffered damage only because his own property is extraordinarily sensitive, or the use he wishes to make of it is in some way unusual or special. If a defendant's behaviour would cause no harm to ordinary plants and vegetation, then there is no cause of action for a plaintiff who has suffered harm only to his extrasensitive orchids. But if the defendant's behaviour would have damaged even the daisies on the lawn, then the plaintiff can recover for the damage to his sensitive property as well as to any ordinary property. It is said that you cannot increase your neighbour's liability by using your own property in some special or extraordinary way.

When the court is assessing the reasonableness of the defendant's behaviour it will take into account that he may be doing something which is of value to the general public, for example making early morning deliveries of milk. A rather greater degree of noise and disturbance may then be acceptable before the behaviour amounts to nuisance. This does not mean that such behaviour can never amount to nuisance. Where it does, the public utility or public interest question may be relevant in determining whether an injunction should be granted. That point was in issue in two instructive cases, *Miller v. Jackson* and *Kennaway v. Thompson*.

In *Miller v. Jackson*, the case turned on the playing of cricket on a village pitch which had been in use since 1905. Adjacent land was developed for private housing and Mr and Mrs Miller purchased a house directly in line with the wicket. They then discovered that they had to live under very trying conditions during the cricket season, when it was impossible to use their garden if play or practice was taking place. Although balls had come into the garden and bounced off the house, no one had yet been struck. On these facts there was indeed a nuisance but, partly because of the public interest, an injunction was refused.

In *Kennaway v. Thompson*, the nuisance arose out of water sporting activities on a lake adjacent to the plaintiff's house. The noise from powerful motor boats was excessive and the court agreed that the activities did indeed constitute a nuisance. Taking into account the public interest in taking part in such recreations, the court decided that some balance could be achieved between the conflicting interests of the plaintiff and the club users. An injunction was granted, not in terms of a total restraint on water sports but limiting the size of boats which could be used and the number of times each year when competitions could be staged.

If the defendant can be shown to have acted out of malice, it will usually be difficult for him to prove that he was acting reasonably. In one case where the defendant lived next door to a music teacher, whenever a music lesson took place he would bang tin trays, whistle and shout. His acts were shown to have been done only for the purpose of annoying and interrupting the plaintiff, and were held to amount to a nuisance.

Liability for nuisance

Where a potential nuisance situation exists, problems arise as to who can bring an action, and against whom that action must be brought. Private nuisance is designed to protect a person's use or enjoyment of land. A plaintiff must, therefore, be able to show that he has some legal interest in the land, whether as owner or tenant. No action in private nuisance is available to a mere licensee (a person who only has permission to be on the land but no legal rights to the land itself). A mere lodger or guest cannot sue, although if either has suffered personal injury he may have a right of action in another tort, for example negligence. Actions in public nuisance are not restricted by this 'interest in land' requirement.

Who can be sued

The occupier of the land from which the nuisance arose is the obvious person on whom to impose liability. But there may be a difficulty if the occupier did not actually cause the nuisance. It seems that any of the following persons may be liable:

1   The actual creator of the nuisance. What is more, he remains liable even if he has disposed of the land and is no longer in a position to put the matter right. The reasoning behind this is that he committed the wrong in the first place and should remain liable.

2   The occupier of the land, if the nuisance was created by himself or his employees, in which case he is vicariously liable for their actions. It is often said that an employer is not vicariously liable for the acts of independent contractors, but this is not always the case. An occupier who engages a contractor to do construction work on his land may well be liable for any nuisance that the contractor creates, if the occupier should have realized that the work was likely to cause a nuisance.

3   A trespasser who creates the nuisance is liable but he may not be easily found or identified. The occupier will be liable for a nuisance created by a trespasser, or resulting from an act of nature if, once he knows about it, he adopts it or continues it. In effect this means that if the occupier fails to take reasonably prompt and sensible steps to stop the nuisance, he will be liable. An example which shows how the occupier can become liable for an act of nature is a case involving a tree which was struck by lightning and which then caught fire. The occupier called someone in to chop it down, but took no steps to put the fire out, leaving it to burn itself out. The fire spread to the plaintiff's property. The defendant was liable in nuisance for the damage caused.

4   The tenant occupier. Where premises are leased by a landlord to a tenant, the tenant as the occupier seems the obvious person to be liable for a nuisance arising from the premises. However, the landlord is also made liable in a number of circumstances, particularly where the nuisance existed when he let the premises or where it is caused by disrepair of the premises for which he is responsible.

Unlike trespass, where a plaintiff does not need to prove damage, an action in nuisance is only possible where damage can be proved. The damage may be to the property itself, (e.g. some nuisance which causes windows to break, or masonry to crack) or may consist of interference with the plaintiff's enjoyment of his property. Neither of these heads of damage includes mere depreciation of the land.

Even where all the various elements of the tort of private nuisance can be proved by the plaintiff, a defendant may escape liability if he has a valid defence. For example, he may be able to plead that the conduct complained of is authorized by an Act of Parliament. This defence can often be used by local authorities, or public authorities who have been authorized by statute to conduct certain operations. Whether the defence of statutory authority will succeed depends partly on whether the statute lays down a duty or merely a power. Much will depend upon the precise wording of the particular piece of legislation. However, in 1981 the House of Lords showed themselves prepared to give a wide interpretation to the words of the statute in the case of *Allen v. Gulf Oil Refining Ltd*. In that case, the Act granted the authority to acquire land and build an oil refinery there. It was held that the defendant's powers must be taken to include the power to operate the refinery on the land and such operations would not, therefore, establish any liability in nuisance unless negligence could be proved.

A defendant may also be able to show that he had a prescriptive right to do the act complained of. Rights to commit a nuisance may be acquired under the Prescription Act 1832 if the defendant can show that he has committed the nuisance openly and continuously for more than twenty years. This is limited to those cases where the right is capable of existing as an easement, which is a question to be determined in accordance with land law principles.

A plaintiff may also have consented to the state of affairs (*volenti non fit injuria*), but this defence would not operate where a plaintiff acquired the land with knowledge of an existing nuisance. It is no defence to argue that the plaintiff came to the nuisance – in other words that he must accept the state of affairs prevailing when he arrived. A defendant's behaviour will still be tested by the stated principles and could be found to amount to nuisance.

Remedies

It is true that the law allows a person affected by a nuisance to take appropriate steps to put a stop to it, but this form of self-help should not be lightly undertaken. The judges have said that this is not a remedy which the law favours and is usually inadvisable. The sort of problem a plaintiff could face is shown in one case where branches from the defendant's apple trees encroached over the plaintiff's land. The plaintiff cut off the branches, stripped off the apples and then sold the fruit. Although he was within his rights to lop the branches, he had no right to keep them, or the fruit. He was successfully sued by his neighbour for having misappropriated the fruit!

It will usually be much safer for a plaintiff to seek an injunction where he wants to put a stop to a nuisance. The granting of an injunction is entirely at the discretion of the court and may be refused.

That may happen where the nuisance occurs only very infrequently or in circumstances where the injunction would cause undue hardship to the defendant. Damages are always available as a remedy to compensate the plaintiff for harm suffered as a result of nuisance.

This account of the rules of private nuisance will be sufficient to convince many people that they would be foolhardy to embark on private litigation. Bringing an action may well prove costly in terms of time and money. If the action is against a large company or organization, a private individual may well feel that he is at a disadvantage because of the resources and expertise available to the other side. There can be significant problems of proof, especially in cases where it is hard to show a link between 'cause' and 'effect'. If these arguments are valid in small-scale instances of nuisance, they will be all the more so when the nuisance complained of is creating extensive environmental damage. In such a case it may be especially unrealistic to expect one private individual to sue, and the rules of statutory nuisance may then be more than ever relevant.

Statutory nuisance

Most plaintiffs simply want to put an end to the state of affairs causing the nuisance, but may be put off by the thought of bringing a costly and time consuming individual court action, which may not improve relations with their neighbours. In many cases, the state of affairs about which they wish to complain may also constitute a statutory nuisance under the Environmental Protection Act 1990, which came into force on 1 January 1991. The act replaces many of the rules previously found in the Public Health Act 1936 and the Control of Pollution Act 1984. Examples of nuisance covered by the new act include: premises in such a state as to be prejudicial to health or a nuisance; accumulations or deposits or animals which are prejudicial to health or a nuisance; emissions of smoke, gas, fumes, dust, steam or other effluvia; noise or vibration. The key phrase from the legislation is 'prejudicial to health or a nuisance'. A state of affairs is prejudicial to health if it is likely to cause injury to health. The nuisance element of the phrase can only be satisfied by showing what amounts to a nuisance at common law (see page 20). A statutory nuisance cannot exist where there is merely an interference with the personal comfort of the occupiers.

A local authority is under a positive duty to make inspections within its area to establish whether any statutory nuisance exists. Additionally, the local authority must take such steps as are reasonably practicable to investigate complaints of statutory nuisance made by persons living within the local authority's area. The inspections are made by Environmental Health Officers, who have the right of entry to property for detection purposes.

Where a statutory nuisance exists, or is likely to occur or recur, the local authority may serve an abatement notice on the person creating the nuisance or, in some cases, on the owner of the property from which the nuisance emanates. The notice indicates what must be done and a time limit for action. Non-compliance with such an abatement notice is a criminal offence, for which the offender can be fined on a continuing daily basis until compliance. Alternatively, the local authority may undertake the work necessary and recover its expenses.

The 1990 Act has introduced a new right of appeal against an abatement notice. The appeal must be lodged within twenty-one days and will be heard by the Magistrates Court.

Where there is evidence of a statutory nuisance and the local authority declines to act, or is itself responsible for the nuisance, any person aggrieved may bring proceedings in the Magistrates Court. In such instances, the aggrieved person must give at least twenty-one days' notice in writing to the defendant, stating his intention to bring proceedings, and outlining the matters complained of. When the case comes before the Magistrates Court, the court has power to make a nuisance abatement order, as well as imposing a fine and ordering reimbursement of necessary expenses. It is also possible for the court to make a criminal compensation order in favour of the aggrieved person, up to a maximum of £2,000. Failure to comply with a nuisance abatement order is in itself a criminal offence. The court may order the local authority to perform the necessary work under the order where a defendant has defaulted.

The rules under the Environmental Protection Act do not give rise to any liability in tort. A person suffering harm from a nuisance would still need to pursue a claim in private nuisance if a large claim in damages was in issue. However, in smaller problems, the possibility of an award of criminal compensation under the 1990 Act may suffice. The advantage of the statutory rules is that, where the local authority is prepared to take action, the state of affairs constituting the nuisance can be put right without any need for individual action.

The rule in *Rylands v. Fletcher*

The type of liability created by this tort is strict liability. This means that if a set of given facts fits the requirements of the rules, then the defendant will be liable, whether he took care or not. This tort is always known by the name of the case which gave rise to the particular form of liability. An occupier who engages in hazardous activities on his property will be liable where those activities injure or cause harm to someone. The same set of facts may also give rise to an action in negligence. The importance of the *Rylands v. Fletcher* rule was that it pre-dated the general development of negligence principles. Nowadays, it is often suggested that the rule is of decreased significance, and certainly, its technical requirements mean that it is difficult to prove.

The rule is usually stated as follows:

> Where a person, for his own purposes, brings on to his land, and collects and keeps there anything likely to do mischief if it escapes, he must keep it at his peril, and if he does not do so, he is liable for all the damage which is a natural consequence of the escape.

The use if the word 'escape' is naturally suggestive of animals, which could come within the rule. But liability in respect of animals may also exist under the Animals Act 1971 and the torts of negligence and nuisance.

The rule involves a number of points:

1   The dangerous 'thing' must be brought by the defendant onto his land. It follows that no liability can arise from an escape of something which is naturally on the land, e.g. weeds or rocks.

2   The 'thing' must be likely to cause harm if it 'escapes'. The rule has been applied to a wide range of substances and items from oil, gas and explosives to flagpoles and fairground equipment. There is no requirement that the 'thing' must be intrinsically dangerous.

3   There must be an escape, i.e. the person injured must show that he was not on the defendant's land at the time when the harm occured.

4   The escape must cause damage. This may be injury to the person or damage to property.

5   The defendant must bring the 'thing' onto his land for his own purposes, and in doing so must be making a non-natural use of his land. This latter point is probably the most difficult and contentious. It appears that the defendant must be using his land in some extraordinary and unusual way. The idea of non-natural use is closely bound up with public benefit (or lack of it) and will tend to change with changing social needs. In the actual case *Rylands v. Fletcher*, the non-natural use was bulk storage of water in a reservoir. That was in 1868. Would the court still decide the case in the same way today? In *Rickards v. Lothian*, a non-natural use was defined as: 'Some special use bringing with it increased danger to others, and not merely the ordinary use of land, or such a use as is proper for general benefit of the community.' It has been said that

where planning permission has been granted for a particular use of land, it would be difficult to argue that such a use was non-natural.

Although liability is said to be strict, i.e. not dependent on whether the defendant took reasonable care, a number of defences may be available to the defendant.
These include:

1 *Fault of the plaintiff* – if the damage is caused by the plaintiff's own wrongful act, he cannot recover.
2 *Consent by the plaintiff* – presumably tenants on different floors of a building impliedly consent to the presence of a water supply running through the building. If flooding occurs on an upper floor causing damage to a lower floor there will be no liability.
3 *Statutory authority* – a defendant may be able to point to an Act of Parliament which excuses his behaviour which would otherwise be tortious.

In some ways this tort is wider than nuisance, in that it protects persons even though they cannot show an interest in land, and even if they suffer only personal injuries; but in other ways, it is narrower in that it requires something to be brought onto the land which is a non-natural use. Finally, it must be remembered that the same set of facts could give rise to liability in both nuisance and *Rylands v. Fletcher*.

Liability for the spread of fire

Fire may be one of man's greatest discoveries but its potential for causing harm is obvious. A person may start a fire which he fails to control and which then spreads, or a fire may begin accidentally on his land, which he then fails to check. Such circumstances can give rise to liability in nuisance, *Rylands v. Fletcher* or negligence, according to the facts of the case.

Not surprisingly, some rules were developed at an early date to deal with harm caused by fire. The Fires Prevention (Metropolis) Act 1774 is still in force, and provides that no action can be brought against a person on whose land a fire accidentally begins. The word 'accidentally' is very restrictively interpreted. If the fire is caused by nuisance or negligence, it cannot then be said to be 'accidental'. Moreover, the defence afforded by the Act is lost if an accidental fire is negligently allowed to spread.

The hazards of the spread of fire have been recognized for so long that a large number of cases exist on the point. Some newer hazards, which are potentially far more harmful, have been dealt with by specific Acts of Parliament. Particular examples are:

- Nuclear incidents.
- Oil pollution.
- Poisonous waste.

The specific acts sometimes create civil liability and allow injured persons to claim damages.

These torts so far considered all relate to land, in that they either protect an interest in land or concern liability arising out of the use of land. Negligence as a tort is not so confined, and can compensate for harm caused in a wide range of circumstances.

Negligence

Negligence as a tort consists of the breach of a duty owed to the plaintiff to take reasonable care, which results in damage of the right type which is not too remote. Many more people are injured by careless acts than by acts which are intentional. As the law of tort developed, a number of specific situations in which liability would be imposed on a person for his negligent behaviour were recognized by the law, (e.g. where an employer fails to take reasonable care to ensure the safety of his employees; or where an occupier fails to take reasonable care to ensure the safety of his visitors), but there was no general principle established which could be applied to any and every set of circumstances.

Such a general principle began to emerge in 1932 from the famous 'snail in the bottle' case, *Donoghue v. Stevenson*. In that case, a manufacturer of ginger beer distributed his product in opaque bottles. One bottle was sold by a café owner to a customer who shared it with his friend. A decomposed snail slithered out from the bottle, causing the friend to become seriously ill. As she had not bought the ginger beer, the friend had no claim in contract. She successfully brought a claim against the manufacturer for negligence. The House of Lords decided that a manufacturer owes a duty to take reasonable care to see that his products are not contaminated. The prime importance of the case is that it tried to formulate some principles which would link together all the previously separate instances of negligence and by which new sets of circumstances could be tested.

Over the past fifty years, the separate tort of negligence has overtaken all other torts in importance; first, in the number of actions which are brought under this head, and second, in the way that the tort of negligence has begun to take over some of the liability which would previously have been covered by torts like trespass or nuisance.

The tort of negligence is usually analysed under three main headings:

- A duty of care owed to the plaintiff.
- Breach of that duty.
- Damage resulting of the right type which is not too remote.

The duty of care

Liability in negligence can only arise if a duty to take care is owed. When a court is faced with a situation which has been considered previously, it may be able to follow a precedent from an earlier case in determining whether a duty exists. Alternatively, an Act of Parliament may impose a duty, e.g. the Occupiers' Liability Act 1957. In either case, establishing the existence of the duty is relatively straightforward.

Where the court has to consider an entirely novel situation, how does it decide whether or not a duty to take care exists? One of the judges in *Donoghue v. Stevenson* suggested the 'neighbour test' for answering this question. He said that it was impossible in law to have a rule which states that you must love your neighbour. But there could be a rule that you must not injure your neighbour – you must take reasonable care to avoid acts or omissions which you can reasonably foresee would be likely to injure your neighbour. Your 'neighbour' for this purpose is any person who is so closely and directly affected by your act or omission that you ought to have him in mind when directing your mind to the act or omission in question. This 'neighbour principle', as it is usually described, has often been thought to rest exclusively on reasonable foresight of harm. In a simple example, if you run a bath for a baby, you can reasonably foresee that the baby will be injured if you do not take reasonable care to test the temperature of the water before putting the baby into the bath. It is clear from the cases that mere foresight of harm is not now to be regarded as establishing a duty of care, without more. Emphasis nowadays is more on a test of proximity. Is there a sufficient degree of proximity between the parties so that the plaintiff should reasonably have contemplated injury to the defendant? The advantage of using a test of proximity is said to be that it can be more stringent where the circumstances require it. Certainly, the very wording of the 'neighbour principle' contains the test of proximity. A neighbour is a person 'closely and directly affected by the act or omission.'

The House of Lords subsequently refined the neighbour principle in *Anns v. Merton London Borough Council* in 1977, by the addition of a 'public policy' element. This consisted of the court weighing factors such as social conditions, a balance of interests and fear of inflicting excessive liability. This produced a result that in establishing whether a duty was owed, the test became a two-stage process. First, apply the neighbour principle, and if a duty appears to be owed, then ask whether there are any policy considerations which may justify the exclusion of, or restriction of the duty.

By the mid 1980s, it had become clear from the cases that the judges were no longer happy with this two-stage formulation of the test for establishing duty. It left the introduction of policy considerations until too late a stage in the assessment of whether a duty existed. It would be more appropriate to take account of such factors when deciding whether the relationship between the parties was sufficiently proximate. A key factor to be taken into account by the court is whether it is just and reasonable to impose a duty. The use of this new approach is made much easier by the fact that the Anns case has now been overruled by *Murphy v. Brentwood District Council* in 1990.

In the light of recent cases, it is therefore better to state that before a duty of care can exist, it must be shown that there is foresight of harm, that there is a proximate relationship between the parties, and that it is just and reasonable to impose a duty. Although it is convenient to list the elements in this way, it should be borne in mind that they are inevitably interrelated. Moreover, in determining what is just and reasonable, account may be taken of factors which previously were considered under the 'policy' head.

In essence, the purpose of requiring a plaintiff to establish a duty of care is simply to determine whether the defendant will have to pay for the harm he has caused. In cases where it is not considered appropriate for a defendant to have to pay, he can be insulated from the need to do so by manipulation of the duty concept, which is inherently flexible when expressed in the three-fold way seen above.

There are certain well-recognized situations where the courts have faced particular problems in establishing whether a duty should exist because of policy considerations.

These include:

● Cases involving pure economic loss.
● Cases involving negligent mis-statement.
● Judicial immunity situations.
● Nervous shock situations.
● Negligent exercise of statutory powers.
● Pure omissions to act.

It should be remembered that these areas constitute 'problem' areas of the law of negligence, and may well prove to be the fields where new developments occur.

1   Cases involving pure economic loss

As a general rule, no duty of care is owed where a plaintiff suffers only pure economic loss. An example can be found in the case where a research institute negligently allowed a virus to escape which caused foot and mouth disease, and as a result cattle needed to be slaughtered over a wide area. Markets were closed to stop the spread of the infection. The plaintiff was a cattle auctioneer who lost profits as a result i.e. his only loss was pure economic loss. He could not recover damages for negligence. No doubt the court feared that if his claim was allowed, every cattle transporter, supplier of cattle food and dairyman would come forward to claim. Liability would have been excessive in terms of the numbers of claims and the possible amounts involved (*Weller v. Foot and Mouth Disease Research Institute*).

The judges are particularly anxious not to create liability 'in an indeterminate amount for an indefinite time and to an indeterminate class'. They also keep in mind that a person who suffers mere economic loss can frequently correct the situation, for example by accepting a smaller level of profit or by increasing charges. This may justify treating economic loss differently from personal injury which is usually irreparable. They may also be taking a realistic account of which party could more easily have insured against the loss.

The rule can undoubtedly be very harsh, and sometimes almost illogical in application. Take, for example, the case of *Spartan Steel and Alloys Ltd v. Martin and Co. (Contractors) Ltd*. The defendants had negligently cut the electric power cable under a road. This resulted in power being cut off in the plaintiff's metal foundry. Work was in progress (a 'melt') which had to be aborted, resulting in damage to the metal. That was physical damage and the plaintiffs could recover for that harm plus the resulting loss of profit on that 'melt'. As there was no power, they lost the possibility to carry out other 'melts' on which they lost profits. That was classed as pure economic loss for which the plaintiff could not recover damages.

Pure economic loss therefore means loss which is not injury to the person or damage to the plaintiff's property. However, there have inevitably been cases where the courts have sought to 'stretch' the definition of the phrase, sometimes with disastrous results. One such infamous case is *Dutton v. Bognor Regis UDC*. In that case, the defendant's negligence had caused a house to be built with defective foundations. The foundations were defective from the very moment of building. When a subsequent purchaser bought the house, could it be argued that the purchaser was suffering from physical damage to his property as a result of the negligence, or alternatively was he merely suffering loss which was purely economic. The house was damaged from the outset. The subsequent purchaser did not therefore 'suffer' damage to the property itself, but only to its value. Yet in the Dutton case, the damage was accepted as damage to property. No doubt the court in that case was anxious to allow the house owner to recover, but in achieving that result, the case created many problems and was clearly wrong. Fortunately, it too has been overruled by the House of Lords decision in Murphy.

During the period when Dutton was regarded as good law, it had to be seen as an exception to the usual rules about pure economic loss. The courts appeared to have created another exception in the very difficult case of *Junior Books Ltd v. Veitchi Co Ltd* which came before the House of Lords in 1982. The plaintiffs had nominated the defendants as sub-contractors to lay a new factory floor. The floor laid by the defendants was defective and the plaintiffs claimed to have suffered losses totalling in excess of £200,000. The figure consisted largely of loss of profits while the factory had to be closed for the floor to be relaid. No one had been injured by the floor being defective, and no harm had been caused to the property, i.e. the losses were pure economic loss. Nevertheless, the court thought that the plaintiffs should recover damages. This decision seems to have been based largely on the 'close relationship' between the plaintiff and the defendant. There was no contract between them but the defendant was a nominated sub-contractor. The court also took account of the fact that making the defendant liable would not open up liability to 'an indeterminate class'. It is certainly true that, in nominating the defendants, the plaintiffs knew of them and relied on them, and although they had no direct contract with the defendants, the defendants were doing their work under the main contract so that was the next best thing. But it could be argued that by allowing the plaintiffs to sue in tort in this case, when they could not sue in contract because of the privity of contract rules, the courts may be undermining the very rules of the law of contract – and that in itself may be a policy consideration for not allowing recovery for pure economic loss in a situation such as the Junior Books case!

Any idea that the Junior Books decision might see the beginning of the end of the economic loss rules has not been borne out by subsequent court decisions. In *Leigh and Sillivan v. Aliakmon Shipping* in 1986, where a shipper damaged goods through his negligence, the buyer of the goods (to whom ownership of the goods had not yet passed) sued in respect of the damage. As the goods did not yet belong to the buyer, the harm was not damage to his property, but mere economic loss. The buyer's problem was that under his contract to buy the goods, he had to undertake to bear the risk of their loss or damage. The House of Lords would not allow the buyer to succeed against the shipper. Although the shipper had been negligent, he had caused the buyer only pure economic loss. Choosing not to try to bring this case within any exceptional principle, the court found that as an aspect of policy, it would be a bad thing to allow the buyer to recover, as that would effectively render useless the protection which the shipper enjoyed under his contract with the seller. In other words, allowing the buyer to succeed would undermine the rules of the law of contract.

In a trio of cases concerning building and building work, (*Simaan General Contracting Co. v. Pilkington Glass Ltd* (No.2), *Greater Nottingham Co-op Society Ltd v. Cementation Piling and Foundations Ltd* and *D & F Estates Ltd v. Church Commissioners for England*), all decided by the Court of Appeal and the House of Lords, it seems clear that the possible trends suggested by Junior Books have been halted. Great emphasis in these cases is laid on the role of the contracts, and claims should be pursued down that route where possible. Within contracts, the parties have the opportunity to establish their responsibilities. Once they have done that, then it would be wrong to impose any further liability.

The difficulty created by Dutton's case, and perpetuated by the decision in Anns, can best be illustrated by reference back to the facts of *Donaghue v. Stevenson*. In that case, the negligent act (putting the snail into the ginger beer) caused harm to the plaintiff. What if, instead of complaining about harm she had suffered, the plaintiff were merely complaining about some harm to the ginger beer itself, e.g. that the presence of the snail had turned it sour? That would have been a complaint about the quality of the product, in which case the plaintiff would not have succeeded in her action in tort. Now translate that example into the building situation. A builder builds a house with defective foundations. When this is discovered by the owner, it has not caused him any physical injury, nor has the house damaged other property. The house merely suffers from a defect (defective foundations – snail in bottle) which damages the property itself (damaged house – damaged ginger beer). Yet in the Dutton and Anns cases, the courts chose to draw a distinction, and to allow the plaintiffs to recover.

The halt to this line of cases drawn by *Murphy v. Brentwood District Council* is greatly to be welcomed. In that case, Lord Keith said of the Anns case: 'It has engendered a vast spate of litigation, and each of the cases in the field which have reached this House [the House of Lords] has been distinguished. Others have been distinguished in the Court of Appeal. The result has been to keep the effect of the decision within reasonable bounds, but that has been achieved only by applying strictly the words of Lord Wilberforce and by refusing to accept the logical implications of the decision itself. These logical implications show that the case properly considered has potentiality for collision with long-established principles regarding liability in the tort of negligence for economic loss. There can be no doubt that to depart from the decision would re-establish a degree of certainty in this field of law which it has done a remarkable amount to upset.' The facts of the Murphy case are considered on page 223.

2   Negligent mis-statements

The policy of excluding pure economic loss claims caused particular problems in those cases where the negligence consisted of a negligent statement rather than a negligent act. In such cases economic loss is the most likely form of harm to result. For example, if a firm wishes to do business with a new and unknown customer, it may have reservations about extending credit to that customer. To protect itself, the firm may ask permission to approach the customer's bank for a credit reference. If the reference is negligently given by the bank and the firm relies on it, extends credit, and sustains heavy economic loss as a result, can the firm sue the bank for negligence when the loss it has suffered is purely financial?

In a case in 1964, *Hedley Byrne v. Heller*, where the facts were similar to the example given above, the courts drew a distinction between negligent acts and negligent statements. If the negligent statement results in physical damage, the normal rules of negligence operate. So, in one case where an architect negligently stated that a wall was safe to be left standing, he was successfully sued in negligence by a workman who was injured when the wall collapsed (*Clay v. Crump*). Where the negligent mis-statement causes economic loss, liability may now arise either under the principles set out in the Hedley Byrne case or by virtue of the Misrepresentation Act 1967. (Liability for false statements in the law of tort had previously been covered only by the tort of deceit. In order to succeed in an action for deceit, it is necessary to prove that the false statement has been made knowingly, without belief in its truth, or recklessly, careless whether it be true or false. There has to be dishonesty, mere carelessness was not enough. Some relief can also be obtained from the law of contract in cases where the false statement does not amount to a term of the contract, but induces the plaintiff to enter the contract. In those circumstances, the plaintiff may be permitted to rescind the contract. It would be useful at this point to refer to the relevant material on misrepresentation in the law of contract.)

The general effect of the Hedley Byrne case is that certain negligent mis-statements are now actionable, even if the only loss is pure economic loss. The judges in the case were no doubt cautious in view of the sizable step they were taking to change the law. In consequence, they wanted to impose restrictions on those negligent statements causing economic loss which should be actionable. Not only should the maker of the statement reasonably foresee that it was likely to cause harm; there must also be a special relationship between the plaintiff and the defendant. The judges in the Hedley Byrne case were not at all clear exactly what would amount to a special relationship. It seemed it would exist if the party making the statement knew, or ought to have known, that the other was trusting him and was going to rely on what he said. Much of the need to establish a special relationship under the Hedley Byrne case is caused by the judge's desire not to open up too wide a potential liability.

The possible scope of the Hedley Byrne principle is very wide. It could apply, for example, to professional advice given by architects, surveyors, engineers, accountants, lawyers or doctors, amongst others. It is clear from the cases that some considerable overlap can occur between the rules of the law of tort and the law of contract. Most professional people are likely to have a contract with their client, so it is more likely that they will be sued for breach of contract in respect of any negligent service. However, two recent cases serve to illustrate how reliance on a negligent mis-statement made outside the context of any contract can cause extensive loss. In *Smith v. Eric Bush*, a prospective purchaser of a house sought a mortgage. The building society instructed a surveyor to carry out a house valuation for them, and on the strength of that survey, the building society loaned money to the purchaser. Relying on the survey, the purchaser decided to go ahead with the purchase. There was no contract between the purchaser and the surveyor, who had been engaged by the building society. However, the court held that the surveyor was liable to the purchaser, as the situation was akin to contract, in that the surveyor knew that the consideration he received derived from the purchaser. He also knew that the purchaser would rely on his report in determining whether to buy the house. The valuation report was negligently prepared, and in consequence, the purchaser was successful in a claim for damages against the surveyor. The surveyor sought to rely on a disclaimer of liability, but the court further held that it would not be fair and reasonable to allow reliance on the disclaimer, as the surveyor must have known that the purchaser would be supplied with a copy of the valuation report and would be likely to rely on it.

In *Caparo Industries plc v. Dickman*, the auditors of a company issued inaccurate and misleading accounts for a company, Fidelity, in which Caparo held shares. Caparo bought further shares on the strength of the audited accounts, which were circulated to all shareholders. Later the same year, he mounted a takeover bid for Fidelity, but once he acquired the company, Caparo discovered the true state of its finances. He alleged that the auditors owed him a duty of care when making statements, both as a shareholder and as a potential bidder to take over the company. In the House of Lords, it was held that no duty was owed to him in either capacity. As a member of the general public, looking at the audited accounts with a view to takeover, there was no sufficiently proximate relationship between the auditors and Caparo. As a shareholder wishing to buy more shares in the company, no duty was owed as an individual shareholder should be in a position no different from that of a member of the general public. The accounts were prepared and circulated to members of the company to enable them to better manage the company, not to permit them to make a personal profit. To find otherwise would be to impose a virtually unlimited and unrestricted duty on the auditors, and would suggest that foresight of harm, without more, was sufficient. Such a finding would run contrary to all the other recent decisions.

Looking back to the Hedley Byrne case itself, the actual claim of the plaintiff failed because the defendants had expressly disclaimed responsibility for their reference. The possibility of using such a disclaimer successfully is limited now by the provisions of the Unfair Contract Terms Act 1977. Under s. 2, where a person seeks by a notice to exclude or restrict his liability in negligence which results in loss or damage other than personal injury, he may only rely on that disclaimer if it satisfies the requirements of reasonableness. It should be noted, however, that the Unfair Contract Terms Acts 1977 applies only to a business liability situation.

The law relating to negligent statements is complicated because of the overlap of the rules of the law of tort and the law of contract. Certainly the Hedley Byrne principles can be important where a false statement has been made which does not induce a contract. Where a contract has resulted it seems likely that a plaintiff would prefer to use the rules of the Misrepresentation Act 1967, to take advantage of a more favourable burden of proof which would then lie with the defendant. The law is probably much more confused than it need be, due in part to the fact that the Misrepresentation Act 1967 was passed on the basis of earlier Law Revision Committee reports and suggestions, made at a time before Hedley Byrne was decided in the courts. The legislators went ahead with the Act, making no attempt to blend in the developments which had occurred subsequently in the Hedley Byrne case.

3   Judicial immunity situations

As a result of Hedley Byrne, the courts have recognized that there are times when there will be liability in tort for negligent mis-statements. Nevertheless, no liability attaches if the statement is made by a judge, or barrister, or arbitrator in the course of legal proceedings. Quite simply, the reason for this is public policy. It is regarded as being against the public interest to have the constant possibility of litigation being reopened. Take the case of a person accused of criminal offences who is represented by a barrister. The accused is found guilty and sent to prison. He believes his barrister handled his case negligently. If the accused could now sue in tort for negligence, this would in effect reopen many of the issues considered in his criminal trial, and would run counter to the principle that there must be an end to litigation.

The immunity of arbitrators was considered in the case of *Sutcliffe v. Thackrah*, where an architect who had negligently certified work claimed to be acting as an arbitrator in the certification process. That claim was not accepted by the court but, had it been correct, no action in negligence would have lain against the architect.

4   Nervous shock situations

Nervous shock in this context means actual illness like psychiatric disorder or depression. Nervous shock as a consequence of negligent behaviour causes no problems where the victim has also sustained physical injuries. So, a victim of a road accident, run over by a negligent motorist, may be claiming in respect of broken limbs, fractured skull, punctured lungs *and* nervous shock. The cases which cause problems are those where the only harm is the nervous shock. The problem is more acute in those cases where the victim of the nervous shock was never in any danger himself of suffering physical harm.

Take the example of the mother who looks out of her bedroom window and sees her small son run over by a reversing lorry. No doubt it is likely she will suffer nervous shock but she was in no personal physical danger. Or, take the example of the person who sees nothing of an accident to a loved one, but reads of it later, or hears of it from a third party. Are such people owed a duty of care by the defendant? Inevitably, these cases raise the usual policy issue, that liability may come to be owed to an 'indeterminate class'. Moreover, the courts may be anxious that these cases could give rise to false claims, as medical knowledge about shock and mental illness is not a particularly exact science.

Many of the issues in this area were clarified by the House of Lords in 1983, in the case of *McLoughlin v. O'Brien*. A horrendous road accident had occurred, in which the plaintiff's husband and children were badly injured, and one child was killed. A friend came to tell the plaintiff the news of the accident and took her to the hospital. There, the plaintiff learnt the full extent of the tragedy and saw her family in harrowing and distressing circumstances. It was held that her nervous shock was reasonably foreseeable, and she should be permitted to recover damages.

A significant number of the anxieties about the development of this area of negligence were aired in the McLoughlin case. Should claims be limited to those people who saw an accident or its immediate consequences? Or should claims be limited to those people who had some reasonably close relationship with the victims of the accident? (If this point is regarded as significant, that could eliminate claims from persons who suffer nervous shock as a result of assisting in an accident or disaster, where they might see and experience dreadful injuries and suffering). Should claims be limited to those people who are reasonably close in time or place to the accident?

If damages for nervous shock are dependent on reasonable foresight of harm to the plaintiff in question, that in itself will act as a significant filter to ensure that only a proportion of cases are likely to succeed. In a recent action brought by relatives of spectators killed in the Hillsborough football stadium disaster, in respect of nervous shock suffered as a consequence of watching the events unfold on television, the Court of Appeal rejected their claim for damages. It seemed that watching TV miles away from the catastrophe could not satisfy the test of proximity.

5   Negligent exercise of statutory powers

Dutton v. Bognor Regis UDC opened up a significant development in the law of negligence, when an owner of a building sued the local authority, alleging negligence with regard to the inspection of the foundations of the building. In many of these cases, the builder himself will not be worth suing if he has gone into liquidation or where there are doubts about his solvency. Local authorities look like richer pickings in these circumstances!

Where a local authority acts under statutory powers, as for example in the building inspection processes, there may be liability for negligence if, once having decided to inspect, the inspector fails to carry out the inspection properly. Of course, where there is merely a statutory *power* to act, as opposed to a statutory *duty*, the local authority has some discretion about whether to do anything at all. Its resources may be so scarce that it has to determine priorities about which inspections it will make. In these circumstances, if it decided to make no inspection, the question then arises whether the authority could be negligent for failing to inspect. It seems that there would be no liability in negligence, so long as the local authority has given proper consideration to the question of whether or not to inspect.

These issues were all considered in *Anns v. Merton London Borough Council* in 1977. This was another case involving defective foundations. Although the decision has now been overruled, some consideration of the approach taken by the House of Lords in Anns is vital to an understanding of the later developments. So far as local authorities are concerned, Anns appeared to decide that a local authority may be liable in tort to a building owner in relation to its statutory control over building operations. The extent of the liability would be the cost of remedying a dangerous defect in the building which had resulted from a negligent failure by the local authority to ensure that the building was constructed in conformity with the appropriate standards laid down in building regulations.

The difficulty created by this broad-ranging approach can best be illustrated by comparing a defective chattel with a defective building. If you make a chattel which contains some latent defect which causes damage or injury to persons or property, you may be liable in negligence if you made the chattel negligently – *Donoghue v. Stevenson*. But if the chattel is merely defective in quality, then your liability in that regard lies only in contract. Anyone acquiring the chattel who has no contract with you may suffer economic loss as a consequence of having to have the chattel repaired or having to simply abandon it, but of course, you would owe no liability in tort in respect of mere economic loss.

Now apply these same principles to a defective building. If a builder constructs a building with a latent defect (e.g. defective foundations), the builder may be liable in tort for injury to the person or damage to property arising from the dangerous defect. But if the owner of the house gets to know about the defect before it causes any injury or damage, then the owner would have rights in contract if the house had been built for him, but would have no rights in tort, because his loss would be mere economic loss – i.e. the cost of the repair, or the cost of abandoning the building if it cannot be repaired. To hold otherwise would be to impose on the builder a warranty as to the quality of his work which would be owed not only to the original owner but also to all who subsequently acquired an interest in the property.

The Anns case, following the earlier decision in Dutton, erred in failing to take account of this distinction between defects causing external harm and defects which merely harm the product itself. If, however, the distinction is a proper one, then it raises the question about liability of local authorities. If the builder's duty should be limited as suggested above, then it seems altogether wrong to make the local authority liable to a greater extent than the builder. The function of the local authority in inspecting building work is to ensure that there is compliance with building regulations. If the local authority were to negligently fail to ensure compliance with those regulations, it seems absurd that it would then incur a liability greater than that of the builder himself. In the Murphy case, overruling Anns, the Lord Chancellor, Lord McKay, makes the point that it is not a proper exercise of judicial power for the courts to create large new areas of responsibility on local authorities in respect of defective buildings. That, properly, is the role of Parliament. He was strengthened in his view by the consideration he gave to the Defective Premises Act 1972 (see page 237).

During the period whilst the Anns case was still good law, it was clear in a number of other cases that the judges were anxious not to let the Anns principles in relation to the exercise of statutory powers run too far. In *Curran v. Northern Ireland Co-Ownership Housing Association Ltd* a house extention on the plaintiff's home had been financed by a grant provided by one of the defendant organizations. It was allegedly so badly built that the work had to be completely redone. The plaintiff argued that he had bought the house in reliance on the fact that a grant had been given, assuming that a grant would only have been paid to the previous owner if the work had been done properly. The defendant organization had a statutory power to make grants to improve houses. A grant could only be made if the property was in stable structural condition on completion of the work, and if the work had been done to the satisfaction of the defendant organization. If the work was defective, could a subsequent owner of the property hold the defendant liable for negligence? Their Lordships found no negligence here, and indicated that caution should be exercised about extending duties of care to statutory bodies exercising their statutory powers to control third parties. Such an extention should only occur if:

1   The statutory power was directed to safeguarding the public, as would be the case in situations like Anns where the building regulations could be seen to have such a purpose;
2   it is clear that a proper exercise of the statutory power would have prevented the danger; and

3   if the negligent exercise of the statutory power created a latent defect which could not have been discovered and remedied before harm occurred. The whole object of the power in the Curran case was to protect the public purse, not to protect the health and safety of the general public. In consequence, the case could be easily distinguished from the Anns case.

Thankfully, the Anns case has now been overruled by *Murphy v. Brentwood District Council*. This case again arose out of defective foundations. A pair of semi-detached houses had been built on an infilled site on a concrete raft foundation to prevent damage from settlement. The local authority approved the plans. Some years after the house was completed, the owner noticed serious cracks, and he then discovered that the raft foundation was defective, and had become distorted. Necessary repairs would have cost £45,000, which the plaintiff could not afford. Instead, he sold the house, and realized £35,000 less than the market value, had the house been in sound condition. The plaintiff sued the local authority to recover that sum. The House of Lords held that the plaintiff was unable to recover from the local authority, as his loss was mere economic loss.

Although the Murphy decision has been greeted with relief, in that it seems to take the law back to a point from which it should never have moved, the case does still leave some questions unanswered. For example, would the local authority be held liable in negligence if a defect in a building, which their negligence has failed to prevent, then caused actual physical injury to someone, or physical damage to some other property? This point was not decided in the Murphy case and must await a future decision.

Inevitably, these complex cases are often the result of an aggrieved person looking for someone who is financially worth suing. It has already been suggested that the erring builder may be insolvent, but the other difficulty which a plaintiff faces is the problem of limitation periods. In all tort actions, a claim must be commenced within the appropriate time limit laid down by the Limitation Act 1980. An action relating to damage to property must be commenced within six years of the cause of action accruing. Usually, this is the moment when damage occurs. That does not necessarily mean when the defective building was constructed. Since the decision of the House of Lords, in *Pirelli General Cable Works Ltd v. Oscar Faber and Partners* in 1983, the cause of action arises when physical damage actually occurs to the building, and it is matterless whether the plaintiff knew or could have known about it. This rule is undeniably harsh, especially as it fixes the date for the cause of action accruing for subsequent as well as present owners.

It runs counter to an earlier test proposed by the courts, that time should only run from a point when the plaintiff could have discovered the defects. Some help with this problem has now been given under the Latent Damage Act 1986. In those instances where damage cannot be discovered immediately, (i.e. defective foundations), the plaintiff must bring his action within three years from the time when he discovers the damage, or when he should have discovered it, if he had been using reasonable care, subject to an overriding rule that the action must be commenced within fifteen years of the building being completed.

6 Omissions to act

As a broad general rule there can be no liability in negligence for a pure omission to act. If a road accident occurs where victims are trapped in a car, a passer-by commits no legal wrong if he makes no effort to save those trapped. This is described as pure omission, pure in the sense that there was no existing duty to act. If there is some existing duty, then an omission can be as wrongful as a negligent act. So, a parent of a small child has a duty to care for the child. If he omits to feed the child, such behaviour could be actionable.

If there is no duty to act, but someone decides to act as may be the case in the example above, where the passer-by decides to try to release the crash victims from the car, then if he behaves negligently, the law generally takes the view that there will be no liability for the negligence unless the passer-by makes matters worse. As there is no duty to act, then if you do act, there is no duty to effect an improvement.

This principle can be regarded as being subject to a most important exception in relation to the exercise of statutory powers. In such a case, although there is no duty to act, the defendant had a duty, if he chooses to exercise the power, to effect an improvement.

Breach of the duty of care

If a duty to take reasonable care is owed to the particular plaintiff, the next stage is for the plaintiff to prove that the defendant was in breach of the duty, i.e. that the defendant failed to take reasonable care. The obvious question must then be asked – how much care should the defendant have taken? What would amount to reasonable care in the particular circumstances? If the defendant falls short of a reasonable standard, then he is in breach of his duty.

Inevitably, there is no absolute precision in measuring what amounts to reasonable care in any given situation. A court will need to weigh up factors like the degree of risk involved in the defendant's behaviour; how serious was the harm which was likely to be caused; was there any particular social value or utility in the defendant's activities; and how costly and inconvenient would it have been to take precautions to eliminate or reduce the risk? The standard of care expected is the care of a reasonable man, although no such person may exist in fact! This means that the defendant's behaviour must be assessed against an objective standard, and it is matterless that the defendant tried hard or did his best. Of course, where a defendant holds himself out as possessing a particular skill or capability, he will be expected to display reasonable amounts of that skill or capability. So a surgeon must operate with the care that a reasonable surgeon would take; a builder must build with the care a reasonable builder would take; and so on. If there is a suggestion that a child has been negligent it may be appropriate to ask whether the defendant child took the care that could be expected of a reasonable child of the same age.

It is important to remember that, in formulating a standard of reasonable care, everyone is assumed to have knowledge about common facts, e.g. fire burns, water can drown, knives cut. In particular fields, a person with expert knowledge will be expected to display a reasonable amount of such knowledge. When judging whether a defendant has taken reasonable care, some guidance may be given by looking at what is usual or common practice in the activity or industry or operation in question. So an employer who fails to provide protective clothing for employees may be doing exactly the same as other employers in the same line of business. Arguably, all the employers may be being negligent, so general practice is not an absolutely reliable guide!

In assessing how much risk is involved in the defendant's activities, one judge has said that 'people must guard against reasonable probabilities, not fantastic possibilities'. If you can only conceive of harm occurring in some obscure or bizarre turn of events, then the risk may be so small that you are justified in ignoring it. After all, the law only requires reasonable care, not an absolute guarantee of safety in all circumstances.

In practice, it may be very difficult to separate questions like degree of risk from seriousness of harm likely to be caused. Obviously, even in cases where a very small risk is involved, it may be necessary to take more elaborate precautions where the harm caused, if any, would be very serious. If an employee has huge tanks full of liquid, he may be able to foresee that employees may fall in, or objects may fall in causing the liquid to splash out. If the liquid is cold water, some barrier to prevent employees falling in may be all that is necessary in order to show reasonable care. If the liquid is some caustic solution, likely to burn on the slightest splash, then the employer may have to consider some protective cover for the tanks. The precautions which are reasonably necessary may also be determined by asking whether employees are meant to be in the vicinity of the tanks or not, and whether employees have been issued with protective clothing.

It will already be apparent that reasonable care will fluctuate according to the exact circumstances of the case. Failing to test the temperature of the bath water may well be negligent if the bath is intended for a baby or someone lacking the mental ability to perceive the dangers of scalding water for themselves; in other circumstances such a failure may not be negligent, because the user of the bath should have checked for himself. A defendant engaging in some activity designed to save life and limb may well escape liability for negligence even though his behaviour may amount to a failure to take reasonable care in less socially useful circumstances. In *Watt v. Hertfordshire County Council*, firemen rushed to the scene of an accident where a jack was needed in order to free a woman who was trapped. Because of the emergency nature of the call, the jack was transported on an unsuitable vehicle, and was not secured during the journey. It shifted on the lorry, and a fireman was injured. There was held to be no negligence here, but it was made clear that if the jack had been transported in a similar way in a commercial enterprise, there would have been a failure to take reasonable care.

Even in those cases where some minute risk is foreseen, it may be possible to eliminate that risk entirely, but only by massive expenditure. The law does not impose such an impossible standard. If the risk could be eliminated or reduced by reasonable expense or practicable precautions, then the defendant should have done what he could. But again, it must be emphasized that he is only required to behave reasonably. In *Latimer v. AEC Ltd*, oil normally ran away in channels in a factory floor. It had been spread over the surface of the floor when the factory was flooded. The factory occupier scattered some sawdust, mopped up as much of the oil as possible, and gave a warning to employees to take care as the floor was slippery. The plaintiff slipped and was injured but the defendants were held not liable as they had taken reasonable care. The risk was not particularly great, any harm they could foresee was not likely to be particularly serious, and short of closing down the factory (which would have been extremely costly), there was nothing more they could have done.

The discussion of reasonable foresight of harm may raise the idea that what the courts are actually concerned with is hindsight! Inevitably, when a court tries to consider what the defendant should have foreseen, the judges will be influenced by policy factors, as they are in so many aspects of the development of the rules of negligence. So, for example, in cases involving motoring accidents, the fact that the defendant is insured could well have a quite distorting influence on the judgement of what amounts to reasonable behaviour. In *Nettleship v. Weston*, it was held that a learner-driver must achieve the standard of a reasonably competent driver. Likewise, in medical negligence cases, policy factors like a fear of encouraging defensive medical practice may play a part in determining what is reasonable.

It has already been indicated that it is up to the plaintiff to show that the defendant was in breach of duty, i.e. that the defendant had failed to take reasonable care. The plaintiff may be assisted in proving negligence by s.11 of the Civil Evidence Act 1968. If the defendant has been found guilty of a criminal offence involving negligence, that fact may be used as evidence of negligence in subsequent civil proceedings. This is obviously a very useful rule where a person has already been convicted of certain driving offences, but it could also be relevant where an employer had been found guilty of offences under the health and safety legislation.

A plaintiff seeking to prove negligence may also rely on the maxim '*res ipsa loquitur*', the facts speak for themselves. This could be pleaded in cases where the facts argue of no explanation other than negligence. In one case, a man was walking along past a warehouse when sacks of sugar fell on his head. What other explanation could there possibly be than that someone was being negligent? It is only appropriate to plead *res ipsa loquitur* if the defendant had management or control of the thing which caused the harm. This tends to depend on whether there was any possibility of some external interference. Where a plaintiff relies on the maxim, it is open for the defendant to rebut the finding of negligence, if he can do so.

Damage resulting of the right type which is not too remote

The type of harm which must be suffered in order to succeed in a claim for negligence has already been considered. The two significant issues which must now be addressed are the question of causation and remoteness. Causation is concerned with the problem of whether the defendant's conduct caused the plaintiff's damage. Remoteness is concerned with the cut-off point at which the law regards the defendant as no longer liable to compensate the plaintiff. If such a cut-off point were not established, a defendant could owe limitless liability.

1   *Causation* – a defendant may behave negligently towards a plaintiff
and yet still not be the cause of his injuries. In *Barnett v. Chelsea and
Kensington Hospital Management Committee*, a doctor was negligent
in failing to examine a patient who had been brought into casualty,
complaining of feeling sick after drinking tea. In fact, the patient
was dying from poison and nothing could have saved him, so the
doctor's negligence did not *cause* his death. It is usual to approach
the causation question by using a 'but for' test. But for the
defendant's negligence would the plaintiff have died in the Barnett
case? Unfortunately, this test is by no means conclusive, and it may
be particularly ineffective in giving an answer where the harm
caused to the plaintiff was inflicted by two or more people, in quite
separate incidents.

2   *Remoteness* – assuming there is no difficulty in proving causation,
the plaintiff must then show the harm he suffered was not too
remote from the defendant's negligent act. Any act can give rise to
endless consequences, and one can often remark with hindsight
that if only a particular event in the past had not happened, none of
the later events would have resulted.

As a feature of not imposing excessive liability, the law has created
the rule that a plaintiff can only recover for harm which is not too
remote a consequence of the negligent act. As soon as such a rule
comes into existence, there must be principles which will assist in
finding the 'dividing line'. The test used by the court is that a
defendant is only liable for such consequences of his negligent act as
could reasonably be foreseen. An objective test is used. Would a
reasonable man reasonably foresee a particular consequence? As an
example, if it is intended to light a bonfire, it is reasonably foreseeable
that people may fall into it, or that a spark from the fire may set alight
nearby fencing, trees or property. But is it reasonably foreseeable that
fumes from the bonfire will choke to death battery chickens being
reared on adjoining land?

In a case which is accepted as establishing the approach to issues of
remoteness, the Wagon Mound, a ship called the *Wagon Mound*
negligently discharged oil into Sydney Harbour as it was sailing out.
By the action of the wind and tide, the oil eventually floated all around
the wharf area where the plaintiffs were carrying out welding
operations. The welding work was suspended until the plaintiffs
checked whether the oil would ignite. They discovered that this was
unlikely as it was furnace oil with a high ignition point. Welding work
recommenced and an extensive fire was caused when the oil did in fact
ignite. The defendants, the owners of the *Wagon Mound*, were held not

liable. Although they owed a duty to take care in relation to the plaintiffs, and were in breach by negligently discharging the oil, the damage they had caused was not a reasonably foreseeable consequence of their negligence.

The damage caused must, therefore, be of a reasonably foreseeable type. In the Wagon Mound, no doubt, the ship owner would have been liable if the plaintiffs had been complaining about oil fouling their slipways. This refinement can only be pursued so far. Take the example of *Bradford v. Robinson Rentals Ltd*, where a van driver was sent on a long journey in the depths of winter in a defective and unheated van. The employers owed him a duty, and were in breach. Could the employee recover for his injuries, which consisted of frostbite? No doubt that is quite an unusual complaint in this country but nevertheless some harm to his health was reasonably foreseeable and frostbite was therefore in the same class of risk. Compare that example with *Doughty v. Turner Manufacturing Co. Ltd* where the employer had a vat of acid maintained at a very high temperature. It was reasonably foreseeable that employees might be injured by falling in or by being splashed if any object fell in. The employer would certainly be liable if an accident had occurred in either of those ways. What actually happened was that the lid of the vat, made from asbestos, slid into the acid. A chemical reaction was caused which resulted in an explosion and employees were injured by the acid erupting. The employers were held not liable, the damage was too remote. It had occurred in a manner which was not reasonably foreseeable.

When deciding the remoteness question a court will bear in mind the following points:

1 *The defendant must take the plaintiff as he finds him* – if a defendant driver is unfortunate enough to knock down a plaintiff who suffers from a weak heart and dies as a result, he may argue that, whereas the plaintiff's injury has proved fatal, any normal victim would only have been shocked and bruised. Again, he may crash into the back of another vehicle, which may be old and rusty or an expensive Rolls-Royce. But in each example the defendant will be liable to the full extent of the injury or damage caused, if injury or damage of that type could have been foreseen.

2 *The consequences of the defendant's breach of duty may have been 'overtaken' by some act which intervenes* – the defendant's breach may satisfy the 'but for' test, yet another event is regarded as the sole cause of the plaintiff's damage. For example, an employer's breach of duty towards his employee causes the employee a slight injury, and an ambulance is called to take the injured man to hospital. The

ambulance driver is negligent, causes a crash and the employee is killed. The crash is then the new act intervening.

If the court takes the view that the harm which the employee has suffered is not too remote from the employer's act, it would consider the question of contribution, if more than one person is liable to the plaintiff. The situation is governed by the Civil Liability (Contribution) Act 1978. The Act provides that where two or more persons are liable in respect of the same damage, each may recover from the other, or others, a contribution of an amount regarded as 'just and equitable', taking into account his or her share of responsibility for the damage.

Even if the plaintiff has satisfied all the above aspects of proof, his claim may still fail if the defendant has a complete defence (e.g. volenti). More usually his claim may fail in part, if it could be shown that the plaintiff was partly to blame for his own injuries, i.e. contributorily negligent. The present rules are to be found in the Law Reform (Contributory Negligence) Act 1945. If a plaintiff suffers damage partly through his own negligence and partly through the negligence of the defendant, the compensation will be reduced to the extent which the court thinks just and equitable, taking into account the plaintiff's share of the responsibility.

To use the defence, the defendant must show that the plaintiff failed to take reasonable care for his own safety. As with negligence itself, the standard of care varies according to the circumstances. Thus, an experienced mature workman can be expected to take more care when carrying out his work than a new apprentice. There has been a modern extension of the use of this defence in motoring cases when an injured plaintiff has failed to wear a seatbelt or crash helmet. In such cases, he may well find himself regarded as contributorily negligent (*Froom v. Butcher*).

If the plaintiff has consented to the risk, he should have no claim if injured. The scope of the defence is very limited and a defendant is more likely to plead contributory negligence. The defence can be relevant, however, when a defendant alleges that the plaintiff impliedly consented. Common situations where it may be raised arise in relations to sporting events, both for spectators voluntarily sitting there to watch, and participants in the sport.

Any account of the rules of negligence shows that there are many obstacles in the way of a successful claim. Often, cases turn on their own individual facts and there are numbers of conflicting precedents. The present process of claims through the courts has been called 'a lottery' and the time may be approaching when a different method should be found to compensate injured persons. The question was considered by a Royal Commission on Civil Liability for Death and Injury, which reported in 1978. Changes recommended by the Commission have not been made, but it was suggested in its report that motor vehicle injuries should be dealt with on a 'no fault' basis. This would mean that an injured person could be compensated out of a central fund, regardless of whether he could prove anyone to be at fault. Naturally, such a system removes the vagaries and imponderables always likely to be present in a negligence action. Despite the introduction of such rules in other countries, e.g. New Zealand, there seems to be no current intention to change the law in the UK.

Occupier's liability

Although the law can now be said to have general principles relating to negligence, there are some categories which pose their own special problems and for which particular rules have been created. An important example is the liability of occupiers of premises, whose duties are now laid out in the Occupiers' Liability Acts 1957 and 1984. The importance of the rules is obvious. Where a person enters premises and trips on a worn stair or collides with an obstacle because the lights are not working, liability can occur under the Acts. The main duty under the 1957 Act is a common duty of care owed by occupiers to their visitors. This requires the following analysis:

- Who is an occupier?
- What are premises?
- Who are visitors?
- What is a common duty of care?

The occupier

This word is not defined by the Act, but is generally understood to mean the person who has occupational control of the premises. He is the person in the best position to know who is likely to be using the premises, and to know about, and be able to put right, anything wrong with the premises. The occupier does not need to be exclusively in occupation; it is possible for premises to have more than one occupier. For example, in *AMF International Ltd v. Magnet Bowling Ltd*, a building contractor was held to be a joint occupier.

The premises

This word is wide enough to include not only buildings, but also land itself. What is more, by s.1(3) the Act extends its meaning to cover vessels, vehicles or aircraft.

The visitors

The range of people 'using' premises can be very wide, from a canvasser, a postman, an invited guest, a gasman, a deliveryman, even a burglar. The most important point is to distinguish between people lawfully on premises and trespassers. A person's presence on premises could be lawful because:

1 He has express or implied permission given by the occupier.
2 His entry is authorized by law (e.g. a policeman with a search warrant, an electricity official to turn off the supply, or factory inspector to investigate a work accident).
3 His entry is by virtue of a contract (e.g. going into a cinema after buying a ticket).

Even where entry on to premises is initially lawful, a visitor can subsequently become a trespasser if the permission to be there is withdrawn. For example, a shopper might enter a department store in a drunken state, create a disturbance and then be asked to leave. If he refuses to go, he becomes a trespasser. What is more, a visitor must only use the premises for the purposes for which he is invited or permitted to be there.

It should be noted that persons who enter under a public or private right of way are not visitors for the purposes of the 1957 Act.

The common duty of care

Under s.1 of the 1957 Act the occupier's duty is owed in respect of dangers due to the state of the premises themselves *and* due to things done or omitted to be done on the premises.

By s.2(2), the duty owed under the Act consists of taking such care as is reasonable in all the circumstances of the case to see that the visitor will be reasonably safe in using the premises for the purposes for which he is invited or permitted to be there.

The Act also sets out a number of factors to be taken into account when determining whether or not there has been a breach of duty:

1 When an occupier is considering how careful a visitor can be expected to be, he must be prepared for children to be less careful than adults (s.2(3)).
2 He can, however, expect visitors who use the premises in the

exercise of their calling (e.g. where a window-cleaner comes to the premises to clean the windows) to appreciate and guard against risks incidental to such calling (s.2(3)). For example, if the occupier asks a lift engineer to repair his defective lift, he will not be liable for damages caused to the engineer by that lift, but he will be liable if the engineer cuts his hand on an already broken pane of glass in the front door when entering the premises.

3   If the occupier has given warning of a danger (e.g. by a notice stating 'cliff edges crumbling – danger of collapse') this is not enough, in itself, to protect him from liability (s.2(4)). But it may in all the circumstances be sufficient to enable the visitor to be reasonably safe, and by this means the occupier may therefore have discharged his duty.

4   The occupier may know of a state of affairs on his premises which he cannot personally remedy, which will involve him in asking a contractor to undertake work of construction, maintenance or repair. Section 2(4) provides that a visitor injured as a result of the faulty execution of such work by a contractor will not succeed in a claim against the occupier so long as:

(a) The occupier acted reasonably in entrusting the work to a contractor, and

(b) the occupier had taken reasonable steps to satisfy himself that the contractor was competent, and

(c) the occupier has taken reasonable steps to satisfy himself that the work had been properly done. Note that this could require the occupier to employ someone to supervise or check the contractor's work e.g. where building work is being carried out, by the employment of an architect.

This section was extensively considered by the House of Lords in *Ferguson v. Walsh and others*. The plaintiff had been injured while working for Walsh, the first defendant, on a demolition job. Walsh had been asked to undertake the work by X, who in turn had been given the job by the district council who owned the site in question where the demolition was to be carried out. By the terms of the contract between X and the district council, X was not allowed to sub-contract the work without the council's permission. Nevertheless, that was exactly what X had done by his contract with Walsh. The first issue in the case was to decide if Ferguson was a visitor for the purpose of the Act. It was decided that he was, because he was effectively there by X's authority, and X was a joint occupier. Whether the council as joint occupiers were liable to Ferguson depended on s.2(4). The council had acted reasonably in entrusting the work to X and were held not to be liable. On its wording, s.2(4) appears to be limited to construction, maintenance or repair, but the House of Lords said that those words should be construed broadly and purposively, by which interpretation they were sure that 'construction' would embrace demolition.

5   The liability of the occupier may be limited or excluded, to the extent permitted by law. Section 2 provides that the occupier owes a common duty of care 'except in so far as he is free to do, and does, restrict or exclude his duty by agreement or otherwise'. There are two principal limitations to an occupier's right to exclude liability:

   (a) Even where he can successfully limit his liability he can only cut it down to the level of responsibility he would owe a trespasser (see page 235). Otherwise a person entering lawfully could have less protection legally than a trespasser.

   (b) More important, any limitation of liability must be read subject to the Unfair Contract Terms Act 1977. In a 'business liability' situation an occupier cannot exclude or limit his liability for death or personal injury caused by negligence. Nor can he limit his liability for other damage caused by negligence unless the restriction satisfies the requirement of reasonableness.

6   When a person enters or uses premises by virtue of a contractual right, then unless the contract states otherwise, it is implied in it that the occupier owes a common duty of care. If the contract does contain express terms about the occupier's liability, these may be subject to the Unfair Contract Terms Act 1977.

A visitor to premises may suffer injury to himself or his property, or both. When he claims against the occupier, the defences which may be pleaded are:

1   Consent – s.2(5) expressly preserves consent as a defence.
2   Contributory negligence.

Occupier's liability to trespassers

As the 1957 Act extends protection only to visitors, it has no relevance when the person injured on premises is a trespasser or non-visitor. The rules which had been developed by the courts, culminating in the House of Lords decision in *British Railways Board v. Herrington*, have now been overtaken by the Occupiers' Liability Act 1984. Cases like Herrington had determined that an occupier owed a lower standard of care to a trespasser, a standard described as a duty of common humanity. The lower standard took account of the fact that a trespasser was uninvited. Nevertheless, common humanity was a variable standard, depending on factors such as whether the occupier knew of the likely presence of the trespasser; the kind of trespassers they were likely to be, e.g. children, burglars, poachers, squatters; the seriousness of the risk or danger; and whether or not the occupier knew of the risk.

The interplay of these factors can be seen in a case like Herrington. A child trespassed on the railway line and was electrocuted. The fence guarding the line was in a state of disrepair. The stationmaster knew that children were trespassing and had alerted the police. The line was something of an enticement, as the broken fence allowed children to take a short cut by that route to the nearby park. It was held that British Railways Board had failed to show common humanity. In view of the high level of danger, the likelihood of trespass, and the relative ease and cheapness of eliminating the danger for an organization with such resources, the child succeeded in an action for damages.

Under the 1984 Act, 'premises' and 'occupiers' are defined in the same way as for the 1957 Act. The duty under the Act is owed to persons 'other than visitors', and the duty consists of taking such care as is reasonable in all the circumstances of the case to see that the non-visitor does not suffer injury on the premises by reason of the danger concerned. For these purposes 'injury' is not to include loss or damage to property; it covers personal injury only. In this respect, the scope of the act in relation to a non-visitor is narrower than the scope of the 1957 Act to a visitor.

The duty under s.1 is only owed by the occupier of premises if:

1 He is aware of danger or has reasonable grounds to believe it exists.
2 He knows, or has reasonable grounds to believe, that the non-visitor is in the vicinity of the danger or may come into that vicinity.
3 The risk is one against which, in all the circumstances of the case, he may reasonably be expected to offer the non-visitor some protection.

As the occupier owes a duty to take such care as is reasonable in all the circumstances, factors which were previously relevant like the age of the trespasser, the nature of the premises, the character of the entry and the extent of the risk, will all still play a part in determining whether there is a breach of duty. One significant difference now is that the subjective element under the old common humanity rules may have gone. It used to be the case that the trespasser had to take the occupier as he found him, so if an occupier had limited financial resources, that might have been relevant in determining whether he had exercised common humanity. However, in determining what care is reasonable in all the circumstances, it is no doubt still open for the court to consider how burdensome it would be for the occupier to eliminate the risk.

Section 1(5) allows the occupier to discharge his obligations in appropriate cases merely by giving warning notices. It is doubtful if a notice saying 'keep out' would suffice, as it would merely alert persons entering the premises to the fact that they were trespassers, and not to the fact that there was some danger. Warning notices may be totally ineffective if the trespassers are children. And of course, as the Act is concerned largely with trespassers, they may choose to enter premises at some unconventional place where no notice is displayed. The Act specifically retains the defence of *volenti* (consent).

One unsatisfactory feature of the Act is that it does not make clear whether it is possible to exclude or limit the liability it creates. If an occupier puts up a notice stating that he is excluding all liability under the 1984 Act, it would be normal to test such a notice against the rules of the Unfair Contract Terms Act 1977. That Act seems not to be relevant here, as it limits its definition of negligence so far as the statutory duty of care is concerned to the Occupiers' Liability Act of 1957. This aspect of the 1984 Act awaits clarification.

It is widely believed that the 1984 Act will make little difference to the sort of trespasser plaintiff who will succeed against an occupier. In cases like *Pannett v. McGuiness & Co.*, decided on the old 'common humanity rules', demolition contractors were occupiers of a site in a busy urban area where it was reasonably to be expected that there would be large numbers of children. It became necessary to burn large quantities of rubbish and, realizing that this would attract children, three workmen were employed to keep them away. Children, including the plaintiff aged five, were chased away from the site on a number of occasions. While the fire was still burning, the three men left the site and the plaintiff re-entered and was injured by the fire. The nature of the activity was hazardous, the likelihood of trespass was great and the attraction to children was obvious. Applying the principles of the 1984 Act, the defendants would be aware of the danger, would know that trespassers were in the vicinity of the danger and in all the circumstances the risk would surely be one against which the contractor could reasonably be expected to offer some protection. The defendants were held liable under the pre-Act rules and the same outcome would be likely to occur today.

Liability of non-occupiers

For complicated reasons connected with the overlap of duties in contract and tort, the law has been slow to develop protection in tort for the person who suffers damage because of a defective building, where the defects are due to a non-occupier. A simple example of this is the case of a builder who built a house in 1970 for X. X sold the house to Y in 1980. The house has defective foundations and Y now discovers cracks appearing and distortion of door and windowframes. Y has no contract with the builder – he bought the house from X. The builder had been negligent. Can Y succeed in a claim against the builder?

In 1972, the Defective Premises Act was passed, imposing a duty on persons who take on work for the provision of dwellings. That duty is owed to the person ordering the work and to any person who subsequently acquires an interest in the dwelling. The extent of the duty is to see that the work is done in a workmanlike and professional manner with proper materials so that the dwelling will be fit for habitation when completed.

Some very significant limits operate, however, to cut down the apparent effectiveness of the protection given by this Act.

- The protection does not apply to dwellings already protected by an approved scheme of the National House Building Council.
- The Act only applies to dwellings, not to all types of buildings.
- Any action based on the Act must be speedily brought as there is a limited period of only six years, which runs from the date of completion of the dwelling.

Although the protection afforded by this Act is useful, the very limited extent of it has encouraged claimants to seek alternative ways of obtaining redress. Earlier cases such as Dutton and Anns demonstrated a willingness of the courts to allow claims against local authorities to succeed, based on negligent inspections of defective foundations, despite the loss in these cases being properly classifiable as pure economic loss. The trend in those cases, already discredited as they were in *D & F Estates Ltd v. Church Commissioners for England*, has now been halted by the decision of the House of Lords in *Murphy v. Brentwood District Council*.

In that case, one of the judges, Lord Mackay, the Lord Chancellor, said: ' . . . I am of the opinion that it is relevant to take into account that Parliament has made provisions in the Defective Premises Act 1972 imposing on builders and others undertaking work in the provision of dwellings obligations relating to the quality of their work and the fitness for habitation of the dwelling. For this House in its judicial capacity to create a large new area of responsibility on local authorities in respect of defective buildings would in my opinion not be a proper exercise of judicial power'. Lord Mackay was supported in this view by Lord Jauncey, who added: 'Parliament imposed a liability on builders by the Defective Premises Act 1972, a liability which falls far short of that which would be imposed on them by Anns. There can therefore be no policy reason for imposing a higher common law duty on builders, from which it follows that there is equally no policy reason for imposing such a high duty on local authorities'.

It seems now that a first purchaser of a defective building is therefore limited to contractual remedies and/or the protection provided by the 1972 Act. A subsequent purchaser of the property will have no contract with the original builder, and will therefore have to rely exclusively on the 1972 Act.

Breach of statutory duty

Many Acts of Parliament create obligations or duties, where a breach may result in the imposition of a penalty, very often a fine. For example, the Factories Act 1961 imposes a duty to fence certain machinery, and an offending factory occupier can be prosecuted and fined. Sometimes, the courts have allowed the Act of Parliament to be used as the basis for a civil action in tort. Such an action is called breach of statutory duty. The difficulty lies in knowing which Acts of Parliament can be used in this dual way. Most industrial safety legislation e.g. Factories Act 1961, has been so used, yet by contrast the Health and Safety at Work etc. Act 1974 makes it clear that its duties give rise to no civil liability (s.47). To succeed in an action for breach of statutory duty a person must, therefore, show:

1   The act in question was intended to create a civil action. This is the biggest hurdle unless a plaintiff can rely on a precedent showing that the Act has been used before as the basis of a civil claim.
2   The act imposes a duty on the defendant which he has broken.
3   The breach of duty has caused harm which is not too remote.

In general, this action is most used by employees in relation to Acts of Parliament concerning industrial safety, when the result is often to give an injured employee two heads of claim – an action based on negligence, and an action based on breach of statutory duty. The attraction of this tort for the employee is that the standard of behaviour expected from the employer is prescribed by the particular statute.

An example of breach of statutory duty of particular relevance to the construction industry is to be found in the Building Act 1984. This is the Act under which the Building Regulations are made. These regulations relate to the design and construction of buildings and are designed to secure the health, safety and welfare of people in the building. Section 38 specifically provides that where a breach of any duty imposed by the Building Regulations causes damage, including death or personal injury, a civil claim for breach of duty will lie. This is in addition to any action in negligence which may be available in relation to the construction of the building. (Note that this section is not yet operative.)

Defective products

Where a person is injured by using a defective product and is looking for some legal redress, there can be considerable overlap between the law of contract and the law of tort. If the injured person purchased the product himself, then he may sue the seller under the Sale of Goods Act 1979 if there has been a breach of any of the implied terms relating to reasonable fitness for purpose and merchantable quality. Moreover, in a consumer transaction, the seller cannot exclude or limit his liability for breach of these implied terms, because of the provisions of the Unfair Contract Terms Act 1977. In exceptional cases a buyer of defective goods may also have some limited contractual rights against the manufacturer, where there is a guarantee in operation. This 'contract route' to gain legal redress is limited to persons who can prove that they bought the goods, so it cannot assist a person who receives the goods as a present, or who is injured when using borrowed goods. Moreover, it is rather inefficient, in the sense that it may set in motion a chain of legal actions – buyer v. seller, seller v. wholesaler, wholesaler v. importer, importer v. manufacturer. Several costly actions may thus be necessary to lay liability at the door of the manufacturer. Moreover, the 'contract route' relies on suing a retailer who owes a strict liability, who will be liable whether he is at fault or not. This does nothing to ensnare the manufacturer, who is the person best placed to remedy such faults for the future, and who could redistribute his losses much more widely if made liable for the defective product.

The 'tort route' for damages in respect of defective products finds its origins in *Donoghue v. Stevenson*, where the defective product was contaminated ginger beer. It was consumed by a friend of the purchaser. The friend had no contractual rights. The House of Lords recognised in that case that a manufacturer owed a duty to take reasonable care to the ultimate consumer of his product where he could foresee injury and it was unlikely that there would be any intermediate examination of the goods. Of course, under this rule, the range of people who can sue is potentially much wider and the manufacturer's liability is not strict. He owes a duty to take reasonable care. The plaintiff will bear the burden of proving negligence against the manufacturer. That may not prove easy, although the plaintiff may be able to rely on the *res ipsa loquitur* principle. A plaintiff's claim may be defeated or reduced if the manufacturer proves that the plaintiff was contributorily negligent, e.g. by failing to follow the instructions issued with the product. And of course, a plaintiff needs to show that he suffered harm of the right type. In an action for negligence, we have already seen that the harm must normally be physical harm, such as personal injury or damage to property. A plaintiff will not usually succeed if he has suffered mere economic loss. But earlier discussions in the area of negligence have already focused on the fine dividing line between physical injury and economic loss. In some cases, there has been a suggestion that a plaintiff can recover for economic loss e.g. *Junior Books Ltd v. Veitchi Co. Ltd*; but that case turned on a peculiarly proximate relationship between the parties which is not usually likely to exist between a manufacturer and a consumer.

Thus the tort and contract routes can both be seen to be problematical. This area is now also governed by legislative controls. This is particularly important as there are inevitable policy decisions to be taken into account. Moreover, English law has had to come into line with the European Community which issued a directive in 1985 requiring member states to harmonize their rules on product liability. This has been achieved by the Consumer Protection Act 1987 which imposes strict liabilities which cannot be excluded or limited, contractually or otherwise (s.7) The Act provides that a producer of defective products is liable for any damage caused by the defect (s.2). The terms 'producer', 'product' and 'defect' are all defined by the Act.

The producer is defined by s.1 as the person who manufactured the product; or in the case of a substance which has been won or extracted, the producer is the person who won or extracted it; or in the case of a product where its essential characteristics are due to an industrial or other process being carried out, the person who carried out the process.

A product, defined by s.1, means any goods or electricity, and includes a product which is comprised in another product as a component part.

The Act recognizes that it may be easy to identify the person who sold goods but not so easy to establish who is the producer. This problem is met by s.2(3), under which a supplier of a product is liable if the plaintiff asks the supplier within a reasonable time of damage occurring to identify the producer, in circumstances where it is not reasonably practicable for the plaintiff to identify the producer, and the supplier fails to satisfy the request within a reasonable time.

A defect in a product is defined by s.3. There is a defect if the safety of the product is not such as persons generally are entitled to expect. In determining what persons generally are entitled to expect, a court could take account of:

1 The manner in which, and purposes for which, the product has been marketed, and any instructions for use, or warnings in relation to the use of the product.
2 What might reasonably be expected to be done with, or in relation to, the product.
3 The time when the product was supplied by its producer to another.

Nothing in this section is to be taken to infer that a product is defective merely because a later issued product adheres to an even higher safety standard. The factors specifically listed in s.3 are not necessarily exhaustive. In determining whether a product is defective a court is bound to take account of a balance which needs to be struck between manufacturing a product with some deficiencies, and the cost of eliminating those deficiencies. If that cost is so great, it may not be reasonable. The type of product will no doubt also be relevant when weighing up such a balance. Any cost may be considered necessary when manufacturing toys for very young children. Conversely, a drug with known adverse side effects may well still be better than no drug at all.

Where a producer is sued in respect of a defective product, s.4 provides that it is a defence for him to show (amongst other things) that at the relevant time (usually when the producer supplied the product to another) the state of scientific and technical knowledge was not such that producers could have been expected to discover the defect. This is often described as 'the state of the art' defence. It is thought to be vital if technical and scientific innovation is not to be discouraged. It was one aspect of the Directive where member states had some choice about whether to incorporate such a defence.

In order to sustain a claim under the Act, a plaintiff would need to prove damage. This is defined by s.5 as including death or personal injury or any loss or damage to any property including land. It expressly excludes loss or damage to the product itself. The property lost or damaged must be property intended for private use or consumption. Where the harm to property is valued at less than £275, no claim lies, but this restriction does not operate where the damage is personal injury.

The Act provides rights which are in addition to existing common law rights. Section 2 specifically states that it is without prejudice to any liability arising otherwise than by virtue of the Act. This could be relevant in cases involving pure economic loss. The Act places an embargo on recovery for such loss but cases on the common law rules of negligence may develop differently. (See Junior Books v. Veitchi.)

An action under the 1987 Act is obviously advantageous to a plaintiff because the burden of proof is primarily on the manufacturer.

Vicarious liability

The word 'vicarious' means 'in place of another person', or 'in substitution for the proper person'. A rule has emerged in tort that an employer is vicariously liable for torts of his employees committed in the course of their employment. The rule is one of policy. Its importance is that is ensures that an injured person can sue the employer instead of suing the employee. The employer is likely to have greater financial resources, and may have taken out insurance against such claims. There is no particularly satisfactory justification for the existence of the rule, although it is often said that an employer profits from his employee's work and should, therefore, bear the risk of it. The two main criteria for the operation of the rule are:

1   The person who commits the tort must be an employee. This, however, can be misleading, as there are a number of important situations in which an employer will also be vicariously liable for the torts of an independent contractor.
2   The employee must commit the tort in the course of employment.

The course of the employment

There is no single test to determine when an employee is in the course of his employment. The decisions of the courts tend to turn on the individual facts of the case. Certain situations seem definitely to be covered.

1   Torts committed while the employee is doing what he is employed to do. For example, a man employed to drive a bus does so negligently and injures a pedestrian.
2   Torts committed while the employee is doing what he is employed to do, but doing it in a manner forbidden by his employers. For example, a petrol tanker driver is forbidden by his employers to smoke while making deliveries. He disobeys this order and causes an explosion which injures a passer-by.
3   Torts committed while the employee is doing what he is employed to do, but doing this in a criminal manner. For example, a solicitor's clerk employed to advise clients, fraudulently advises the client to transfer property to him.
4   Torts committed while the employee is doing acts which are reasonably incidental to his work. For example, an employee opens

his office window for ventilation and in doing so negligently knocks a potted plant out of the window onto a passer-by below.

5   Torts committed while the employee is acting in an emergency for the protection of his employer's person or property, when his actions would normally be outside the scope of his employment. For example, an employee negligently moves a vehicle which he has no authority to drive, but which he reasonably fears is about to be damaged in a fire.

Where the employee's behaviour has amounted to a 'frolic of his own', the employer will not be vicariously liable. Reported cases cover the bus conductress who decides to drive the bus, the delivery driver who varies his proper route to visit a friend, and the garage attendant who assaults a customer with whom he has had an argument. In all of these cases, there is (at least temporarily) no course of employment.

The rule of vicarious liability is often said to be one of the distinguishing features of an employer/employee relationship. Generally, an employer is not vicariously liable for the torts of an independent contractor. If I enagage a builder to build me a house, he is liable for any acts of trespass or negligence he may commit, but I am not. However, in some cases either the liability imposed is strict, or the duties owed by a person are so onerous that there can be no delegation to someone else. Then the employer is liable in addition to the contractor. Although these are often spoken of as examples of vicarious liability, it is more appropriate to regard them as examples of an employer continuing to be personally liable. This can arise in the following situations:

1   When the employer is negligent in choosing the contractor, he remains personally liable. For example, an occupier might need repair work of a technical nature undertaken on his premises. He knows that the work involves electrical rewiring and yet he appoints an 'odd-job-man' with no training or expertise in this sort of work. The job is not properly done and causes a lawful visitor to the premises to receive a severe electric shock. The occupier would be in breach of his duty under the Occupiers' Liability Act 1957 and could not plead the benefit of s.2(4) of the Act, because he has not taken reasonable steps to satisfy himself that the contractor was competent.

2   When the liability of the employer is strict (e.g. as in the tort of *Rylands v. Fletcher*) and can occur even if he has taken reasonable care, the employer is liable whether he commits the tort personally or through an independent contractor.

3   When the employer undertakes a particularly hazardous activity,

especially when it is on or near the highway, he is liable for torts committed personally or by his independent contractor. In one case, a heavy lamp suspended over a footpath fell into disrepair. The employer was held liable when a passer-by was injured by the activities of the contractor called in to repair it. In another case, a contractor was engaged to thaw out frozen pipes and chose to use a blow-lamp. The employer was held vicariously liable when a fire broke out as a result of the contractor's negligence.

4 When the employer authorizes or instructs the contractor to do something involving the commission of a tort, he remains liable. When a gas company engaged a contractor to dig up part of a street over which they had no such authority, the gas company was held liable when a passer-by fell over a heap of earth left by the contractor.

Contractors' acts of collateral negligence

Even in the above cases where both employer and contractor are laible, the former will not be held responsible for the contractor's collateral acts of negligence. In other words, an employer will only be liable if the risk of harm arises from the work itself, rather that the negligent performance of the work. For example, if an employer engages a competent contractor to install replacement frames on windows overlooking the highway, he will be liable if injury to a passer-by is caused by the glass being knocked out of the old windows (injury due to the work itself) but he will not be liable if the injury is caused by a workman negligently dropping his hammer (injury caused by the performance of the work).

10

Health and safety

The background to legislation

The following comment from a report published by the Health and Safety Executive on safety in the construction industry sets the scene for the problems of accident prevention in the industry:

> Construction management has to contend with a number of problems which vary enormously from site to site during the life of the site – climate, regional attitudes, geology, the time of year, the type of contract, the scale of the job, the methods of payment, the type of employment, the rapid turnover of labour. There is also the very complex problem of the relationship between a main contractor and an ever-changing group of sub-contractors. All these factors affect management in all its aspects, including the management of safety.

For a long time the law has played a part in controlling how employers must 'manage' safety. Acts of Parliament laying down duties and standards in specific working places date back to 1802. The earliest rules related to the employment of the very young in the mills, where the particular evil was the importing of large numbers of pauper children and engaging them in appalling working conditions. The procedure of making rules to control specific workplaces was established, and it will be seen that this became one of the worst features of the safety legislation.

With the pattern set, whenever a new loophole, crisis or new hazardous work area was discovered, special rules would be made to cover the situation. The end result has been piecemeal legislation covering mines, factories, offices and shops, agriculture and so on, culminating in a series of specific workplaces each governed by its own Act of Parliament. The Acts were not sufficiently detailed in themselves to cover every conceivable situation, so they all had various sets of regulations (delegated legislation) made under them. The Factories Act 1961 alone has more than 200 sets of regulations made by virtue of its authority.

The main aim of the safety legislation was to establish standards and duties for the workplaces covered. Failure to abide by the prescribed standards and duties would lead to employers being prosecuted and fined. By operating in this way the rules could, therefore, be seen to fulfil an accident prevention role. When an employer's breach of duty led to a workman being injured the various Acts were interpreted by the courts as giving the injured workman the right to sue for compensation.

The defects in the system of piecemeal legislation ultimately led to new thinking on health and safety – implemented by the passing of the Health and Safety at Work etc. Act 1974. Although the intention is for this Act to replace all previous specific legislation, this process will take time. Currently the 1974 Act must, therefore, be read in conjunction with all the earlier Acts and Regulations.

About 1000 people are killed at work annually and about half a million suffer injury as a result of accidents at work. Over 20 million working days are lost each year because of industrial accidents and diseases. The number of fatal accidents in the building industry is reducing. The principal cause of non-fatal accidents in the industry is falls. In 1905 57 per cent of accidents were attributable to falls and disappointingly that figure still stood at 54 per cent at the start of 1980. Diseases caused by work processes include skin diseases and cancers, pneumoconiosis and asbestosis, hearing impairment, bursitis and disorders of muscles, tendons and joints.

The health and safety question can be seen to have three dimensions:

1 *The point of view of an injured employee* – he will want to know the answer to several questions. Should he report the accident? Can he get compensation? Is his employer insured? Will he get state benefits? Does it matter that he was partly to blame?

2 *The point of view of the employer* – he will want to know whether he will be prosecuted? Will his insurance premiums be increased? Will the employee claim damages? Should he alter existing safety arrangements?

3 *The point of view of the state* – here the issues will include the cost of health care for the injured person, lost productivity, the cost of state benefits and whether there are any lessons to be learnt for

future safety policy. The answers to some of these questions come from the interaction of:

- The employer's duty in common law to take reasonable care for the safety of his employee. This is concerned exclusively with compensation.
- The employer's duties imposed by various specific Acts and Regulations e.g. Factories Act 1961, Construction (Working Places) Regulations 1966. These Acts and Regulations are concerned with accident prevention and compensation.
- The general duties imposed upon employers, employees, the self-employed and others under the Health and Safety at Work etc. Act 1974, which are concerned with accident prevention.
- The rules governing the Industrial Injuries Scheme, which is part of the system of social security and primarily concerned with compensation.

The Robens Report

At present, the 1974 Act has to operate side by side with the old Acts and Regulations but eventually these will be repealed. The Act was based on recommendations contained in a report on safety and health at work (The Robens Report). That report found the following major defects in the pre-1974 situation:

1 There was too much law. The sheer mass of rules, far from advancing the cause of safety, had sometimes reached the point of being counter-productive. The system relied too much on state regulation.
2 The rules themselves were badly structured, and written in a style which made them almost unintelligible to those who should be operating within them. The sheer mass of rules made it virtually impossible to keep everything up to date.
3 Because of the piecemeal way the rules developed, they were administered in a fragmented way. There were nine sets of statutes under the control of five separate government departments, administered by seven different inspectorates, as well as by local authorities. Much time could be spent arguing who should enforce the different rules.
4 The drawbacks of the system led to a feeling of apathy about safety questions amongst workers. Indeed the Robens Report thought apathy was the greatest single factor contributing to accidents at work. It was considered important to foster safety awareness and

awaken the same degree of interest and concern in safety issues as in industrial relations.

5   Emphasis on particular workplaces meant that many other places had no specific statutory coverage, and as a result some 5 million employees enjoyed no statutory protective rules.

The question of compensation for accidents was not within the terms of reference of the Robens Committee, but it is interesting to note that they found:

1   The possibility of a civil claim for damages had an inhibiting and distorting effect on accident prevention.
2   So far as insurance against liability was concerned, negligent employers appeared to be no worse off than careful employers.
3   There should be a thorough review of the system of compensation for accidents. (That review occurred when a Royal Commission was subsequently appointed to look into the issue, its report being published in 1978. However, it recommended no change in the compensation system for work-based accidents.)

The Health and Safety Commission

It is worth remembering that safety is not just an issue affecting those in employment. The general public is awakened to safety issues from time to time when a major disaster occurs such as the Kings Cross tube station fire in 1987. At such a time, there are often demands for safety standards to be improved, and a public inquiry (held by virtue of s.14 of HSWA 1974) may highlight changes that are necessary. The government has overall responsibility for introducing legislation to promote health and safety, and several of its departments, such as Transport and the Environment, will see this as a significant part of their work. Other organizations (e.g. the Royal Society for the Prevention of Accidents) exist to promote health and safety, and although their work may be more general, it can have useful implications for health and safety in employment.

The most significant organization, the Health and Safety Commission, was established by the Act in 1974. It has up to nine members, who are required by the Act to be representative of employers, trade unions, local authorities and other bodies, such as RoSPA, concerned with health and safety. The role of the Commission is to undertake, by whatever means it considers appropriate, to secure the health, safety and welfare of people at work, and to protect other people from risk to their health and safety created by work activities. The Commission may carry out research, provide training, disseminate information and advice, and submit proposals to the Minister for new regulations.

The Commission's accident investigation or inquiry role is significant, as it tends to have a high public profile and creates significant pressure for change or some government action. An investigation is less formal than an inquiry, so whereas the latter is the proper method to adopt in the Kings Cross situation, an investigation may be more appropriate for, say, a serious accident at a fairground. The person appointed to conduct an inquiry is given formal powers to compel the attendance of those he requires to be present. Inquiries are usually held in public and may well involve visits to the site.

One major initiative of the Health and Safety Commission has been to establish advisory committees on issues such as major hazards, nuclear safety and toxic substances, as well as industry-based advisory committees designed to promote the health and safety of workers in a particular industry. One example is the Construction Industry Advisory Committee. This kind of specialist committee can play an important role in assisting the Commission in tasks such as drawing up guidance. For instance, the booklet *Managing Health and Safety in Construction* (HMSO 1987) was drawn up in consultation with the Construction Industry Advisory Committee.

The most significant development which resulted from the establishment of the Health and Safety Commission was the new unified focus for safety issues and policy-making, which had previously been lacking. The Commission operates on a day-to-day basis through the Health and Safety Executive, which is the enforcing authority. Some enforcement duties are allocated to local authorities, and to avoid duplication between Health and Safety Executive inspection and local authority inspection, some types of premises e.g. shops, catering establishments and offices, have been specifically allocated as the responsibility of the local authorities. However, local authorities do *not* inspect their own offices! That task is performed by health and safety inspectors.

The Health and Safety at Work etc. Act 1974

The 1974 Act adopted the recommendations of the Robens Report, placing emphasis on greater involvement and self-regulation rather than reliance on state regulation. The Act provides the framework of a new system, and under this 'umbrella' new codes of practice will be created. As this happens, the intention is that old Acts and Regulations will gradually be repealed.

The main objectives of the Act are set out in s.1:

1 To secure the health, safety and welfare of persons at work.
2 To protect persons other than persons at work against risks to health and safety arising out of work activities.
3 To control the keeping and use of dangerous substances.
4 To control the emission of noxious and offensive substances.

To achieve these objectives, the Act lays general duties on employers (s.2), employees (s.7), the self-employed (s.3) occupiers of workplaces (s.4) and manufacturers and suppliers (s.6).

Duties owed by the employer – sections 2 and 3.

So far as is reasonably practicable, an employer must ensure the health, safety and welfare of his employees at work. This broad generalist approach is certainly a remarkable contrast with the detailed format previously adopted by safety Acts and Regulations. Perhaps unnerved by the 'baldness' of the duty, the Act goes on to spell out its nature more specifically. The employer must (so far as is reasonably practicable):

1 Provide and maintain plant and systems which are safe and without risk to health.
2 Make proper arrangements for the safe handling, storage, use and transport of articles and substances.
3 Provide necessary information, training, instruction and supervision.
4 Maintain the place of work and access to it so that it is safe and without risk to health.
5 Provide and maintain a safe and adequate working environment.

The Act does not define the terms 'health', 'safety' or 'welfare' nor the phrase 'so far as is reasonably practicable'. The latter phrase is familiar to the lawyer, because it is also used to qualify certain duties created by the Factories Act 1961. For example, s.28 of that Act provides that floors and stairs must, so far as is reasonably practicable, be kept free from obstruction. The meaning of this phrase has been judicially considered and has a narrower meaning than 'physically possible'. It implies that: 'A computation must be made in which the quantum of risk is placed on one scale and the sacrifice involved in the measures necessary in averting the risk is placed on the other. If the risk is insignificant in relation to the sacrifice, the defendants discharge the onus on them.' The following case provides an illustration. As a result of an accident at work, the Health and Safety Inspector issued an Improvement Notice, requiring a dairy to provide protective footwear free of charge to all employees involved in operating hydraulic trolley-jacks. The employer successfully appealed against the notice. The expense of providing the footwear free of charge was disproportionate to the risk to the employees. The dairy's existing arrangements, whereby employees could buy the footwear at cost price and pay by instalments, were adequate to satisfy the firm's duty to secure its employees' safety so far as was reasonably practicable (*Associated Dairies v. Hartley*).

Nothing in the Act allows these duties to be used as the basis for a claim for compensation. The sanctions for their enforcement are criminal. However, an injured workman would be able to proceed against the employer under ordinary negligence principles.

Section 2(3) provides that an employer must prepare and, when necessary, revise a written statement of his general policy with regard to health and safety, and he must bring the statement to the notice of his employees. The introduction of such written policy statements is seen as an important application of the ideas about greater involvement and self-regulation expressed in the Robens Report. If employees are to be involved, they must know what the safety policy is. The Act gives no guidance on the form or content of the safety policy. This will naturally vary with the size and type of organization and the specific hazards involved. The lack of a model form is sensible, as it compels employers to think positively about safety problems. Failure to abide by the rule about issuing a safety policy is an offence usually punishable by a fine.

Section 3 imposes on employers and self-employed persons a duty to conduct their undertakings in such a way as to ensure, as far as is reasonably practicable, that persons not in their employment who may be affected are not exposed to risks to their health and safety. This section is a valuable protection for members of the public but an unusual application of it can be seen in *R. v. Swan Hunter Shipbuilders Ltd*. In that case a fire broke out on board a ship being built by Swan Hunter. In one part of the ship the fire became particularly intense because a sub-contractor had left an oxygen hose there. Swan Hunter was aware of the dangers of using oxygen equipment, particularly because oxygen enrichment could occur in confined spaces. In order to alert its own employees to this danger, Swan's had distributed a booklet to them, setting out practical safety rules. These booklets were not given to all sub-contractors as a matter of course. As a result of the fire, eight men died. Swan Hunter was convicted of a breach of its duties to provide a safe system of work and to provide information and instruction (s.2). It was *also* convicted of a breach of its duty under s.3. By not providing information to non-employees, Swan Hunter had failed to ensure that persons not in its employment were not exposed to risk to their health.

Duties laid on controllers of premises (s.4)

Section 4 imposes duties on controllers of premises, where the premises are used by persons who are not employees, and where those persons may use plant or substances provided there for their use. A frequently quoted example of such premises is a coin-operated dry cleaners. Here, the controller must take such measures as are reasonable to ensure that the premises, plant and substances are safe and without risk to health so far as is reasonably practicable. (This is the criminal law provision corresponding with an occupier's duties at civil law under the Occupiers' Liability Act 1957.)

Section 4 can also be significant where a site is in the control of the main contractor. That site will be used by sub-contractors and their employees, i.e. people who are not employees of the main contractor. In one case a prosecution was brought in London under s.4. The employee of a sub-contractor was driving a small dumper truck out of a service lift when the lift suddenly rose as he was half way out. The driver was killed when he became trapped between the dumper truck and the lift shaft. The tragedy could have been avoided if the interlock on the lift had not been jammed with pieces of timber, thus tricking the machine into believing that the lift gates were shut. The main contractor was fined £1,000.

Duties laid on manufacturers and suppliers (s.6)

These duties are regarded as among the most important methods of securing an improvement in safety standards at work. Generally, manufacturers or suppliers of any article or substance for use at work must, so far as is reasonably practicable:

1 Ensure that the article or substance is safe and without risk to health when properly used.
2 Carry out such tests and examinations as are necessary to achieve (1) above.
3 Take such steps as are necessary to ensure that adequate information is available about how to use the article or substance, so that when properly used, it is safe and without risk to health.

These duties allow faults and defects to be traced back to their source, and prosecutions can be brought against persons with the ability to remedy them. The effect of s.6 is not to absolve the employer from his duties, but it is recognized that the power of the employer to do much is often limited. These duties do not create any new civil liability. Any civil proceedings must be brought under ordinary negligence rules. However, the possibility to prosecute under s.6 is a significant increase in the scope of the inspectorate's power. Note also that similar duties are imposed on designers, importers, erectors and installers.

Duties laid on employees (s.7)

Under the old Acts and Regulations duties were placed directly on employees, and this section merely extends an old principle. The duties which an employee owes while at work are:

1 To take reasonable care for his own health and safety.
2 To take reasonable care for the health and safety of others affected by his acts or omissions at work.
3 To cooperate with the employer where necessary to enable the employer to fulfil his duties.

As with the other duties under the Act, s.7 cannot give rise to a civil claim for compensation but an offending employee can be prosecuted. Employees are most likely to be prosecuted in those cases where the employer has fully complied with his duties. The most notable feature about prosecutions brought against employees is that fines tend to be smaller than those imposed on employers, although the maximum fine in the Magistrates Court is £1,000. In a case brought against two nurses under s.7, where they had put an elderly patient into a scalding bath without testing the water, and the patient had died as a result of the accident, both were fined £1,000.

Although s.7 relates specifically to employees, they could also, with others, be prosecuted under s.8 which provides that no person shall intentionally or recklessly interfere with, or misuse, anything provided under the Act for health and safety purposes.

Safety representatives

In safety matters, the Robens Report considered that management and employees had an 'identity of interest' which should lead to 'participation in working out solutions'. Indeed they found evidence in some working situations of existing participation by employees, e.g. the representatives appointed by coalminers to inspect mines. Many firms and organizations had also established voluntary safety committees before 1974. This voluntary effort needed statutory support, and the

1974 Act permits regulations to be made providing for the appointment of safety representatives and for the establishment of safety committees. Such regulations have been in force since 1978 and provide for recognized trade unions to appoint safety representatives from amongst the employees. Generally, representatives must have been employed for two years by the employer or have two years' experience in similar employment. The main tasks of the representative are:

1   To be consulted on safety matters.
2   To inspect plant and premises, usually at three monthly intervals but more often if there has been a change in work methods, or an accident.
3   To investigate complaints from employees with regard to health, safety and welfare.
4   To investigate potential hazards and dangerous occurrences.

To perform these functions effectively, the representative needs time and training. The Regulations provide for time off with pay for carrying out their responsibilities.

The appointment of safety representatives is a step designed to overcome the apathy on safety matters which had been identified by Robens. This can be regarded as enforcement through cooperation. Two points may be noted, however:

1   The representatives have no obvious 'teeth' for enforcement. Given that they are appointed by recognized trade unions, it could be argued that any necessary 'teeth' would be the usual forms of industrial pressure or action. If this is what is envisaged, it seems to contradict the idea of a 'common interest' in safety matters.
2   By limiting the power to appoint safety representatives to recognized trade unions, no statutory machinery exists to appoint representatives in non-unionized areas of employment. Presumably, employees in these areas are to be left to 'flourish' in the state of apathy which the Robens Report identified. The initiative in these cases may need to come from management.

Safety committees

Regulations made under the Act provide for the establishment of safety committees if the employer receives a request in writing from two safety representatives. Once a committee is established, s.2 lays down that it should keep health and safety measures under review. The recommendation about health and safety committees is that they should not be given any other functions or responsibilities. There are no prescribed rules about membership, but the make-up of the committee, and the seniority of the management representatives chosen to sit on it may well give a good indication of a firm's general attitude to safety questions!

One useful function which a safety committee can fulfil is to monitor the advice available which is disseminated by bodies like the Health and Safety Executive. That advice can then be pursued and applied more specifically to the particular work situation. For example, in demolition work, an area notorious for the number and seriousness of accidents, the committee might consider the Executive's guidance notes, and then recommend to the employer that he should adopt a policy of drawing up a 'written methods statement' for each demolition job. This would focus the employer's attention on the hazards of the particular job to be undertaken (e.g. the presence of asbestos, unusual structures, toxic chemicals, safe access for work to be carried out at height, dust levels, and the need for protective clothing). If this is prepared after a site visit and at tender stage, it will allow the contractor to tender at a price level which takes account of doing the job safely.

By monitoring all the reports and advice available, the safety committee can also play a useful role in alerting employers to wider health and safety issues. Again, taking demolition as the example, it may be thought that the hazards are all too obvious. But this type of work may be even more hazardous than conventional construction work because of hidden dangers. It may seemingly have been fungal spores which caused severe pulmonary illness in Lord Caernarvon and some of his team who had excavated the tomb of Tutankhamun. Indeed, the illness was referred to as the 'curse of the Pharaohs'! Some old buildings could present similar hazards, calling for breathing equipment or protective clothing.

It should be remembered that the inspectors employed by the Health and Safety Executive have always seen advice giving as one of their key functions, and a safety committee can act as an impetus to the employer to take the benefit of their advice.

Enforcement of the act

A system of inspectors for the enforcement of safety legislation has existed for more than 150 years. Indeed it is the oldest established inspectorate in the world. With the establishment of the Health and Safety Executive, all inspectors have been brought together under one umbrella, but there are still different branches of the inspectorate. The factory inspectorate, which has responsibility for construction, is by far the largest branch. Its inspectors are responsible for almost half a million sets of premises, and the focus of their work has been dramatically broadened by the 1974 Act. In one of their publications for young people who may be contemplating a career with the inspectorate, they say:

> As well as gaining an awareness and understanding of the practical problems that industry faces, a Factory Inspector must be able to deal firmly and diplomatically with a wide range of people. Many situations will require delicate handling and the successful inspector is one who is able to adapt his approach and meet the needs of the situation without losing sight of his main objective – an improvement in health and safety conditions. The Factory Inspector has to be conversant with a wide range of technical issues, ranging from the nature of toxic chemicals to the techniques for guarding a whole range of machinery. He must also have a thorough understanding of health and safety law, as well as having the tact and diplomacy to deal with the sensitive issues that arise from time to time.

Training for new inspectors is partly 'on the job' and partly by formal training courses. A warrant is issued immediately to a new inspector. This is his authority to act. It specifies the powers conferred on him and he must produce it on request when seeking to exercise those powers.

Although inspectors have always had power to prosecute, there has been internal conflict over their role, which they have seen to be the improvement of standards of safety, rather than the mere enforcement of the law. Indeed, the time and effort needed to mount a prosecution was often felt to be wasted because of the low level of fines imposed. The inspectorate was fragmented with separate inspectors for factories, mines and quarries etc. Valuable time was often wasted making routine inspections of places where there was no great danger, leaving insufficient time to concentrate on places where there were real hazards. In its analysis of the problem of enforcement and the inspectorate, the Robens Report found that:

1 There should be a unified inspectorate.
2 The principal objective of the inspectorate should be to give impartial advice to industry.
3 The services of the inspectorate should be more selectively used foregoing the system of routine visits.
4 Where sanctions needed to be used by inspectors, the penalties imposed should be more severe.
5 A range of alternative procedures should be available to inspectors,

allowing them to use sanctions which were immediate and constructive.

These proposals were implemented by the Act, and the scope of an
inspector's powers is now set out in s.20. To enable him to perform his
duties effectively, he may:

1 Enter premises (if necessary with a constable) taking necessary
   equipment with him.
2 Make investigations and examinations.
3 If necessary, order the premises to be left undisturbed.
4 Take photographs and measurements or recordings, and if necessary take away samples.
5 Question persons whom he believes can give him information
   relating to his investigation.
6 Inspect records, accident books, test certificates etc.

When establishing how his time can best be spent, an inspector
involved in the construction industry might prioritize as follows:

1 Investigating fatal accidents and large incidents.
2 Visiting demolition sites and sites where steel erection is taking
   place. This is seen as particularly important, not only because of
   the high level of accidents, but also because these may involve
   examples of employers using untrained employees.
3 Investigating any site involving asbestos. This takes a high priority
   because of public perceptions of likely harm.
4 Investigating non-fatal accidents, where there has been a breach of
   law.
5 Investigating complaints from the general public. Very few of these
   come from trade unions. Some come from groups such as parents
   who are worried about an adjacent building site. Others come from
   rival contractors, possibly disgruntled that they failed to get the
   job!

Each year, the inspectorate focuses on one particular type of
inspection, for instance roofing or transport. This is seen as an
important part of their preventative role. The inspectors also lay
considerable stress on their instruction role and point to guidance
notes issued e.g. on use of ladders, or demolition practice. These
guidance notes are less formal than codes of practice, of which there
are very few. Ironically, codes and guidance are not always popular
with 'customers' who actually seem to prefer strict regulations!

Most inspectors emphasize that, by and large, they get a good
reception from employers, who accept how wide the powers of the

inspector are. This may be due in part to their training in the skills necessary to present new ideas and persuade people to make changes in their working practices. The inspectors deal with people from the shop floor and people at director level, with back-street garages and multinational corporations. In all these dealings, they hope to advise and persuade. Often the threat of action by an inspector is the only 'enforcement' necessary.

If that fails, or the situation otherwise merits it, an inspector may use the powers granted by ss.21 and 22 to serve either an improvement notice or a prohibition notice. The advantage of both of these notices is that they can be issued by the inspector immediately.

Improvement notices (s.21)

The inspector may discover a breach of HSWA 1974 or the old Acts and Regulations and decide to serve an improvement notice on the person in breach. This notice will set out the breach of duty which the inspector thinks is occurring, specify the Act or Regulation in question, and give the inspector's reasons for his opinion. The notice will also set out the time limit for correcting the breach, the matters to be put right and the way in which this is to be done.

The earliest date which an inspector can set for compliance is twenty-one days after service of the notice. This is to allow time for an appeal to be lodged but it creates the biggest drawback about improvement notices – it means that it is impossible to get something done immediately. This can sometimes undermine the inspector's authority. Take the example of a site with no welfare hut. This is certainly not likely to be a situation warranting the use of a prohibition notice, but if the inspector serves an improvement notice, the employer can continue to 'cock a snook' for the next twenty-one days.

There is a right of appeal against the notice:

- Against the time limit imposed.
- Against the substance of the notice.

The effect of lodging an appeal is to suspend the operation of the improvement notice. On appeal, which is heard by the Industrial Tribunal, the notice may be affirmed cancelled or modified. The most frequent modification is an extension of the time limit. There must be proper grounds for an appeal. Mere lack of finance to carry out the improvements is doomed to failure as an excuse. Similarly, arguments that there has never been an accident, that the employees have not complained, or that the breach is trivial, have not found favour with tribunals.

Prohibition notices (s.22)

This type of notice can be served when activities being carried on involve a risk of serious personal injury. Unlike an improvement notice, no specific breach of the Acts or Regulations need be specified, but the inspector must give reasons to support his decision. The notice directs that the activities in question must stop until matters have been remedied. One significant difference about a prohibition notice is that lodging an appeal does *not* suspend its operation. The repercussions of a prohibition notice are serious for an employer, as his business may be brought to a standstill. In consequence, these appeals are usually heard as a matter of urgency.

Anyone served with either variety of notice who fails to comply with it commits an offence for which he may be prosecuted. As well as imposing a fine, the court may order him to attend to the matters specified in the notice.

Prosecutions (ss.33–42)

The two types of notices already mentioned may not be considered appropriate by the inspector. His knowledge of an employer's past record may convince him that immediate prosecution is necessary. Prior to 1974, proceedings were always summary in the Magistrates Courts, and the levels of fines tended to be quite low. The Act has now created the possibility of summary proceedings in the Magistrates Court or proceedings on indictment in the Crown Court.

Prosecutions in the Magistrates Courts must be brought within six months of the date of the offence, but there is no time limit if a case is tried on indictment. In the Magistrates Court, the inspector will conduct the prosecution himself. Commonly, the charge may be failing to comply with s.2 of the 1974 Act. On summary conviction, the employer can expect to be fined up to £1,000 in respect of each offence. If he is charged with contravening a prohibition notice, he can also be fined £100 per day in respect of continuing offences. In addition to imposing a fine, the court may order the employer to take specific steps to remedy the matter. Breach of such an order is punishable by a fine of up to £100 per day.

Where the prosecution is brought on indictment in the Crown Court, the court has the power to impose unlimited fines and in certain circumstances can also impose a term of imprisonment not exceeding two years.

Prosecutions are only brought in extreme cases. In any one year, less than 1000 employers may be prosecuted, whereas in excess of

15,000 prohibition and improvement notices will be issued. In an industry where more people are killed each year than in all the rest of manufacturing industry, weapons such as notices and prosecution form a useful part of the inspector's tools.

The Factories Act 1961

It has already been seen that the Health and Safety at Work etc. Act 1974 provides a framework which will eventually operate with new Codes of Practice and Regulations. Until the intended changes are completed, the Health and Safety Executive created by the Act is also responsible for enforcement of the old Acts and regulations, which remain in force. The Factories Act 1961 is a useful model serving to show the distinction between the old format and the new approach. It is also the parent Act under which important Regulations for the construction industry derive their authority.

The duties created by the Factories Act 1961 and the Regulations made under it have been interpreted to give rise to both criminal and civil liability, with the result that the provisions have been the subject of much judicial interpretation. The civil action is in respect of breach of statutory duty.

What is a factory?

It is not surprising that the Robens Report did not like the existing system of legislation for specific places when the committee members encountered the definition of a factory! It covers almost two pages and has ten sub-sections. Moreover, it is recognized that the main definition is neither adequate nor exhaustive, because s.175 of the Factories Act 1961 also lists as factories an assortment of places, in case they do not fall within the general definition. Basically to constitute a factory there must be:

1 Premises,
2 in which persons are employed,
3 in manual labour,
4 for a variety of listed purposes (e.g. making articles, altering articles, adapting articles for sale),
5 where the work is carried on by way of trade or for purposes of gain,
6 where the employer has the right of access or control.

The definition can produce some odd results, e.g. a florist's shop, where the back part was curtained off and flowers were made into wreaths and bouquets. The front part of the premises was a shop and the back part was a factory. This breakdown of premises into parts which are covered by different statutory requirements can occur frequently. For example, a factory is also likely to have parts which are offices, and these will be covered by the Offices, Shops and Railway Premises Act 1963.

Once it is established that the place is a factory, the duties owed in those premises fall under three main headings: health, safety and welfare. Generally, the duties are owed by the 'occupier'. This term is not defined, but in most cases the occupier will be the employer.

Health provisions cover cleanliness, overcrowding, temperature, ventilation, lighting, drainage and sanitary conveniences.

Safety provisions cover fencing of machinery, safe places of work and safe means of access to them and fire escapes. The fencing provisions require that prime movers, transmission machinery and other dangerous parts of machinery must be securely fenced while in motion or in use. The problems of interpretation of these rules are obvious. What are dangerous parts of machinery? What does 'securely fenced' mean? When is a machine in motion or in use?

Welfare provisions cover washing and sitting facilities, first aid, accommodation for clothing and provision of drinking water. Many of these duties are duplicated by more detailed provisions in the Construction Regulations.

Construction regulations

The vast range of workplaces and working situations covered by the Factories Act 1961 means that the rules, though detailed, cannot be very specific. Each working situation will tend to have hazards peculiar to it. In the construction industry statistics show that many accidents are caused by falls – from ladders, scaffolds, platforms, or roofs – or by materials falling. Another significant cause of accidents, sometimes fatal, is the use of lifting equipment and machinery. Significant numbers of less serious accidents occur when employees step on, or strike against, objects. There is extra danger for workers in the industry when excavation and tunnelling takes place. To take account of these special risks, there are several sets of Regulations in the construction industry:

- Construction (General Provisions) Regulations 1961.
- Construction (Lifting Operations) Regulations 1961.
- Construction (Working Places) Regulations 1966.
- Construction (Health and Welfare) Regulations 1966.

These Regulations are made by the Secretary of State for Employ-ment under powers granted by the Factories Act 1961. In any situation covered by the Regulations, an employer will owe duties under the Health and Safety at Work Act 1974, the Factories Act 1961 and the Regulations. The same breach of duty could, therefore, constitute an offence under all of these different provisions.

General provisions regulations

These Regulations apply whenever there are building operations or works of engineering construction. The two terms are used in all the sets of Regulations and their definitions are contained in the Factories Act 1961.

'Building operations' means the construction, structural alteration, repair or maintenance of a building (including repainting, redeco-ration and external cleaning of the structure), the demolition of a building and the preparation for, and laying the foundations of, an intended building.

'Works of engineering construction' means the construction of railway lines or sidings or the construction, structural alteration or repair or demolition of things such as docks, harbours, tunnels, bridges, viaducts, reservoirs, pipelines, sewers or gas holders.

Where more than twenty persons are employed, the Regulations require the appointment of safety supervisors, whose duties include promoting safe conduct of the work generally. These supervisors are a specialized example of the use of safety representatives well before the 1974 Act took effect.

The Regulations principally cover:

1   Excavations, shafts and tunnels.
2   Coffer dams and caissons.
3   Use of explosives.
4   Work in dangerous or unhealthy atmospheres.
5   Dangers connected with transport.
6   Demolition.
7   Miscellaneous protections, e.g. fencing, protection from falling materials, lighting, or lifting excessive weights.

The duties are imposed on contractors and employers of workmen, and their nature varies according to the form of words used. For example, a strict duty is imposed by the regulation that 'Explosives shall not be handled or used except by, or under the immediate control, of a competent person . . . ' Compare 'In any excavation, shaft or tunnel where there is reason to apprehend danger to persons employed therein from rising water, there shall be provided, so far as is reasonably practicable, means to enable such persons to reach positions of safety'. In the latter case the duty is qualified.

Lifting Operations Regulations 1961

These are also made by the Secretary of State to apply in building operations and works of engineering construction. The rules cover:

1 Lifting appliances – these must be of good mechanical construction, sound material, adequate strength and free from patent defect, properly maintained, and inspected at least once a week by a competent person who must make a report in the prescribed form. The rules go on to deal with the support and anchoring of the appliance, with safe working loads, and the testing and certification of appliances.
2 Chains, ropes and lifting gear.
3 Hoists.
4 Carrying people on lifting appliances.
5 Secureness of loads.
6 Keeping of records.

Again, the strictness of the duty depends on the exact words used e.g. 'no crane which has any timber structural member shall be used', imposes a strict duty, whereas 'Where reasonably practicable, the cabin shall when in use during the cold weather be adequately heated by suitable means', imposes a qualified duty.

The Working Places Regulations 1966

Scaffolding is one of the principal matters covered by these Regulations. The accident statistics for the industry show that a high proportion of accidents and deaths involve scaffolding, and the importance of the Regulations will be obvious. Their scope again includes building operations and works of engineering construction. Among the duties imposed are:

1 Providing safe and suitable access to places of work so far as is reasonably practicable.
2 Providing scaffolds or ladders where work cannot be safely done from the ground or from another part of the building.
3 Erecting and dismantling scaffolding under the supervision of a competent person.
4 Providing scaffolds of good construction, suitable and sound

material, and adequate strength for their purpose. The timber used
for the scaffolds must be of suitable quality in good condition.

5   Properly maintaining the scaffolds and ensuring that they are
stable.
6   Special duties providing for sling scaffolds, suspended scaffolds,
cantilever scaffolds, bosun's chairs etc.
7   A number of duties relating to working platforms, gangways and
runs. These should be closely boarded, planked or plated with
material of specified thickness and width resting on sufficient
supports and if the boarding projects at an end, precautions should
be taken to prevent tipping.
8   Duties with regard to guard rails and toe-boards.
9   Duties with regard to the construction, maintenance and use of
ladders.
10 Duties relating to work on sloping roofs.
11 Where there is special risk of workmen falling, duties with regard
to safety nets and safety belts.

The Health and Welfare Regulations 1966

The main duties under these Regulations relate to matters such as:

1   First aid equipment and training in first aid treatment.
2   Shelters and accommodation for clothing and taking meals.
3   Washing facilities and sanitary conveniences.
4   Protective clothing for persons required to continue working in bad
weather.

It is undoubtedly the case that all of the rules stated above will be of
little effect without proper attention by employers and employees to
safety questions. The reports of the Health and Safety Executive
indicate that accidents are more frequent in smaller firms, which may
take a less positive interest in safety. Motivating employees to be
safety conscious is an especially difficult problem if the workplace is
constantly changing and at some distant location, making constant
supervision impossible. One suggestion of the Executive may have
some impact. Clients about to engage a contractor are advised not only
to satisfy themselves about his technical and financial ability to do the
job, but also to enquire into the contractor's health and safety record!

Compensation for injuries at work

Where a workman is injured or is killed in an accident at work, he or
his dependants may wish to sue for damages. Damages are only

available where an employee can show that the employer was in some way at fault. Generally, this means that the employee must prove the tort of negligence. Although negligence is still developing as a tort, the example of the duty owed by an employer to take reasonable care for the safety of his employees was recognized very early. Not only may the injured employee be able to sue in negligence, he may also have a claim for damages for breach of statutory duty. Negligence and breach of statutory duty are considered in detail in the chapter dealing with tort. Apart from claims for damages, the injured employee may also be entitled to disablement benefits under the Industrial Injuries Scheme. He may be entitled to benefits under his own private insurance arrangements, or from his trade union.

When the court is considering a claim for damages from an employee, it will expect the employer to have taken reasonable care, given the state of knowledge and recognized practice in particular industries and trades. An employer will be expected to keep abreast of developing knowledge. The duties owed are not absolute so the employer must weigh up the risks involved and set these against the effectiveness of precautions he could take, bearing in mind the cost and inconvenience of taking those precautions.

An employer owes the duty to take reasonable care to all of his employees as individuals. Where some of his employees are inexperienced or do not easily understand English, or are newly recruited, he may have to take more precautions in their case than for other workmen. However, the courts have said that they do not see the relationship of employer and employee as that of nurse and imbecile child!

The employer's duty to take reasonable care has been analysed regularly by the courts and they have been inclined to break down the duty into a number of broad heads:

- A duty to provide reasonably safe plant, equipment and premises
- A duty to provide reasonably safe fellow workers.
- A duty to provide a reasonably safe system of work.

In all of these aspects the duty is on-going. A safe system of work, once introduced, must be regularly checked and monitored. It may need to be changed to meet new standards created by new knowledge.

An employer is in breach of his duty if he fails to take reasonable care. The duty is not absolute; he does not guarantee an employee's safety. It will be for the injured employee to prove negligence. In some cases this will be admitted by the employer and the subsequent court action will concern itself only with the measure of damages. The employer may seek to defend himself by pleading that the employee was partly to blame – contributory negligence. If that plea is successful, it will operate to reduce the damages payable by that proportion which the employee is found to be at fault.

Inevitably, employers have insurance cover to provide for the damages in such cases. Large sums may be awarded to the employee, but that is not, in itself, a particular reason for an employer wanting to improve his accident record. The employer may be embarrassed by the publicity given to the case but more often than not, potential civil claims by employees may encourage the retention of bad practices, as the employer may not want to change his practices in case such steps are seen as an admission of negligence.

11
Land law

Classification of property

Land is one of a number of kinds of property which can be owned, so it is useful to establish the meaning of the word 'property' and then to attempt to classify types of property. When considering sale of goods we saw that the word 'property' was used in the special sense of 'ownership'. The more general meaning of the word is, simply, anything capable of being owned.

The various categories of property are so diverse (e.g. land, jewellery, cars, stocks and shares, patents, money) that it is not surprising that the law has needed to develop different rules for each type to cover buying, selling or other transfer. Of course, if you buy a loaf of bread, it can be handed over to you. The same is not true when you buy land. A transaction involving land may be far more complex, especially when several people may have different rights over the same property at the same time. A person may own a house in which a tenant is currently living. The house may be mortgaged to a building society, and the owner may have leased shooting and fishing rights on the land and granted rights of way. This is a simple example but it serves to illustrate why the rules relating to land can be complex.

Obvious ways to divide property of all types are into things which are movable or immovable, or things which are tangible or intangible. Unfortunately, English law has not used either of these classifications, but instead divides all property into that which is real and that which is personal. This might be simple, if real property consisted of land, and personal property was everything else. But real property consists only of freehold interests in land, so (for historical reasons) leasehold interests are classed as personal property. As the terms 'real' and 'personal' do not conjure up as clear a picture of what they cover as the other classifications, it is interesting to note the derivation of the names. Historically, English law has always given preferential treatment to land and interests in land. If a person had his freehold land wrongfully taken from him the law would ensure that he could recover it by means of a 'real' action. If any other type of property was wrongfully taken from him the law merely allowed him to make a claim for damages against the wrongdoer, by means of 'personal' action. So property came to be classified according to the type of court action needed to protect it, which accounts for the anomalous classification of leasehold interests in land.

What is land?

Land is the surface of the earth, the airspace above it and the ground below. An owner of land could expect the law to protect his interests if someone unlawfully tunnelled under the land. However, Acts of Parliament limit a landowner's rights in this respect. Certain mining and mineral rights have been granted by statute to public corporations e.g. coal mining rights to British Coal, formerly the NCB.

As for the airspace above the surface of the earth, it used to be assumed that the landowner owned the space up to the heavens. This rather romantic idea has now been restricted by cases such as *Bernstein v. Skyviews and General Ltd* where it was held that an owner owns only as much of the airspace above his land as is reasonably necessary for his ordinary use or enjoyment of the land. In that case, a firm specializing in aerial photography flew over the plaintiff's house to photograph it. This act was held not to constitute a trespass, given the height at which the aeroplane flew. Most normal aircraft activity is excused under the Civil Aviation Act 1949, which precludes actions for nuisance or trespass if the aircraft flies over at a reasonable height.

It is difficult to think of airspace as being a valuable commodity but it may have significant commercial worth. For example, it may be possible to rent out space for erection of an advertising hoarding. The commercial value of airspace was at stake in a case, *Woollerton and Wilson Ltd v. Richard Costain Ltd* where a builder was using a tower crane. The arm of the crane swung over adjacent land, trespassing to the owner's airspace. The builder had not sought permission for this activity. When it became clear that he was trespassing, he offered to pay a weekly sum to the landowner. The landowner obviously thought he could hold out for more. However, his greed was 'rewarded' when the court granted him an injunction to prevent the builder using the crane, but its operation was postponed for several months, by which time the need for the crane had disappeared! An injunction was granted with immediate effect in similar circumstances in *Anchor Brewhouse Developments Ltd v. Berkley House Ltd*.

Is it clear that the law now sees some limit on the extent to which land extends into the air. The precise limit will depend on the type of land and the sort of use to which it could be reasonably expected to be put. An owner of a grouse moor may need a considerably greater height of air than the owner of a suburban bungalow where the only likely use for airspace will be for the erection of a TV aerial.

On the surface of land there are likely to be structures such as houses or factories. Buildings form part of the land, and so too do fixtures. A fixture is something on, or attached to, the land for its improvement, which is then regarded as forming part of it, e.g. a garden gate, rose bushes, a dry-stone wall. The item in question need not be permanently fixed. Compare a dry-stone wall and a pile of stones in a builder's yard; the wall is a fixture but the pile of stones retains its character as 'goods'. The distinction is important because the dry-stone wall is real property and the pile of stones is personal property. In that example, the point may not seem very significant. But suppose there is a dispute over a valuable tapestry fixed to battens on a wall. If the owner dies, and in his will, leaves his real property to X and his personal property to Y, naturally Y will be keen to show that the tapestry is not a 'fixture'.

The first stage in determining whether an item has become a fixture is to establish whether it is physically attached to the land. If so, that raises a presumption that the item has become a fixture. A fireplace mounted into a wall, or a statue which is cemented in place would be presumed to be fixtures. It is possible to rebut this presumption by showing that the item in question was fixed only to allow it to be enjoyed as a chattel and not for the improvement of the land as land. In the tapestry example given earlier, how else would it be possible to display and enjoy such an item without fixing it in some reasonably robust way appropriate to its considerable weight? By contrast, the dry-stone wall would clearly be regarded as a fixture, because it is there to improve the land, although unattached other than by its own weight.

These problems relating to fixtures are usually most relevant when buying and selling houses. They are an important issue on which the parties should reach agreement. Which items are to be included in the purchase price, and which does the vendor intend to remove? If such an agreement was always reached, there would be fewer disputes over greenhouses and sheds, TV aerials, dishwashers, carpets, and garden ornaments! In the absence of agreement, fixtures form part of the land and pass with the land to the purchaser.

Fixtures can also be an issue in relation to leases and tenancies. When a lease or tenancy comes to the end of its term, which items can the tenant remove? Generally, the tenant may remove tenant's fixtures which were attached to the property by him. These will vary according to whether the tenancy is commercial, agricultural or domestic. A domestic tenant is likely to want to take away items like fitted kitchen units and fitted bedroom furniture. Much may depend on whether they can be removed without substantially damaging the property. In commercial lettings some of the fixtures may be the tenant's plant and equipment, which he is entitled to take. Where a lease has run for some considerable time, the fixtures installed by a tenant may have substantially improved the property, e.g. the installation of air-conditioning or central heating. The tenant is entitled to make such improvements as long as they are not expressly forbidden by the terms of his lease. The tenant cannot take away such fixtures but, in strictly controlled circumstances, he may be eligible for compensation.

The question of whether an item has become a fixture can also be relevant if the landowner becomes insolvent. In the case of *Lyons Co v.London City Bank* the owner of chairs had hired them out to the owner of a hall. In order to comply with local bye-laws on safety, the hall owner had fixed the rows of chairs to the floor. He then became insolvent and the receiver was keen to show that the chairs formed part of the hall owner's land, as fixtures. The chair owner was equally keen to show that they were still his chattels, as he would be limited to a fairly hopeless claim for their value in the insolvency proceedings unless he could take the chairs back.

As ownership of land includes the surface and the ground below, a landowner might imagine the he owes everything in or on the land. The special position of mineral rights has already been mentioned, but it is also worth noting that any 'treasure trove' found on the land belongs to the Crown. Objects will only be held to be treasure trove if they consist in large part of gold or silver which have been deliberately hidden, and the true owner is unknown. If necessary, the coroner must hold an enquiry into findings of treasure trove. Items of value do get found from time to time, particularly where land was previously occupied by the Romans. Discoveries are more likely nowadays because of the use of metal detectors. In 1981 a farmer in Lincolnshire was approached by a man asking if he could go over the land with a metal detector. The farmer agreed but insisted that anything found should be brought to him. The man found several thousand Roman coins and a broken Roman pot but he handed over only the pot to the farmer! He was subsequently found out and convicted of theft. The farmer was allowed to keep the coins because they contained only trace amounts of silver and were held not to be treasure trove. (*Attorney General v. Overton*).

Wild animals living on a person's land are incapable of being owned. Once the animals are dead, they belong to the landowner, so a poacher should hand over the fruits of his labours! Percolating and flowing water cannot be owned, but a landowner is permitted to abstract quantities of it for uses connected with his land. Similarly, if his land is adjacent to a river, he may take water for domestic purposes but if he takes it for other purposes connected with the land, he must be careful to observe the rule that landowners further downstream are also entitled to the flow of the river unaltered in quantity and quality. If a landowner pollutes the water which he returns to the river he can be sued in nuisance.

Freehold and leasehold estates

People are often surprised to learn that in England individuals do not own land. All land belongs to the Crown, and the greatest interest which a landholder can own is the freehold interest or estate. This peculiarity of English law is explained by reference to history. When Willaim conquered England in 1066 he claimed all the land for himself, and then parcelled it out to his barons as a reward for their support. In return, they owed allegiance to him and undertook various services, some merely ceremonial, some valuable. This was the feudal system. It was not until 1925 that our legal system was rid of most of the consequences of feudalism. Modern land law is based on the Law of Property Act 1925.

As every landowner is technically a tenant of the Crown, it is common to refer to his interest in land as an 'estate'. The law recognizes two estates – freehold and leasehold. The major difference between a freehold and leasehold is the length of time for which the land will be held.

Freehold is the nearest equivalent to absolute ownership of land, and is more technically described as a 'fee simple absolute in possession'. By its very nature it is impossible to say how long an owner's estate will continue, but it could be enjoyed by him and his heirs in perpetuity.

By contrast, a leasehold is a 'term of years absolute'. This means that a landlord grants to a tenant exclusive possession of property which the tenant is to enjoy for a fixed period. If that period is quite short it is usual to call it a tenancy. Longer terms are usually referred to as leases, but there is no fixed rule.

Interests in land

The law must also make provision within the system for the many other rights and interests which can exist in or over a piece of land. For example, John may buy Blackacre, a farm with a house, farm buildings and 100 acres of land. He acquires the fee simple absolute in possession in Blackacre, a freehold interest. He then raises a loan, using the farm as security, with the Black Building Society. He sells the farm buildings separately to Anne. She intends to convert the buildings into a house, and for that purpose, John has granted her a right of way over his retained land, and the right to lay drains across his land to the main sewer. Anne also covenants that she will use the buildings only as a single private dwellinghouse and not for business purposes. The law recognises these various rights enjoyed by the Black Building Society and Anne over John's land. They are called *interest in land*. Some of these interests are recognized and enforceable in law. These are termed *legal interests*. Others are recognized only in equity – *equitable interests*. This distinction is important because it governs what steps should be taken, if any, to protect the interest in question.

The number of possible legal interests is restricted by s.1 of the Law of Property Act 1925. It recognizes only certain types of easements, rent charges, rights of entry and mortgages as being capable of being legal interests. Even these may not be so classified unless they are made by deed, and otherwise fulfil all the criteria set out in the Act. Any interest in land not legal by virtue of s.1 must necessarily be an equitable interest. The value of proving an interest to be a legal interest is that it is then enforceable against any subsequent purchaser of the land, whether the purchaser had notice of the interest or not. Thus, legal interests are very secure. Where the interest is classified as equitable, it may not be binding on a subsequent purchaser. In some circumstances, a purchaser can take the land free from the equitable interest.

Equitable interests thus create two problems. First, how is the holder of the equitable interest able to protect his rights and make sure they will bind a subsequent purchaser? Second, how is a purchaser to ensure that the land he is buying is not encumbered by numerous third party rights, by which he will be bound? The answer to these questions will depend in part on whether the land involved is registered or unregistered. This classification determines which system of conveyancing (the transfer of the title to the land) must be used.

With *registered land*, details regarding ownership and title to the land are all entered in a Register of Title lodged at the Land Registry. When the land is sold, all necessary checks are made by searching in the Register, which should contain the essential information about the land involved. With *unregistered land*, the details of ownership will have to be gleaned from checking the title deeds to the property. It was originally intended by the 1925 reforms that all land would speedily be brought into the registration system. However, the pace of compulsory registration of title to land has been very slow. As a consequence, the two systems of land transfer have had to operate side by side.

For a prospective purchaser of land, anxious to know if there are any equitable interests by which he will be bound, the way forward is determined by asking the question, is the land registered or unregistered?

Registered land

Registration is governed by the Land Registration Act 1925, which defines possible interests in registered land as 'registrable interests', 'minor interests', 'overriding interests', and 'registered charges'.

Registered interests are separately registered in their own right, and comprise the legal estates, i.e. the fee simple asbolute in possession and the term of years absolute.

Minor interests include equitable easements, restrictive covenants, estate contracts and interests of a beneficiary under a trust. They are entered on the register as restrictions, notices, cautions or inhibitions. As a general rule, a purchaser is bound by minor interests which appear on the register, and takes the land free of any minor interests which are not registered.

Overriding interests, as their name suggests, are not recorded in the register but nevertheless bind a subsequent purchaser of the land. It is a characteristic of this group of interests that they relate to matters which are best discovered by other kinds of checks, e.g. physical inspection of the land involved and enquiries directed to the persons in occupation there. Overriding interests can include legal leases for less than 21 years, and the rights of persons in actual occupation of the land.

Registered charges are the standard method of mortgaging registered land. They take effect as charges by way of legal mortgage, and once registered, the chargee (the lender) will be issued with a charge certificate. While the charge remains in effect, the charger (the borrower) must deposit his land certificate with the Land Registry. This effectively prevents him from having any further dealings with the land until the charge is redeemed.

Unregistered land

Legal estates and interests always bind a subsequent purchaser. Whether he is bound by equitable interests depends on their type. Some are listed as *land charges* and as such, details of them may be entered on to the Land Charges Register. If an equitable interest could be entered on the Register in this way but is not, it is not usually binding on a subsequent purchaser. If the equitable interest is registered as a land charge, then the purchaser will be bound by it whether he bothered to check the Land Charges Register or not.

If the equitable interest is not capable of registration as a land charge, its enforceability against a subsequent purchaser will depend on whether the purchaser had knowledge of the interest.

Formalities for the transfer of land

Any transaction for the sale or lease of land or any interest in land will involve two stages:

1   The agreement to buy and sell or lease – the contract stage.
2   The actual transfer of the legal title to the land – the conveyance stage.

The contract

Contracts for the sale or other disposition of any interest in land are now governed by s.2 of the Law of Property (Miscellaneous Provisions) Act 1989. Such contracts are now valid only if they are made in writing. The writing must embody all the terms agreed and it must be signed by both parties. These rules are considered in more detail on page 78.

The conveyance

Actual transfer of the legal title is required by law to be effected by means of a deed (s.52 Law of Property Act 1925).

Conveyancing

The term 'conveyancing' is used to denote the processes involved in the transfer of title to land. This work is usually undertaken by a solicitor. Once a purchaser has bought land, it would be an unpleasant surprise for him to learn that there were burdensome restrictive covenants over it, or that it is criss-crossed by rights of way, or that a deserted spouse of the seller has the legally protected right to go on occupying the house. Before any legally binding contract is made, it is usual to make *enquiries before contract*. The solicitor acting for the purchaser can then raise any questions, such as ownership of fences, or whether there have been previous disputes relating to the land. False information given at this stage could amount to a misrepresentation (see page 91).

The solicitor will also make 'local searches', to discover any plans for the neighbourhood which might have an adverse effect on the property in question, or its value. These local searches, made in registers maintained by the relevant local authority, might indicate the existence of a tree preservation order, or planning restrictions on the use of the land.

The Local Land Charges Act 1977 requires each local authority to keep a register of local land charges for its area. A local land charge falls into one of two categories:

1 A restriction imposed on the use of the land, e.g. planning permission which restricts the number of houses to be built on the land.
2 A financial charge imposed on land for work carried out by the local authority, e.g. where a road has been made up and the cost has been apportioned among the frontagers.

If the would-be purchaser is satisfied by his preliminary enquiries and searches, he may then wish to have a survey of the property carried out. This is not essential, but may be a prudent step. If the purchaser needs to raise money by a mortgage, the building society would usually insist on a structural survey. (See *Smith v. Eric S. Bush* on page 217 for an example involving a negligent survey.) If the survey is satisfactory, and raising any necessary finance presents no problems, it will then be safe to make a legally binding contract, in accordance with the rules set out above. The vendor must then show that he has the necessary title to the land which he has undertaken by the contract to transfer. Establishing the title to property varies according to whether the title is registered or unregistered.

The actual transfer of legal title takes place by deed, called a transfer in registered land, and a conveyance in unregistered land. Where the land is registered, the purchaser will need to complete his title by registering the transfer at the Land Registry. Only then does he become the legal owner. In transactions involving unregistered land, compulsory registration has now been introduced. The new owner will need to seek a first registration of title, and thereafter the land will be transfered as registered land in any subsequent transactions.

Leases

A lease is a grant of exclusive possession of land for a fixed period, e.g. a lease for 99 years, a tenancy for three years. It might seem difficult to establish what is the fixed period in a weekly or monthly tenancy, but the rule is that it is fixed according to how the rent is calculated. If the rent is quoted at £x per annum, that is a tenancy for a year. If the rent is £x monthly, it is a monthly tenancy. These tenancies are terminated by giving appropriate periods of notice.

A leaseholder only has the right to the land for the period of the lease, but of course, that may be a very long period. Leases for 99 years and 999 years are very common. At the end of every leasehold interest there is always a freehold, for when the lease expires, the land will revert to the freehold owner. As a lease nears the end of its life its value becomes significantly less.

As a leaseholder will have nothing when his lease runs out, that may raise the question why anyone would want to take a lease rather than buy a freehold estate. Commercial and personal considerations will inevitably play a part in such a decision. A businessman may need offices or premises in a very specific area where the only available property is leasehold. The need for the property may be very short term, or a person may lack the funds or the means of raising the funds to buy a freehold property. From the point of view of the freeholder, there may be significant advantages in granting leases rather then selling land outright. Take the example of a person developing land as a shopping arcade. If he sells all the units within it as freeholds, it will be quite difficult to impose positive obligations on freeholders so that the properties can be maintained in a uniform way and common areas kept in order. If he grants leases he can impose conditions more easily, and maintain a greater measure of control.

Types of lease

Leases may be either for a fixed term or periodic:

1 *Fixed-term lease e.g. for ten years* – both parties know at the outset the date of expiry of the lease and there is no need to serve notice to bring it to an end.
2 *Periodic lease or tenancy, e.g. weekly, monthly or quarterly* – the fixed period here is the week, month or quarter. If neither party gives notice to terminate the lease it goes on renewing itself weekly, monthly or quarterly, and will continue indefinitely until such notice is given. (Note that because of modern statutory protections the notice may not be allowed to take effect.) Generally, the

minimum period of notice is fixed according to the length of lease. So, in the case of a quarterly tenancy, at least a quarter's notice must be given. By Act of Parliament, longer and more protective periods of notice may be prescribed, e.g. where premises are let as a dwelling on a weekly tenancy, four weeks' notice is required to terminate.

Formalities for creating a lease

As a general rule, an agreement to grant a lease must be made in writing (s.2 Law of Property (Misc. Provisions) Act 1989) and the lease itself must be created by deed. However, where the lease is for less than three years, and is to take effect in possession, it may be created orally or in writing (s.54 Law of Property Act 1925).

Obligations of the parties to a lease

The obligations of the parties towards each other depend upon:

1   Any express terms of the agreement.
2   Any terms implied by common law.
3   Any obligations imposed by Act of Parliament.

Commonly a landlord and tenant need to know their respective rights and duties concerning:

1   The rent and the means of fixing the amount.
2   Repairs and maintenance.
3   Rights of the landlord to enter and inspect the premises.
4   Assignment of the lease, and sub-letting.
5   Insurance of the property.
6   Notice to terminate and security of tenure.

Nowadays the measure of statutory control in leases and tenancies is formidable, particularly in relation to rent, repairs and protection from eviction. The level of protection afforded depends on the type of tenancy, e.g. private or business.

Lease v. Licence

One of the results of increasing statutory protection and control is that landlords have sometimes wanted to find ways to enjoy profits from their land without creating a tenancy or lease. This has tended to give greater prominence to the licence. A licence is a permission to do something in relation to land which would otherwise amount to a trespass. A licence does not create any interest in the land itself. So, for example, if you visit the cinema, you have a contractual licence to be on the premises. If I give you permission to walk in my fields, you have a bare licence (i.e. you have given no consideration) to be there.

In practice, the critical difference between a lease and a licence is that the former gives a tenant certain statutory protections which do not exist for a mere licensee. In theory, the important difference is that a tenant enjoys an interest in land, a proprietory right which is capable of being binding on a purchaser, whereas a licensee merely enjoys a personal right enforceable against the licensor only.

Many of the cases involving licences have arisen in circumstances involving family arrangements. These cases have proved to be exceptionally difficult. In such arrangements, the parties often fail to make their intentions clear, yet proving intention to create a lease is critical. A typical example where it is hard to establish intention is *Hardwick v. Johnson*. A mother bought a house for her son and his new wife to live in. They agreed to pay her a monthly sum but it was never clear whether this was rent, or in repayment of the mortgage. The subject tended to cause great embarrassment when raised, so the true nature of the arrangement between the parties was never thrashed out. The son deserted the wife who by then had a small baby. Could the mother evict the daughter-in-law? It was held that the daughter-in-law had a licence, but could not be evicted for the time being.

Although these family arrangements can cause problems in relation to licences, it should be remembered that there are many commercial examples of the use of a licence which work perfectly well. For example, when a contractor takes over a site he is usually there by virtue of a licence, and not because he has any interest in the land itself.

The House of Lords has had the opportunity, in *Street v. Mountford* (1985), to consider how a licence may be used merely as a device to evade statutory controls. The agreement between the landlord and Mrs Mountford expressly stated that it was a licence agreement, and expressly indicated that it was outside the control of the Rent Acts. Nevertheless, Mrs Mountford applied to the Rent Officer to fix a fair rent. The landlord objected on the grounds that the Rent Officer had no jurisdiction. The House of Lords did not agree. They found that the reality of the situation was that Mrs Mountford had been granted exclusive possession, and it was matterless what the parties chose to call their relationship. In truth it was a lease. Some of the problems in this area may have been resolved by the introduction of short-hold tenancies.

Joint ownership

It is quite common for one person to share the ownership of land with another. Obvious examples are a husband and wife who buy a house, or parties who buy premises from which to run their business. The law recognizes two types of co-ownership:

- Joint tenancy.
- Tenancy in common.

With joint tenancy, the co-owners are regarded as an idivisible whole, owning the entire property as one, whereas in tenancy in common, the persons involved each own a share. This can be important if one of the co-owners dies. In a joint tenancy, the effect of death is to vest the deceased person's rights in the land in the surviving owners. If a house is owned in joint tenancy by a husband and wife (i.e. as joint tenants), and the husband dies, the wife is then absolutely entitled to the house. If a property is owned equally by four partners (i.e. as tenants in common), each is at liberty to dispose of his share, and if one dies that share may be inherited by someone other than the surviving partners.

One problem with a tenancy in common is that it could result in large numbers of people owning a share in the same piece of land. This would greatly complicate transfers or other transactions, so it is now provided that tenancies in common can only exist within a trust. The legal interest in the land must be vested in trustees, of whom there can be no more than four. Each of the persons entitled to a share will then hold an equitable interest.

If co-owners have not made it clear exactly how they intend to hold the land, rules exist to determine whether there is joint tenancy or a tenancy in common.

1 For a joint tenancy, the co-owners must be granted the same interest in the land. So if the land is given to A and B, they could be joint tenants, but if the land is given to A and B in shares of two-thirds and one-third respectively, they cannot be joint tenants.
2 For a joint tenancy, all co-owners must acquire their title under the same document.
3 For a joint tenancy, all co-owners must acquire their interest at the same time.
4 For either type of co-ownership each co-owner must be as much entitled as the others to possession of any part of the land.
5 If no answer is provided by these various tests, then it becomes necessary to look at the deed creating the co-ownership, to see if it makes clear which type of co-ownership is intended. A grant to A and B jointly is construed as a joint tenancy; a grant to A and B in

equal shares is construed as a tenancy in common. Words such as 'in equal shares', which indicate that owners are to take distinct shares in the property, are said to be words of severance.

6   Where none of the tests is conclusive there are some factual circumstances in which equity will favour a tenancy in common, because it is fairer. These includes cases where land is purchased by co-owners who have contributed in unequal shares, or as partnership property.

Even where these tests indicate that land is held as a joint tenancy it is possible for the parties to alter the arrangement in equity, by severing the joint tenancy. The simplest way to do this is for one tenant to serve notice in writing on the other joint tenants indicating that the server of the notice wishes to sever his share (s.36 Law of Property Act 1925). One example where this could be necessary is where the husband and wife have purchased property as joint tenants. If the marriage breaks down and one party leaves the other, the right of survivorship rule would continue to apply unless the joint tenancy is severed. If a spouse wants to preserve a 'share' in the matrimonial home, severance is a sensible step.

Rights and duties of owners of land

It is difficult to summarize the rights of a landowner. They certainly include the right to occupy the land without interference from others. (Interferences which the law will control include trespass and nuisance.) One important right of every landowner is a right of support for his land from adjacent pieces of land. Any withdrawal of such support, which causes the adjacent land to slip e.g. excavation during building work, may result in a claim for damages. The right of support is a natural right, existing because of the nature of the land itself. A right of support may, however, be acquired, in which case the right is called an easement.

An owner's duties in relation to his land include not only using it in a way which will not constitute a nuisance, but also complying with all the various statutory controls which now exist concerning land use. Significant amongst these are the planning laws contained principally in the Town and Country Planning Act 1990.

The controls on a landowner by statute range from restrictions on killing certain kinds of birds and animals on his land to positive obligations to repair dilapidated property. If an authority wishes to take an owner's land from him, it may be possible to do so under the rules of compulsory purchase. And rights of access may be reserved by statute e.g. for the creation of a long distance footpath. When the range of controls on a landowner is fully examined it is clear that the number of restrictions is far greater then the number of rights.

Easements and restrictive covenants

An easement is a right acquired to benefit one piece of land (e.g. a right of support for a building), which imposes a burden or restriction on another piece of land. The essential feature of easements is that they pass with the land. An example will illustrate how this works.

John owns a farm called East Farm, where one of his fields is inconveniently situated. He would like Bill, the owner of West Farm, to grant him more direct access to his field by a track over a West Farm field. Bill agrees to grant this right, and a price is agreed. Here one piece of land (East Farm) gets a benefit and the other piece of land (West Farm) is burdened. Because this is an easement, if either John or Bill sells his farm, the benefit or burden will pass to the next owner. Compare this with the situation where Bill merely grants John a licence to use the track. If Bill dies, whoever inherits his farm can then withdraw the permission.

Easements can take various forms. Examples of a right of way and a right of support for a building have already been given. Another example is the right to lay and maintain drains under a person's land. An easement is usually created by an express grant (e.g. when property is being sold, the deeds and documents may contain easements), but may be acquired by prescription. This means that the right can be shown to have been peacefully and openly exercised over a very long period without contradiction, when it can be assumed that a lawful grant has been made at some stage.

Restrictive covenants are undertakings to restrict the use of one piece of land so that other land will benefit. An example will show the meaning and operation of a restrictive covenant.

John owns a piece of land adjacent to his own house and garden, and he wants to sell it. Although the money it will realize is attractive to him, he wants to limit the uses to which that land can be put. He would accept its use for the erection of one house but not more, and he certainly does not want to see any trade or business being carried on there. He finds a buyer, Bill, who is prepared to buy the land subject to these restrictions. As part of their bargain, they covenant with each other (i.e. they agree between themselves) that Bill will use the land only for a single dwelling house which will not be used for purposes of trade or business. So far, this arrangement is personal between John and Bill. At a later date John wishes to sell his own house. Any prospective purchaser might be equally keen to see the same restrictions imposed on Bill. On normal contract principles Bill could argue that his agreement to these restrictions was with John, and should not benefit a later purchaser who was not a party to that agreement (the rule of privity of contract). However, when John extracted those promises from Bill, he did so in order to benefit his own land, and effectively this placed a burden or restriction on the use of Bill's land. Where the covenant 'touches and concerns' the land in this way, the benefits and burdens are said to 'run with the land' and in effect become a part of the land. Consequently, if John sells his land to Fred, Bill is under the same restrictions in relation to Fred as he was to John.

Naturally, if land is burdened with numerous restrictive covenants, e.g. not to keep animals, not to park caravans on the land, not to change the external appearance without approval, a prospective purchaser will be anxious to know about them. The covenants may well influence his decision to go ahead with the purchase or the price he is prepared to pay. Restrictive covenants are usually registrable under the land charges rules and Bill's covenant, in the example above, will be entered in the Register against his name by John. Registration is vital to achieve the maximum benefit from such covenants, and they are only binding on a person who has notice of them. If registered under the land charges system, a purchaser is deemed to have notice of the covenants, whether he searched in the Register or not.

Mortgages of land

The enduring quality of land makes it a valuable asset and a superior form of security when needing to raise money. The owner of the land who borrows against it will naturally want to continue to use and enjoy it, but the person lending the money must be given certain rights over the land in the event of the borrower defaulting on payment. These requirements are provided for in the rules governing legal mortgages.

The method of creating a mortgage depends on the type of interest which the landowner holds. If he has a freehold interest there are two possible ways:

1   By a charge by deed, expressed to be by way of legal mortgage.
2   By creating a lease (usually of 3000 years) in favour of the lender (the mortgagee), which provides for the lease to end once the mortgage is redeemed (i.e. the money is repaid), and which permits the borrower (mortgagor) to retain possession, allowing the mortgagee to take possession only on default.

Where the landowner has a leasehold interest (e.g. a lease for ninety-nine years), he can mortgage either by a charge by deed (as in 1 above) or by creating a sub-lease in favour of the mortgagee which is for a period shorter than the unexpired term of his own lease. He usually makes a sub-lease ten days shorter, which leaves it open to create second and subsequent mortgages. This possibility of other mortgages presupposes that the first mortgage is for the sum less than the full value of the property. No one is likely to grant a second or subsequent mortgage if the security provided by the property is exhausted, usually signified in layman's terms by the expression 'mortgaged up to the hilt'.

The rules ensure that a mortgagee has the necessary interest in the land for it to constitute effective security for the loan. They are reinforced by the rights granted to a lender if the borrower defaults. In extreme cases, a mortgagee may need to sell the property in order to realize his security. To enable him to do so, he may rely on:

1 *The right to take possession* – naturally, if a mortgagee has to sell, obtaining vacant possession of the property is a crucial first stage. He is effectively entitled to possession by virtue of the interest in the land granted to him by the mortgage itself, but he can only exercise this right through the court, i.e. a mortgagee must apply to the court for an order for possession.
2 *The right to foreclose the mortgage* – again this right is exercisable through the court. If an order is granted, its effect is somewhat drastic. It removes the right of a mortgagor to redeem his mortgage and vests the legal interest in the land in the mortgagee. In other words, the mortgagor loses all rights to the land. This is so extreme a result that it is unlikely that a court would make such an order. A mortgagee would normally be satisfied to exercise his right to sell.
3 *The right to sell* – the duty of a mortgagee when selling is to obtain the best possible price. He then pays himself what he is due and any surplus is used to discharge subsequent mortgages. If there is any money left, it is paid over to the mortgagor.

Naturally a purchaser of land must be careful to ensure that what he is buying is not the subject of an unredeemed mortgage. A legal mortgage, protected by depositing the title deeds to the land with the mortgagee, is not a registrable interest under the land charges system. However, the purchaser always needs to see the title deeds, and if they are not available, this will obviously suggest that they are being held by someone as security to protect his loan.

12

Planning law

Central and local planning responsibilities

If people are to enjoy and maintain a reasonable quality of life in the place where they live, then issues relating to planning and development should obviously concern them. The very words 'planning and development' suggest change, and the policies developed should aim to maintain and improve the environment as an attractive place to live and work.

Any coherent system of planning control is necessarily dependent on a proper administrative structure. The local government structure was established by the 1890s and the first Planning Act followed in 1909. The emphasis in that early Act was directed towards planning being used as a tool to secure better sanitary conditions but it introduced for the first time the important issues of 'amenity and convenience'. Early planning Acts were based on the idea of local councils preparing planning schemes to control land use in suburban areas. General control of land use was introduced in 1947, creating the modern system of planning law. The main principles are now contained in the Town and Country Planning Act 1990.

The overall structure for administering the rules on planning is headed by the Secretary of State for the Environment who controls the local planning authorities – county councils and district councils vested with planning responsibilities. County councils must draw up a 'structure plan', which is a policy statement concerning land use and the environmental implications for their area.

The concept of the structure plan was only introduced in 1968. Prior to that date there had been Development Plans, consisting of a map and written statement, containing the main proposals of the plan. The written statement would often be quite bald, with little or no supportive reasoning. The philosophy of the new structure plans is quite different in that they concern themselves much more extensively with implementing social and economic policies in relation to land use. A structure plan will only emerge after an extensive survey of the area, covering its size, the population and its distribution, transport and communications, and physical and economic characteristics. The county councils must consult with the district planning authorities within their area and the plan must be approved by the Secretary of State. Inevitably, there are likely to be persons or organizations who object to the structure plan. Adequate publicity must be given to the proposals, and the Secretary of State will only approve the plan once he has held an examination in public to hear objectors.

Once a plan is approved by the Secretary of State, changes within the area may cause a county council to wish to change it. Procedures are available to allow this to happen, subject to adequate safeguards and controls.

District planning authorities are charged with the responsibility of preparing local plans for their area, but of course this is not possible until a structure plan has been approved, as the local plan must be in general conformity with the structure plan. The local plan indicates in detail how the policies of the structure plan will be implemented in that area. Local plans do not need the Secretary of State's approval, but he has power to call in such a plan for approval. The plan can only be adopted once formal procedures have been implemented to publicize the plan, and invite and hear objections. The local authority is not obliged to alter its proposals to take account of objectors, but it may be asked to state its reasons, and this may be sufficient to determine the Secretary of State to call for the plan for his approval.

The local plan will be much more detailed than the structure plan and may relate to one small town or a small geographically identifiable area. It will contain proposals for development and land use, and measures for controlling traffic and improving the environment. It will seek to provide for acceptable levels of change, and will set down allocations of land for particular types of development. In terms of timescale, a local plain is probably geared to a ten-year span. Inevitably, any place or area cannot function in isolation from its surrounding area, and the cumulative effect of decisions taken by private individuals, local and national government, businesses and recreational organizations will all affect how a town, village or area develops.

Take the example of a small country town, supporting a local auction mart with a regular market day, where the town centre is congested and full of buildings of historic significance. A new by-pass opens and the town's one major industrial employer is booming and seeking to expand. It is obvious in such a case that a local plan will need to give thought to issues such as the availability of land for industrial purposes, provision of housing for key workers, expansion of parking facilities within the town and the growth of any tourist industry with attendant demands for accommodation and catering, while still adequately catering for long-established businesses like the auction mart.

Local plans should aim:

- To apply the strategic objectives of the structure plan and relate them to precise areas of land.
- To provide a well-reasoned framework for development control.
- To provide a detailed basis for coordinating development by various agencies.
- To bring detailed planning issues before the public.
- To ensure that planning decisions can be taken in full knowledge of local needs and possibilities.
- To focus opportunities for public and private investment.
- To examine particular social, economic and land use problems and to propose solutions.

The local plan will be especially useful when applications for planning permission are being dealt with.

It should be noted that the whole development plan system has been the subject of extensive recent review and some streamlining of the system can be expected from the Planning and Compensation Bill presently before Parliament.

Development

The key concept in planning control is development. It is defined by the 1990 Act, s. 55 as: 'The carrying out of building, engineering, mining or other operations in, on, over or under the land, or the making of any material change in the use of any building or other land'. If an activity comes within this definition, then as a broad general rule, planning permission is required. The usual way to seek planning permission is to apply to the local planning authority. However, there are instances where no individual planning permission is necessary. This may be because:

1 The operation planned is not within the meaning of the word 'development'.

2 The development is permitted within the terms of the General Development Order, so that no specific application need be made.

The definition of the term 'development' has two aspects – 'operations' and 'uses'. An operation results in changes to the physical form of the land which will have some degree of permanence. Use consists of the activities done in, or on, the land which do not change its physical form. Inevitably, the definition of development has given rise to much dispute and case law. This sometimes happens because a person goes ahead and does something which the local planning authority finds out about, and for which it considers that planning permission should have been obtained, e.g. the erection of a building. The planning authority may then serve an enforcement notice, ordering the building to be removed. The costs involved will usually spur the person who has erected the building to appeal.

The s.55 definition of development is further extended in the Act itself. 'Building' is defined to include any structure or erection, but does not include the plant and machinery within the building. 'Building operations' are defined to include: 'Rebuilding operations, structural alterations of, or additions to, buildings, and other operations normally undertaken by a person carrying on business as a builder'. This at first sight seems to be virtually all-embracing, but s.55 of the Act does say that development does *not* include: 'The carrying out of work for the maintenance, improvement or other alteration of any building, being works which affect only the interior of the building or which do not materially affect the external appearance of the building.'

It is not altogether clear where demolition work stands within the s.55 definition of development. It could be argued that this constitutes 'other operations on land' which would certainly result in the physical alteration of land. If it is within the definition, then planning permission is required. In some cases, where demolition is to take place, e.g. demolition of a building in a conservation area, permission would be required in any event under the 'listed building consent' procedure of the Act. Would planning permission be required too? It is not clear from the cases whether this would be necesary, but recommendations have been made that the legislation should make it clear that such work does require planning permission. In practice, it is not regarded as necessary by planning authorities.

Change of use

Only those changes of use which are 'material' require planning permission. Inevitably, what is material is a question of degree, but the Act aims to give some assistance by laying down certain specific instances of material change of use. These are:

1 Where a single dwelling house is converted into two or more separate dwellings.
2 Where there is to be a display of advertisements on any external part of a building not previously used for that purpose.
3 Where refuse or waste materials are to be deposited, including extending an existing tip.

If the change of use proposed is within the scope of what is permitted by the Use Classes Order, then there is no requirement to seek planning permission. The latest order is the Town and Country Planning (Use Classes) Order 1987. Where a person has obtained permission for one use and implemented that permission, he can then change the use of the land and buildings to any of the similar uses provided for by the order. So, for example, if permission was initially obtained to use premises as an art gallery, and that use was implemented, then those same premises can subsequently be used as a museum, public library, reading room, public hall, exhibition hall, day centre, educational institution or creche without the need to seek further permission. Previous permission to use premises as a casino would allow change of use to a cinema, concert hall, bingo hall, dance hall, swimming bath, skating rink or gymnasium, without further permission.

Of course, if the use for which permission was originally granted is not listed in the Use Classes Order, then its rules cannot assist and a normal planning application will be necessary. Again planning permission for the original use may have been subject to conditions which over-ride the provisions of the Use Classes Order. The order may permit a change of *use* without further permission but if the change of use requires new buildings, or alterations or extension to existing buildings, planning permission is still likely to be required.

Permission under the General Development Order 1988

Instead of seeking permission for development by applying to the local planning authority, there are cases, covered by the General Development Order made by the Secretary of State, where permission is automatically given for all classes of development set out in the order. Some commonly encountered examples of development which are permitted by the order include:

1 Development within the curtilage of a dwelling house. Where it is proposed to extend a dwelling house, then provided that the extension does not increase the overall size of the house by more than 15 per cent (10 per cent in the case of a terraced house) calculated by reference to cubic capacity, such development is permitted. There are other conditions to be satisfied, e.g. that the height of the building when extended must not exceed the height of the original dwelling house.

2 Construction of porches and garages, subject to size and height limitations.

3 Minor operations, e.g. gates, fences, walls, hard-standing for cars, installation of oil storage tanks.

4 Temporary buildings. Where building operations for which planning permission has been granted are in progress, this rule allows temporary buildings needed in connection with the building work such as site huts or workmen's lavatories to be erected. But they must be removed at the end of the building operations.

5 Temporary uses. Land can be used for any purpose for up to twenty-eight days each year. This rule would allow land to be used for an occasional agricultural show, or point-to-point, or as a site for a summer fete. The permission also covers the erection of movable structures (e.g. marquees) for these purposes. If the purpose is to hold a market, or motor racing or speed trials, or clay-pigeon shooting, the temporary use is limited to fourteen days each year.

6 Building or engineering operations required for agricultural purposes may be carried out on agricultural land, e.g. erection of barns and steadings. This permission is restricted in terms of size and height limitations, and distances from trunk or classified roads.

7 Additions to industrial buildings, limited in size and height.

It should be noted that permitted development under the General Development Order can only operate once. Other extensions to a property which have already occurred, even if validly covered by planning permission, may reduce or remove permitted development rights. Even if work looks as though it is covered by the General Development Order, the local planning authority may have made an 'Article 4 Direction'. Such directions are made in the interests of good planning in a particular area. The local planning authority will impose restrictions on development in that area, so that an application for permission must be made, even though it appears that permission already exists under the Order. There is likely to be an 'Article 4 Direction' if the place is a conservation area, or if a particular street has a special character or appearance. Landowners in such areas should have been served with a copy of the direction.

A further situation in which planning consent may be automatically granted is where a 'simplified planning zone' is established by a local planning authority. This is a new idea created by the Housing and Planning Act 1986 and as yet, it is impossible to judge what its impact will be. Within such zones, designated by a local planning authority only after extensive consultative processes, certain developments or classes of development will be permitted without the need for formal application. These simplified planning zones are likely to have particular significance in run-down industrial areas, but it could be argued that the greatest incentive for development in such areas is the type of inducement (e.g. no rates) which was previously available in enterprise zones. The mere relaxation of planning controls is not, in itself, likely to act as a significant inducement. The fact that no formal application need be made, and that no fee is payable are likely to be insignificant details to large developers.

It must be borne in mind that planning permission can do nothing to help in those cases where the type of development is prevented by a restrictive covenant, or where a tenant is precluded from carrying out the development in question by the express terms of his lease.

Making a planning application

One immediate advantage of development which is permitted under the General Development Order is that it costs the developer nothing to get his permission. Since 1980, fees have been introduced in respect of planning applications, and the level of these can be varied from time to time. Currently (1991), they range between £38 and £5,700, usually depending on the size of the development proposed. The fee for an application for permission for a single dwelling house would be £76; for other buildings exceeding a gross floor space of 75 sq. m, it is £76 for each 75 sq. m up to a maximum of £3,750; to carry out operations connected with exploratory drilling for oil or natural gas, it is £76 for each 0.1 hectare of the site area, subject to a maximum of £5,700. In the longer term, the Government intends to increase the fees to cover all of a local authority's development control costs.

Applications are made to the local planning authority, and may be made by anyone, whether or not he owns the land or any interest in it. The actual owner does not need to give his consent, but the applicant has to give notice of his application to anyone with a material interest in the land. The necessary forms are supplied by the local planning authority, and it may be sensible to appoint a surveyor or architect to make the application. A full application will require plans so that the site can be adequately indentified and the development proposals fully understood. Enagaging professional assistance may be costly, and at an early stage a developer may simply want to discover the attitude of the planning authority in principle to what is proposed. In such a case, an outline planning application is appropriate. A developer may still have to acquire the land and commission detailed plans, but he can then go ahead with more confidence in his business venture, armed with his outline permission. This is not usually the best way for private individuals to proceed, as the outline permission, if granted, must be followed by a second application for 'approval of reserved matters'.

Once an application has been submitted, with the correct number of copies and the appropriate fee, one copy will be placed in the planning register, which is a public document available for inspection by anyone. Depending on the nature of the proposed development, some or all of the following procedures may be followed:

1 The planning authority may need to consult with the highway authority or the housing authority or a parish council or the Ministry of Agriculture or the Department of the Environment. This latter consultation may be required if the development proposed would involve some radical departure from the local plan.
2 The planning authority may advertise the application in the local newspaper, or may notify owners or occupiers of adjoining land. This is particularly likely to happen where 'bad neighbour' development is proposed e.g. the construction of a public lavatory, applications for permission to use land as a scrapyard or cemetery, or the construction of buildings for use as a slaughterhouse.
3 The planning authority will have to refer the application direct to the Secretary of State if he has used his power to 'call in' the application. This is likely to happen only in the case of very large-scale, controversial development proposals.

The planning authority must now make a decision on the application before it. It will take account of structure and local plans, the views of any organizations it has consulted, objections received, and any other material considerations, which may in appropriate cases include the need within the area for development of this type. The authority should keep in mind the central government guidance, which is that a positive approach to planning applications should be adopted, and that permission should only be refused in order to protect the public interest. It has been said that planning laws are not concerned with the protection of the private interests of one individual against another.

A decision by the planning authority should be taken within eight weeks. That decision may be:

- Unconditional permission or approval.
- Conditional permission.
- Refusal of permission.

In the vast majority of cases permission is conditional. The conditions imposed can be whatever the planning authority 'thinks fit', so long as the authority acts reasonably and the conditions themselves are within the general spirit and objects of planning law. For instance, permission may be given only for a limited period, or subject to work being commenced within a particular period. Conditions may relate to the materials to be used, or the placing of a building on the site.

If planning permission is refused, or the applicant is aggrieved by the conditions imposed, he may appeal. Before considering an appeal it may be worthwhile negotiating with the planning authority. Its objections may possibly be overcome by design changes or the resiting of the proposed development. In such cases the renewed planning application will be exempt from a fee, as long as it is made within twelve months.

Appeals

An appeal must be lodged within six months of receiving the planning authority's decision. It may be an appeal against refusal of permission or an appeal against the imposition of conditions on the permission. There are two methods for dealing with appeals – written representations or public inquiry:

1 *Written representations* – this procedure can be used where both parties consent. It avoids the expense of an inquiry. Each side must provide the other with a full written statement of its case. Each then has the right to comment on the other's case. All the written material is put before an inspector, who may decide to make a site visit. This written representations procedure is used in the majority of cases.

2 *Public inquiry* – this will be conducted by an Inspector appointed by the Secretary of State. The Inspector makes the decision in the case, unless it is one of a limited class of appeals where only the Secretary of State may give the decision. The Inspector hears the appeal as if it had come to him at first instance. This can result in a case where permission has been granted subject to conditions now being refused permission altogether. Inquiries tend to be formal and legalistic. The Inspector is required to observe the rules of natural justice. He must conduct the inquiry fairly, giving both sides an adequate chance to present their case. The proceedings will usually

be held in public, and they give an opportunity to persons closely affected by the development to put their objections. Once the Inspector (or the Secretary of State in appropriate cases) has made his decision, he must communicate it, together with the reasons for the decision. His decision can only be challenged by applying to the High Court on a point of law to have the decision quashed.

Planning enforcement

The planning rules need to provide for those cases where development is carried without without valid permission, or where a developer breaches the conditions imposed on the permission. Breaches of the planning rules can come to light in a number of ways. Some are reported, often anonymously, by neighbours or persons affected by the development. Others become obvious when a subsequent permission is applied for. The planning officers are regularly out and about making site inspections and they tend to know what is going on and what has been authorized within their 'patch'. They liaise with the building inspectors, who have the opportunity to observe 'unauthorized' development in the course of their work. Breach of the rules is not a criminal offence as such. The planning authority uses an enforcement notice where some action is necessary.

It must be emphasized that where possible, the planning authority will seek to resolve matters without the need to resort to enforcement procedures. For example, the development may be of a type which would clearly have been permitted, if permission had been sought at the appropriate time. In such a case, the developer is encouraged to make a late application, which will be heard in the ordinary way by the planning authority. Steps short of enforcement procedures are to be introduced by the Planning and Compensation Bill 1991. Two new kinds of notice, a planning contravention order and a breach of condition notice, will assist planning officers to seek information and ensure compliance. Only as a last resort, when persuasion has failed, will an enforcement notice be issued. The notice must specify the alleged breach of the planning laws, and the steps which must now be taken to remedy the breach, together with the time limit for taking the necessary steps. The measures to be taken can vary considerably. For example, where a building has been erected without permission, at one extreme the step may consist of ordering it to be demolished, or at the other, may simply require some tree planting or landscaping to disguise the building.

A developer may appeal to the Secretary of State against an enforcement notice on a number of grounds, e.g. the matters specified in the notice do not constitute a breach of planning laws, or the time specified to take the necessary steps is unreasonably short. The appeal has the effect of suspending the enforcement notice until the appeal has been resolved. This means that the operation or change of use can go on as before until the appeal is resolved. That could be disastrous where, by allowing the operation to continue, it would be impossible to subsequently correct matters. In such circumstances it may be appropriate to issue a stop notice. Failure to comply with a stop notice is a criminal offence. If the enforcement notice is quashed on appeal, the local planning authority must compensate an owner or occupier of land for losses occasioned by the stop notice. This can include a contractor who has been held up on a site. In addition to the stop notice, the new rules in the Planning and Compensation Bill 1991 provide for a local planning authority to apply for an injunction to restrain any actual or apprehended breach of planning control.

If an enforcement notice is upheld on appeal, or if no appeal is made against it, then it must be complied with within the prescribed time limits. Non-compliance with an enforcement notice is a criminal offence, with a maximum fine of £1,000 on summary conviction and no limit on indictment. Moreover, in cases of non-compliance, the local planning authority may enter the land and carry out the necessary steps at the expense of the owner.

Planning and the preservation of amenity

A vital part of the planning process is the preservation and enhancement of amenity. That term is not defined by the planning legislation, but the dictionary defines it as 'pleasantness, as in situation and characteristics'. The ordinary planning rules can do much to preserve amenity, by refusing permission in appropriate cases, or attaching conditions to preserve or improve amenity in others. Additionally, certain specific forms of control are particularly geared to protect amenity.

Trees

Local planning authorities may make tree preservation orders in the interests of amenity. These may be designed to protect individual trees or areas of woodland. In such cases, once an order is made, permission must be sought to fell or lop a tree. If such permission is granted, the local planning authority will often require replacement planting. Ordinary planning permission may be granted subject to the preservation of trees on the site, or subject to the planting of additional trees.

Interference with protected trees is a criminal offence, punishable by a fine up to £1,000, or twice the value of the tree, whichever is the greater.

Buildings of special interest and conservation areas

Buildings of special interest are usually refered to as 'listed buildings'. They become listed by the Secretary of State after consultation with experts if they are of special architectural or historic interest. The buildings listed are often proposed to the Secretary of State by the local planning authority. The owner of the building cannot object to its listing. He may know nothing of a decision to list the building until he is notified by the local planning authority. The listing will also be registered in the local land charges register. The local planning authority may give six months protection to a building under a 'building preservation notice' while they initiate the procedures for listing with the Secretary of State.

If a building is listed, any work to alter or demolish it must have 'listed building consent'. If such consent is refused, the owner can then appeal and argue that the building should never have been listed. This argument is significant because the owner had no right initially to object to the listing. Many owners do not welcome listing of their property. Not only is the planning control much more rigorous, but it may also cause considerable loss if it was hoped to sell the building to realize its development value. This was the problem facing the parties in the case of *Amalgamated Investment Co Ltd v. John Walker and Sons Ltd* where a property with development potential was agreed to be sold for £1.7 million. The building on the land was listed before the sale went through, and the value of the land then slumped to £250,000! In exceptional cases, an owner may serve a 'listed building purchase notice' on the planning authority, but generally there is no compensation if listed building consent for development is withheld.

The concept of conservation areas stems from the Civic Amenities Act 1967. Prior to 1967 the emphasis was on the preservation of individual buildings, not areas. Local planning authorities are now required to determine those areas which are of special historical or architectural interest, where it is desirable to preserve or enhance their appearance. Effectively these are areas which are rich, or potentially rich, in listed buildings. Where an area is to be designated as a conservation area, the local planning authority must give notice in the local press, and enter appropriate notices in the land charges register.

When the local planning authority is considering designating a conservation area it will take account not only of individual buildings but groupings of buildings, their relationship to each other, and the quality and character of the space between buildings. The group of houses and shops in a marketplace of a small town may not be particularly worthy of note individually, but the overall impact of the area may be sufficently pleasing to warrant creating a conservation area. Naturally, owners within such an area might consider themselves to be weighed down by the extra obligations relating to development. District councils are empowered to give grants to owners of listed buildings for their repair and maintenance, which may go some way to redress the balance. New development within a conservation area is not forbidden, but it must be sympathetic to the general character of the area.

Advertisements

The Secretary of State can, by regulations, control the display of advertisements so far as it appears to be expedient in the interests of amenity or public safety. This is generally designed to control the display of outdoor advertising, which includes any model, sign, placard, board, notice, device or representation, whether illuminated or not. The definition is wide enough to cover nameplates on shops and professional premises, as well as road signs. The power of the planning authority relates to issues of amenity and public safety; it could not therefore refuse permission on grounds of social desirability.

Under Regulation 6 of the Control of Advertisements Regulations 1989 a number of advertisements may be displayed without express consent. These include functional advertisements of local authorities and statutory undertakers; nameplates for businesses or companies; and advertisements of local religious, cultural, political, social or recreational events. If there is no deemed consent under Regulation 6 planning permission is required.

Wasteland

Where a local planning authority considers that the amenity of an area is adversely affected by any vacant site or wasteland, it can serve a notice on the owner or occupier requiring him to take steps to remedy the condition on the land. Failure to comply is punishable by a fine and the local authority can then enter, carry out the necessary work, and charge the owner.

The Refuse Disposal (Amenity) Act 1978 also gives local planning authorities powers in relation to abandoned vehicles and dumped refuse, which may not strictly be within the law of planning but which are certainly important in the preservation of amenity.

Financial problems – compensation and betterment

When a planning decision has been made (e.g. to create a new motorway, or build a new airport runway) there will be owners of property adjacent to the development whose property needs to be acquired by compulsory purchase for the purposes of the development. For some owners the value of their property will be significantly reduced by the development, while for others the value of the property will be increased by the planning decision.

Local authorities and development corporations have power to acquire land compulsorily for planning purposes. In such a case the appropriate authority or corporation will have initiated the necessary legal steps to acquire the land. There are two situations, however, where a landowner can initiate proceedings to force the local authority to purchase his land:

1   *Purchase notices* – where planning permission has been refused or made subject to onerous conditions, an owner may argue that his land is incapable of reasonably beneficial use in its existing state. He may then serve a purchase notice on the local authority, requiring it to buy the property. Compensation is payable to the owner in the same way as it would be under an ordinary compulsory purchase order. This will only be effective if the adverse planning decision renders the land useless, not where it merely renders it less valuable.
2   *Blight notices* – where an owner is unable to sell his land at a fair market price because the prospect that it may be compulsorily purchased has rendered it virtually unsaleable, he may serve a blight notice on the appropriate public authority requiring it to buy his land. Compensation is again payable as a under a normal compulsory purchase order.

As a broad general rule, no compensation is payable merely because planning permission has been refused. Exceptionally, where a revocation or modification of planning permission results in an existing right being lost (e.g. where the owner of agricultural land could have erected a barn) compensation may be payable.

The problems of taxing betterment is a political issue and approaches to the question have varied according to the government of the day. Most recently this was achieved by the Development Land Tax Act 1976 but this has been abolished by the Conservative government.

13

Highways

Introduction

Even a short journey by road will serve to convince the traveller that the law relating to highways must be complex. Workmen are to be seen digging up portions of the road; part of the road is blocked off for repair; notices indicate the building of a new road; trees adjacent to the road have become a hazard with their overhanging branches; the road has a bad surface which needs repair; builders have deposited a skip and piles of sand and stones on the road by a building site; demonstrators have blocked the road with a march; animals have strayed on to the road; snow is making the road dangerous. Many of these incidents can cause annoyance and, more seriously, delay, injury or loss. Who will be responsible? Against whom can a complaint be made? When can damages be claimed? The answer to these questions can be learned from an analysis of highway law.

The first question to be posed is what is a highway? Simply, the answer is any portion of land over which the public has the right to pass. When it is remembered that many highways have existed for over 1000 years, and that the law on this subject has been developing for almost as long, this may explain some of the complexity. Most of the relevant statutory law on the point is now contained in the Highways Act 1980. The main aim of the Act was to bring together many rules previously contained in Highways Acts passed between 1959 and 1971 and in the Private Street Works Act 1961 but account was also taken of recommendations made by the Law Commission. The enormity of the subject can be grasped when it is seen that the Highways Act 1980 runs to 432 pages.

Although the mental picture which most people have of a highway is a busy road full of motor traffic, the term is far wider than that. Highways can be subdivided, and further definitions of some other common expressions will be useful:

1 *Footpath* – a highway over which the public have a right of way on foot only.
2 *Footway* – a part of a highway which is also a carriageway (see below) where the public have a right of way on foot only. A footway is what is commonly called the pavement at the side of a road.
3 *Carriageway* – a highway over which the public have a right of way for the passage of vehicles, i.e. what is commonly called a road.
4 *Bridleway* – a highway over which the public have a right of way on foot or on horseback.

Certain obvious questions arise in connection with highways:

- How does a highway come into existence?
- Who owns the highway?
- Who is responsible for the upkeep of the highway?

Acquisition and ownership of highways

There are two ways in which a highway can be created: by dedication or by statute.

Dedication

A highway can come into existence if the owner of the land concerned dedicates the right to cross it to the general public, which right is then accepted by the public actually using it. Dedication sounds like a very formal act, but in fact it can occur impliedly. Several points about dedication should be noted:

1 The owner of the land must intend to dedicate it as a highway. He shows such intention in the case where he makes a formal dedication, e.g. if he uses a formal document. Often, his intention will be implied from the circumstances, e.g. he knows people are passing and repassing over his land, and he takes none of the steps available to him to stop the creation of a highway (see below).
2 The highway must be dedicated to the public generally.
3 The person dedicating the land as a highway must be granting a right for all time. Effectively, therefore, only an outright owner of land can dedicate.

4   The right to pass and repass must be accepted, by the public actually using the highway.

Some assistance in proving the existence of a highway created by dedication is given by statute. Section 31 of the Highways Act 1980 provides that where a way has been enjoyed by the public as a right, without interruption for twenty years, then it is deemed to be dedicated as a highway unless the owner can prove that he did not intend to dedicate the way. The owner could best prove lack of intention to dedicate by showing that he had displayed notices to that effect, e.g. 'No public right of way', or 'This land is not dedicated as a public highway'.

The rule created by s.31 is important because it places responsibility on the owner to show that there is no highway, rather than on the public to show that there is. Even if a twenty-year period has not elapsed, it would still be open to a member of the public to try to prove the existence of a highway. It would then be necessary to prove that the owner intended to dedicate it. This might be possible, for example, by showing that the owner had allowed repairs to be undertaken by the highway authority. (Merely because a highway is acknowledged to exist by the landowner it does not necessarily follow that it is maintainable at public expense – see below.)

Creation of highways by Act of Parliament

The main rules are now consolidated in the Highways Act 1980, s.24. Under its provisions highway authorities can build highways including particular types of road (e.g. motorways where access and passage are restricted to certain classes of vehicle).

Who owns the highway?

Although the highway authority, when building new roads, may have acquired the land on which the highway is built, it is quite usual for the land under a highway to remain in the ownership of a private person, possibly the person who dedicates the highway. Often the land-owners on either side of a highway own the land to the centre line of the road. Naturally, the use to which they can put such land is very limited. At common law, owners did have rights, e.g. to tunnel under the land, but many of the common law rights have been eroded by controls in Acts of Parliament. Ownership of a highway may still be important, however, if it is one which is not maintainable at public expense (see below).

Upkeep of the highway

The position with regard to repair and maintenance of highways is more easily understood if a brief mention is made of the historical development of the rules. At common law (before the introduction of any statutory changes), the duty and expense of repair rested with parishes, of which there were originally more than 10,000. The drawbacks of such a fragmented system were obvious, especially once methods of communication and transport were quicker. Changes made by statutes gradually produced the result that 'highway authorities' were created with responsibility for repair and maintenance. Today the position is that highway authorities are either:

1　The Minister of Transport, or
2　County councils.

The responsibility of the Minister of Transport is for trunk roads, i.e. the principal roads constituting the national system of routes for through traffic in Great Britain. However, the work of repair and maintenance is commonly delegated to the county council as agents. The county councils are the highway authorities responsible for all other roads maintainable at public expense. In turn, repair work is commonly delegated by a county council to district councils.

Section 36 of the 1980 Act deals with the question of which highways are maintainable at public expense. Effectively, these are:

1　Those highways in existence before 1835.
2　Highways created since then which have been adopted by the highway authority. Adoption can occur in a number of ways, e.g. by the dedicator serving notice on the highway authority which is accepted within the terms of s.37, or by agreement (s.38). Most important, however, are the adoption procedures with regard to private streets provided for by Part XI of the 1980 Act.

Streets and street works

Although the word 'street' may conjure up a mental picture of a road with buildings on either side of it, the definition provided by the 1980 Act is much more vague. 'Street' includes any highway, road, lane, footpath, square, court, alley or passage, whether a thoroughfare or not (s.329). The Act goes on to define a street as one which is not a highway maintainable at public expense. In order for a private street to be 'adopted', i.e. to become maintainable at public expense, street works as specified by the 1980 Act must be executed, and then the adoption rules applied (s.228). These rules are important to landowners who have done the work specified and now want to rid themselves of responsibility for repair and maintenance. This will be particularly significant for an estate developer.

The private street works code

Street Works Authorities (generally outside London these are the county councils) have power to make bye-laws regulating the building of streets (s.186) and power to execute street works in private streets (s.205). Where this power is used, it is generally referred to as the Private Street Works Code. This involves the council preparing:

- A specification of the street works.
- An estimate of the probable expense.
- A provisional apportionment of those probable expenses between the premises liable to be charged – this means premises fronting the street.

Once these details are approved by the Street Works Authority, it must:

1 Publish notices containing relevant details in local newspapers.
2 Post notices in the street affected.
3 Serve individual notices on the owners of the premises liable to be charged for the work, stating the sum provisionally apportioned to their premises. Generally, this will be decided according to the length of frontage of the premises to the street, but s.207 provides for the provisional sum calculated to be increased or decreased, depending on factors such as the degree of benefit to be derived by the owners of the premises, and any work already carried out by the owners.

Once all the required notices have been given, the owners of premises affected may wish to object. Section 208 sets out possible grounds of objection. These include arguments that:

- The street is not a private street.
- The estimated expenses are excessive.
- The proposed works are unreasonable.
- The provisional apportionment is unacceptable.

Hearings of these objections take place before the Magistrates Court, which has authority to quash the proposals in whole or in part, or amend them.

Once any objections are resolved and the work is completed, the Street Works Authority can then recover the costs in the agreed proportions from the owners, who may be given up to thirty years to pay. The actual amount due becomes a charge on the premises. This means that the agreed cost passes as a liability to any new owner of the premises.

Once the street works have been executed, it is then possible to 'adopt' the street and make it a highway maintainable at public expense under s.228. This is done by the Street Works Authority displaying a notice in the street declaring it to be a highway maintainable at public expense. If no objection is made within a month, the street becomes such a highway. But a majority of owners in the street may object and in that case the Street Works Authority must apply to the Magistrates Court for an order overruling their objections, before the street can be turned into a highway maintainable at public expense.

Advance Payments Code

The standards imposed by Street Works Authorities in the making up of streets mean that this work can prove very costly. The authority operating under the Private Street Works Code is responsible for recovering the sums due after completion of the work and money may be outstanding for long periods. The drawback of this system can be avoided in cases where the Advance Payments Code applies. The purpose of this code is to secure payment of the expenses of executing street works in private streets adjacent to new buildings. Section 219 provides that where (a) it is proposed to erect a building for which plans must be deposited with the local authority and (b) the building fronts onto a private street where the Street Works Authority could execute street works under the Private Street Works Code, then no building can take place until the owner of the land has paid or secured the payment of the sums required to the Street Works Authority under the Advance Payments Code. The sanction for disobeying this rule is a fine. However, s.219 is subject to a number of important exceptions, e.g. where an agreement under s.38 has been made with the Street Works Authority, whereby the person undertaking street works at his own expense will, on completion of the works, dedicate the street as a highway.

If the Advance Payments Code does apply, then the Act provides the machinery for establishing the amount to be deposited – this is 'such sum as, in the opinion of the Street Works Authority, would be recoverable under the Private Street Works Code if the Street Works Authority were to carry out the work'. Provision is made for appeal to the Secretary of State for Transport against the amount proposed.

Once an advance payment has been made, it opens the way for the 'adoption' procedure under s.229. As long as one frontager to the street has paid under the Code then a majority of the frontagers (either in terms of numbers of owners, or length of frontage owned) may request the Street Works Authority to secure the carrying out of appropriate street works and then declare the street to be a highway maintainable at public expense.

Two final points with regard to street works should be noted:

1   Where a private street is in need of repair to obviate danger to traffic, the Street Works Authority can require owners fronting onto the street to undertake specified repairs within a given time. If they fail to do so, the Street Works Authority may proceed with the repairs and recover the cost proportionately from the owners. Where a notice is served requiring urgent repairs, it may be in the interests of the owners to ask the authority to undertake the work of properly making up the street under the Private Street Works Code, as it will, thereafter, be a highway maintainable at public expense (s.230).

2   Section 236 gives power to a Street Works Authority to resolve to bear all or any part of the costs of works under the Private Street Works Code. This then discharges or reduces the liability of the owner.

Standard of the highway

When considering the state of repair of a highway, all highway authorities should bear in mind the words of a judge in the House of Lords:

> It is the duty of the road authorities to keep their public highways in a state fit to accommodate the ordinary traffic which passes or may be expected to pass along them. As the ordinary traffic expands or changes in character, so must the nature of the maintenance and repair of the highway alter to suit the change.

In fact, most highway authorities will wish to improve highways under their care in so far as their budget allows them to do so. The Highways Act 1980 makes extensive provision for such improvements. Part V of the Act contains rules, e.g. with regard to dual carriageways and roundabouts, cycle tracks, footways, guardrails, refuges, subways and footbridges, levelling of highways, improvement of corners, fencing and lighting of the highway, and roadside planting.

Where a person is affected by a failure to repair the highway, he may wish to exercise the enforcement procedure provided by s.56 of the 1980 Act. To use this, a notice is served on the highway authority (or other party alleged to be responsible for maintenance) requiring the repair to be done. If the highway authority disputes the notice, the case is referred to the Crown Court, which may order the highway to be put in proper repair within a specified period.

The failure to repair the highway may have led to injury or damage being caused. Until 1961 it was very difficult to bring a civil action for damages against a highway authority, as the rule was that the authority owed no liability for injury caused by failure to repair, only for injury caused by negligent carrying out of the repairs. That rule is now changed; the present law is that the highway authority can be fully liable for injury caused by its failure to maintain or repair the highway. However, by way of defence, the authority may plead that it took such care as was reasonably required to secure that the highway was not dangerous to traffic (s.58). Naturally, this will involve factors such as the type of highway involved, the usual nature of the traffic using it, and the state of knowledge of the highway authority. People frequently seek to bring actions under these rules when they have been injured as pedestrians by a fall on an uneven or broken pavement.

Heavy traffic

The damage caused to highways is often due to excessively heavy traffic. It seems very unjust that the public should bear the cost of repair and maintenance when the damage is perhaps caused by the vehicles of one person, company or organization. Rules to redress this injustice are contained in s.59. They provide that a highway authority may recover 'excessive expenses' for maintaining the highway from any person causing excessive weight or other extraordinary traffic to pass along the highway. The excess expenses are those incurred over and above the average expenses for maintaining that or a similar highway which have resulted from damage arising from the extraordinary traffic.

Where a person knows that he will be operating traffic likely to cause such damage, he can agree in advance a payment to the highway authority. The advantage of this is that the payment will be a fixed amount, whereas if the operator waits for recovery procedures to be used by the highway authority, the 'excess expenses' are an unknown quantity. There is a significant amount of case law particularly on the meaning of the phrases 'excessive weight' and 'extraordinary traffic' which are not defined in the Act. Given the loads carried by builders and the type of vehicles being brought to sites, it will be appreciated that the section may be relevant to them.

Closing and obstruction of highways

It may be necessary, from time to time, to close or divert a highway e.g. while work is in progress on it. Alternatively, the need for the highway may have disappeared and the authority may wish to close it permanently. The procedure for 'stopping up' is contained in the Highways Act 1980, s.116. Generally, this involves an application to the Magistrates Court by the highway authority. (Where the closure is sought by a person other than the highway authority, he must ask the highway authority to take the necessary steps. There is no appeal if the highway authority refuses to activate the procedure but it must not unreasonably withhold consent.) The magistrates can make an appropriate order once the highway authority has followed through the necessary steps. These include notifying adjoining owners and occupiers, advertising the proposed closure or diversion in the press, and fixing notices at each end of the highway.

Any obstruction of, or interference with, the highway, unless authorized in some way, may constitute a civil and/or criminal offence. The Highways Act 1980, Part IX, contains numerous offences (e.g. in relation to straying animals and unlawful deposits) and also creates various duties and powers.

The highway authority is under a general duty to assert and protect the rights of the public to the use and enjoyment of any highway, and to prevent as far as possible the obstruction of the highway. It may enforce these rules in legal proceedings. Some specific examples of interference with the highway which are relevant to construction work should be noted:

1   Section 133 – if excavation or other work on land adjoining a street causes damage to a footway (pavement), the highway authority can recover the cost of repair from the landowner, or from the person causing the damage.
2   Section 131 – it is an offence, without lawful authority, to make an excavation on the highway, or to deposit anything on a highway that will cause it damage. The penalty imposed in respect of such offences is a fine of up to £20.
3   Section 137 – it is an offence to wilfully obstruct free passage along the highway.
4   Section 139 – builders' skips may not be deposited on a highway

to them. It would not be surprising, therefore, if the owners wished to object to the prescription of the improvement line. This can be done by any aggrieved person appealing to the Crown Court. If the appeal fails, it should be noted that s.73 (9) provides for compensation to be paid to persons whose property is thus injuriously affected.

Section 74 of the Act provides for the highway authority to prescribe a building line. Once such a building line is operative, no new building shall be erected beyond the building line. Rather like the rules in s.73, provision is made to compensate owners whose property is injuriously affected, but unlike s.73 there is no provision in s.74 for appealing against the imposition of the building line. Schedule 9 merely provides that the highway authority must consider objections.

Once either type of line is properly prescribed, it must be shown on a duly authenticated plan which is available for inspection by interested parties. Both ss. 73 and 74 provide means whereby these lines can be removed if they are subsequently seen to be unnecessary.

14

Building Regulations

Purpose and scope of the Building Regulations

Since 1875, the law has imposed controls to ensure that buildings are constructed in a way which is conducive to good health. Originally, local authorities made bye-laws on matters such as the materials to be used, ventilation and sanitation. Relevant legislation is now consolidated in the Building Act 1984 which empowers the Secretary of State for the Environment to make Regulations. New Building Regulations were made in 1985, replacing the 1976 set. There is a significant change in approach in the 1985 version, in that the Regulations now impose much less detailed control. Many specific points previously contained in the Regulations are now covered by guidance documents, a system similar to the codes of practice and guidance issued by the Health and Safety Commission. Section 7 of the 1984 Act provides that a failure to comply with guidance documents does not in itself render a person liable to civil or criminal proceedings, but in any such proceedings a failure to comply may be relied on as tending to establish liability.

Under s.1 of the Building Act 1984, the Secretary of State may make regulations:

1 To secure the health, safety, welfare and convenience of persons in or about buildings and of others who may be affected by buildings.
2 To further the conservation of fuel and power.
3 To prevent waste, undue consumption, misuse or contamination of water.

The regulations may relate to the design and construction of buildings, and the provision of services, fittings and equipment in, or in connection with, buildings. Such regulations are to be known as

Building Regulations. The Secretary of State has power to dispense with or relax a Regulation in particular cases where he considers that its operation would be unreasonable (s.8). When making regulations, the Secretary of State is advised by the Building Regulations Advisory Committee, appointed under s.14.

Enforcement procedures

The Regulations apply to any 'building work' or 'material change of use' of a building. The work done must be supervised, either by the local authority or an approved inspector, i.e. a person approved by the Secretary of State. The approved inspector must have no professional or financial interest in the work. Inevitably, the amount of insurance prescribed to take on work as an approved inspector means that few people are available in many parts of the country. This does not, therefore, represent a real alternative to inspection by the local authority.

When work is to be supervised by the local authority, the builder will provide the authority with a building notice, or he will deposit full plans. Building notices are only appropriate for small and minor works. The local authority can ask the builder for such extra detail as it needs, and will make the same site inspections as in other cases. On a deposit of full plans, these must be passed or rejected by the authority within five weeks. Where the plans show that work will be carried out in accordance with the Building Regulations, the authority must approve them. Appropriate fees are paid on deposit of the plans. These are usually worked out on a sliding scale, depending on the job cost.

Where the local authority is supervising, there are prescribed time limits for notifying the authority about aspects of the work:

1   At least forty-eight hours notice of commencement.
2   At least twenty-four hours notice before covering up foundations, or a dampcourse, or any concrete material.
3   At least twenty-four hours notice before covering up any drain.
4   Notice within seven days of completion of the work.

Many local authorities issue pro-forma notices for a builder to post off to them at relevant times.

Under s.35 of the 1984 Act, contraventions of the Building Regulations render a person liable on summary conviction in the Magistrates Court to a fine of up to level five on the standard scale. The scale is laid down in the Criminal Justice Act 1982. A local authority may also serve notice on an owner requiring him to pull down or remove the work, or make the alterations necessary so that it does comply with the

Regulations. If necessary, the local authority may pull down or remove the work themselves, and charge the owner (s.36). No s.36 notice can be served after the expiration of twelve months from the date of completion of the work in question.

Under s.38 (Which is not yet (1991) in force), breach of a duty imposed by Building Regulations which causes death or personal injury is to be actionable in civil proceedings, unless the specific regulation provides otherwise. This rule is in addition to any rights of action in negligence at common law.

Defective and dangerous buildings

Sections 76–83 of the Building Act 1984 create several important controls regarding defective and dangerous premises and demolition. These are in addition to rules which already exist in the Environmental Protection Act 1990 and the Town and Country Planning Act 1990. Where a building is in such a defective state that it is prejudicial to health or a nuisance, the local authority may serve a notice on the owner indicating that they intend to remedy the defective state of affairs. Nine days after serving the notice, the authority may execute the work and recover its expenses from the owner. An owner can serve a counter-notice within seven days, saying that he intends to remedy the situation himself. The local authority can then only intervene if the owner does not make a start within a reasonable time, or does not make reasonable progress. The advantage of using this s.76 procedure is speed. It is only available in cases where it appears to the authority that the procedures under the Environmental Protection Act 1990 would cause unreasonable delay. The drawback of the procedure is that an authority may need to bring proceedings to recover its expenses, and at that point, the court can enquire whether the authority was justified in the assumptions it made and the steps it took. If not justified, the authority cannot recover the expenses or any part of them. Similar rules exist with regard to dangerous buildings (ss.77 and 78), and dilapidated buildings and neglected sites (s.79).

Demolition work is now subject to a measure of control by local authorities by virtue of ss.80–3. Where the whole or part of a building is to be demolished, then no work should commence until a notice of intention to demolish has been given to the local authority and either the local authority has served a s.81 notice, or six weeks have elapsed since they received the notice of intention. If the authority decides to serve a s.81 notice, it may require the demolition contractor to take any, or all, of the following steps:

- Shore up adjacent buildings.
- Weatherproof surfaces of adjacent buildings exposed by demolition.
- Repair and make good any damage to adjacent buildings caused by the demolition.
- Remove rubbish or material resulting from the demolition.
- Disconnect and seal sewers or drains.
- Make good the surface of the ground.
- Make arrangements for disconnection of services.
- Take such steps as the authority considers necessary for the protection of the public and preservation of public amenity.

A contractor can appeal to the Magistrates Court against a s.81 notice, particularly against the shoring-up and weatherproofing requirements, where he may argue that the adjacent owner ought to pay or contribute to the costs.

For the effective operation of many of these rules, it is essential that authorized officers of local authorities have power to enter premises. Powers are granted by s.95, and must sometimes be exercised with the authority of a justice's warrant. Officers must ensure that they have appropriate authority to enter, otherwise their actions constitute the tort of trespass.

Index